The GREAT BOOK of BAKING

*A Step-by-Step Guide
to Baking Cakes, Cookies,
Breads and Pastries*

Arnold Zabert

The GREAT BOOK of BAKING

A Step-by-Step Guide
to Baking Cakes, Cookies,
Breads and Pastries

Arnold Zabert

Originally published as Backen: Die neue grosse Schule
© 1985, 1987 Verlag Zabert Sandmann GmbH, Hamburg

Published in 1990 by

Galahad Books
A division of LDAP, Inc.
166 Fifth Avenue
New York, NY 10010

Galahad Books is a registered trademark of LDAP, Inc.

Published by arrangement with Ottenheimer Publishers, Inc.
Library of Congress Catalog Card Number: 87-12063

ISBN 0-88365-758-9

Printed in Hong Kong

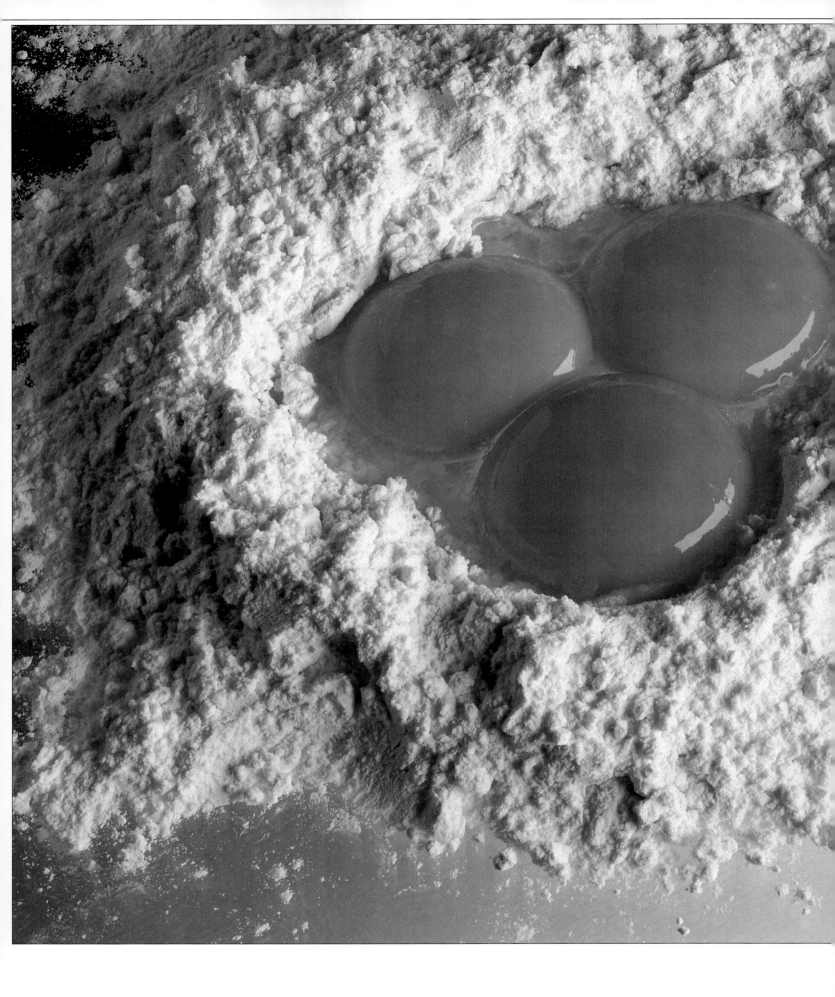

ABOUT THIS BOOK

We think everyone will share our enthusiasm for this book. It includes recipes for all those irresistible pastries, cakes and cookies that we all love and consider delicacies. However recipes for our daily bread are not neglected.

Everyday items such as eggs, butter, sugar, flour, cream, chocolate and fruits are the materials used to create all these delectable items. When the aroma of fresh baked goods fill a room, there's magic in the air; smiles appear, the family gathers in unity around the dining table and bad moods disappear. Try it for yourself—it works!

If baking is new to you, the book will help you get started. It shows, step-by-step, with text and illustrations, how to climb the ladder of baking artistry. You'll learn how to make everything from the simplest pastry to the elegant dessert for an important occasion.

If you are already a baking expert who doesn't need as much guidance, this book will offer you many new ideas. The main purpose of this book is to instill a love for baking.

Our editors and I have done everything possible to provide you with recipes and detailed photos to make your job easy. We think the dishes are simply delicious. We sincerely think you will enjoy this book!

Arnold Zabert

THE TEAM

Arnold Zabert
Publisher and
Photographer

Arnold Zabert was one
of the first German
photographers to
specialize in food
photography. His
photographs have
become well known in
general and women's
magazines, books and
advertisements. He
was the originator of
the idea for this book
and also did the
photography.

Martina Meuth
Food Journalist

A journalist for almost
all of her adult life,
Martina now special-
izes in writing about
food. She has written a
magazine food column
and written and
translated cookbooks.
She did the recipe
format and wrote the
text for this book.

Sönke Knickrehm
Editor

Sönke has edited
several publications.
He was responsible for
copy editing this book.

Hermann Rottmann
Cooking Expert

Hermann Rottmann
has been associated in
cooking projects with
Arnold Zabert for three
years. An accom-
plished chef and pastry
cook, he previously
worked in a well-known
restaurant in Hamburg,
West Germany. He is
particularly interested in
creating delicious,
low-calorie recipes. He
developed the recipes
for this book and also
did the food styling for
photography.

Walter Cimbal
Assistant Photographer

He has been working in
food photography for
two years. He played a
significant role in the
production of the
extensive photography
for this book.

Hartwig Kloeverkorn
Art Director

A leading force in the
graphic design of top
women's magazines,
he has also been
involved in culinary
publications. He is
responsible for the
book's overall graphic
design.

Jörn Rynio
Photography and
Design Assistant

An enthusiastic
amateur cook, Jörn
assists the publisher in
both photography and
graphic arts.

This Book . . .

. . . is designed to provide detailed instruction, helpful ideas and guidance for all bakers. It is also designed to make baking understandable and easy for beginners. There are a wide variety of recipes; informative text on techniques, ingredients and equipment; step-by-step photographs; and beautiful photographs of finished products all geared to help you become a better baker.

Each chapter starts with a basic recipe. Precise step-by-step photographs take you through every step. Helpful hints and tips are included to take the mystery out of baking.

Once you have mastered the basic recipe, you will have gained the knowledge necessary to move on to the next level in the art of baking. The pages that follow each basic recipe build on it and provide variations that gradually lead you toward more complicated baking, providing necessary skills and many opportunities to practice along the way. And, if you have any problem, you can turn back to the basic recipe for help.

As you progress beyond the basic recipe, you can combine the baking "building blocks" in any way you like, and use them to make your own completely individual creations. All kinds of ideas are illustrated to help you and to guide you toward the ultimate joy of creative baking. But best of all, you will be able to build your baking skills gradually from basic recipes to recipes that require more advanced cooking techniques.

As you use the recipes, if you come across any cooking terms that are not familiar, use the index to locate an explanation of the term or to find detailed and helpful information on the ingredients used in baking.

Table of Contents

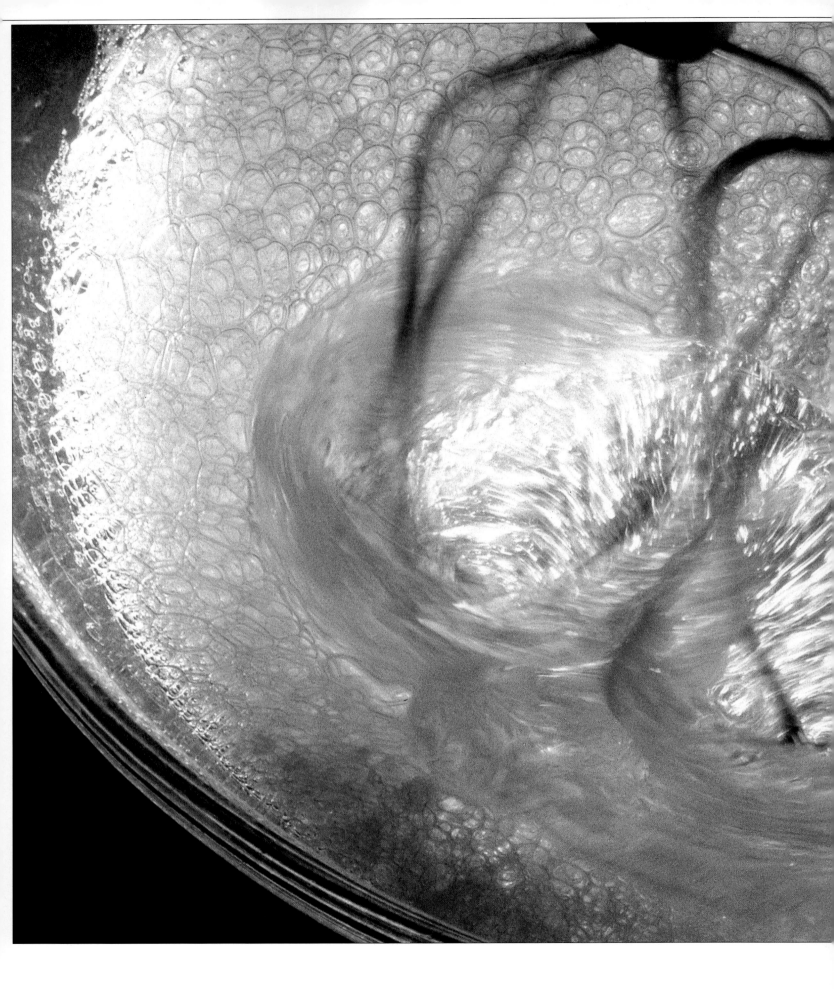

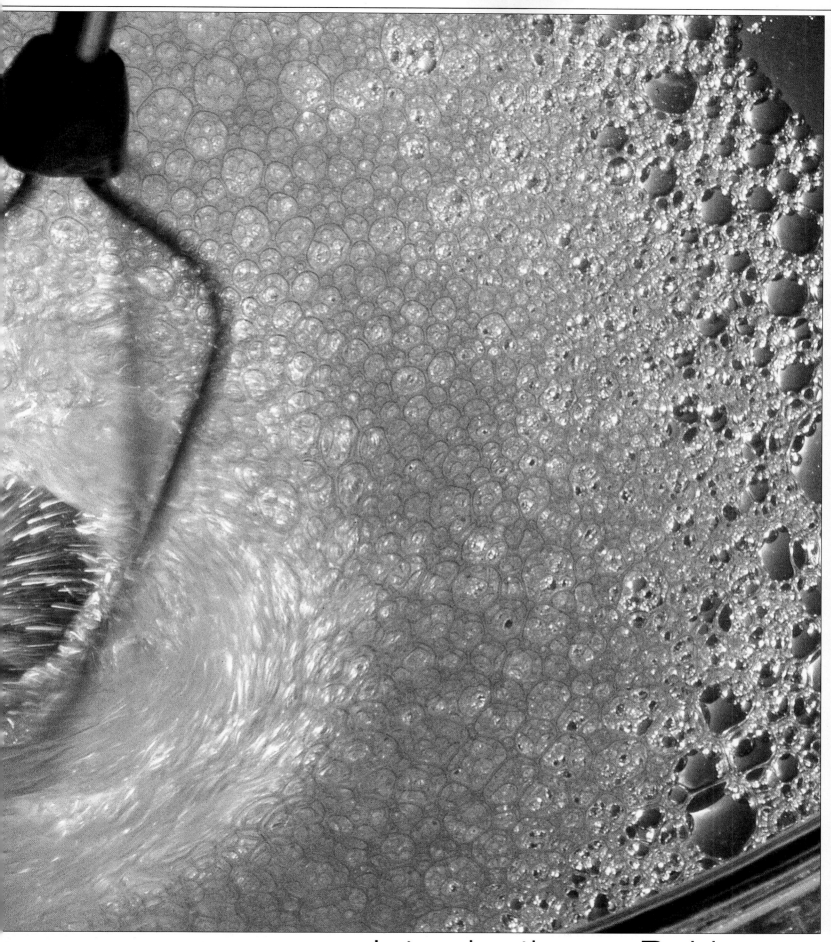

Introduction—Baking
Techniques & Equipment
to Make Baking Easy

The Basics of Baking

No matter what you bake—a cake, delicate tarts, bread or cookies—there are some basic rules that must be followed. Baking rules are not necessarily complicated, nor are they difficult to remember, but they can be the determining factor between success and failure.

The Importance of Recipes

Successful cooking is a combination of many things; a reliable recipe, proper equipment, good-quality ingredients and often a touch of imagination. The recipe comes first. In many instances a confident or adventuresome cook can use a recipe as either a guide to follow or to change as desired. But baking recipes are an exception because they are chemical formulas that must be followed precisely. Obviously there is some room for change in flavoring or for such things as choice of nuts to be added or left out, and there is endless leeway to vary fillings, icings and decorations. But the procedures for making batters or mixtures, and the methods for handling them, must be followed with great care or disaster is almost sure to follow. Measure ingredients carefully, using either dry or liquid measuring cups as appropriate. Follow instructions, when given, on the proper temperature of ingredients and combine them in the order given. Use the correct size pan and follow instructions faithfully for the preparation of the pan. Check the temperature of the oven with an oven thermometer and be sure to preheat the oven. Follow directions for baking and, finally, cool the finish product as instructed in order to be sure it will come out of the pan easily and neatly.

A Word About Ovens

There was a time when the home cook had little or no option about what kind of oven to use. Originally all cooking took place around the fireplace. The brick ovens, usually built next to the fireplace, were heated by wood until the end of the seventeenth century when coal replaced wood. But the real revolution in kitchens took place in the late eighteenth century when Count Rumford invented the cast-iron stove and cooking moved from the fireplace to the stove. It took about a hundred years for the next major change, an oven heated by gas instead of coal, and about fifty years more before electric ovens were introduced. The twentieth century brought us convection and microwave ovens.

Modern cooks have a choice of gas, electric, convection or microwave ovens. They can even choose an oven that cooks by two methods. Ovens are available that combine microwave and convection cooking or combine either microwave or convection with either gas or electric. These ovens can be used to cook by either of the two methods provided, or in some instances by a combination of two methods that alternate as cooking progresses.

The question of whether gas or electric ovens are preferable for baking is academic for anyone who already has a good-working radiant oven in their kitchen. But if a radiant oven must be replaced, it should be noted that electric ovens preheat more quickly than gas, heat more evenly and hold the temperature better—all factors that are important to the serious baker.

Convection ovens were used in commercial bakeries long before they were available for home cooks. They differ from radiant ovens because they have a built-in fan that circulates hot air evenly throughout the oven, a feature excellent for many kinds of baking. Food is baked at a slightly lower temperature than the temperature used in a conventional oven, and baking time is reduced by about 25%. An additional advantage for bakers is that food can be placed on two racks simultaneously during baking without damage to the finished products, something that cannot be done in a conventional gas or electric oven without rotating the pans.

Most baked products benefit enormously from the even temperature and constant circulation of hot air. Exceptions include cakes baked in deep pans such as Bundt cakes, fruit cakes and angel food cakes where the circulating hot air cannot penetrate into the depth of the pan.

Microwave ovens, the miracle of our century, are wonderful for cooking many things. Manufacturers of these ovens almost always include cookbooks with recipes for all kinds of baked products. Although it certainly is possible to bake some things in a microwave oven, the results are never as satisfactory as when a conventional or convection oven is used instead. Among the problems bakers face when using a microwave oven for baking are the inability of the oven to brown food properly and the fact that food is cooked from the outer edge in toward the center, which means a dense cake often is somewhat overcooked on the outer edge while the center of the cake is not fully cooked. Fair results can be achieved for quick breads and for cakes baked in a microwave-safe ring mold.

Combination cooking is not recommended for serious baking.

Baking recipes call for preheated ovens and indicate the temperature at which foods should be baked. But all too often a cook will set an oven correctly at the temperature called for in a recipe and be distressed and surprised to discover the food does not cook in the time it is supposed to cook, or it gets too brown or not brown enough. Why? The answer is very simple. Ovens must be calibrated periodically in order to be sure they heat to the temperature at which they have been set. If your oven is brand new or very old, chances are it will need some adjustment. In order to find out how accurate your oven actually is, all you have to do is invest in a piece of very basic, important and inexpensive equipment—an oven thermometer. Place the thermometer in the center of the oven and check it before you start to bake. If the temperature on your thermometer is not the temperature you want, adjust the temperature setting on the oven accordingly. And, in order to be on the safe side, replace the oven thermometer every few years because it will not remain accurate indefinitely.

Unless a baking recipe tells you otherwise, place the pan in the center of the oven so heat can circulate evenly around the pan. Ideally there should be at least two inches between the sides of a pan or baking sheet and the walls of the oven.

Equipment

The pages that follow show some of the basic equipment necessary for successful baking, as well as an assortment of baking pans. Some of the equipment is inexpensive enough to consider buying in duplicate. Baking is easiest when you have extra measuring cups and bowls and several sets of measuring spoons and rubber spatulas so you don't have to stop and waste time washing equipment in the middle of mixing a batter or dough. Good-quality baking pans, electric mixers and blenders, on the other hand, can be expensive, so it is important to think through the kind of expensive equipment you really need and buy reliable tools that will last for many years. One of the most foolhardy purchases a cook can make is to buy lightweight, inexpensive pans that are likely to cause food to cook unevenly. In fact, a poor-quality pan can cause as great a baking disaster as an uncalibrated oven! Choose your pans carefully and, if necessary, buy one good pan at a time instead of several poor-quality pans. As your interest in baking grows, and your repertoire increases, you can add specialized pans one at a time.

Ingredients

In the next chapter you will find detailed information about many of the ingredients used in baking. Flour, sugar, fat and leavening agents are described and identified in order to help you understand the differences between them. Be sure to use fresh ingredients at all times. The quality of the ingredients used will directly effect the quality of the finished product. It's a shame to put the time and effort into baking, but compromise the final result by using ingredients that cannot provide the best possible flavor and texture.

Baking at High Altitudes

Most people who live at altitudes of 3,000 feet above sea level or higher already know that high altitudes effect cooking and therefore adjustments must be made. This is particularly true for baking recipes. Changes often must be made in oven temperature and ingredients.

There is no exact formula that can be given for the adjustments necessary for high-altitude baking. If you are new to the area, try some of the suggestions that follow, check your local library for guidelines that may have been developed for your area by appropriate agencies, ask your neighbors for advice and, above all, be prepared to experiment. Eventually you will be able to judge what kinds of changes are necessary. Some of the suggestions that follow may prove helpful.

Increase oven temperature between 15F and 25F (-10C and -5C) when baking cakes and quick breads.

Decrease each teaspoon of baking powder by 1/8 to 1/4 teaspoon; decrease each cup of sugar by 1 to 3 tablespoons; decrease each cup of fat by 1 to 2 tablespoons; decrease flour slightly; increase each cup of liquid by 1 to 4 tablespoons; add an extra egg.

High altitudes cause yeast dough to rise more quickly than at sea level. Therefore it is recommended that dough be punched down and allowed to rise a second time before shaping.

Beat egg whites to soft peak stage rather than stiff peak stage.

The Right Tools for the Job

It is difficult, and sometimes all but impossible, to cook successfully without the right tools. This is just as true for home cooks as it is for professional cooks. Of course it is possible, in an emergency, to improvise to some extent. But, if you are interested in cooking successfully without wasting precious time, you will find it worthwhile to take the question of cooking equipment seriously. Choose your equipment with several things in mind: the kind of cooking you do, the dimensions of your oven cavity, the storage space you have available and your budget. And don't forget that well-made equipment, designed to last, is more economical in the long run than poorly made equipment that does not function well to begin with and ultimately must be replaced.

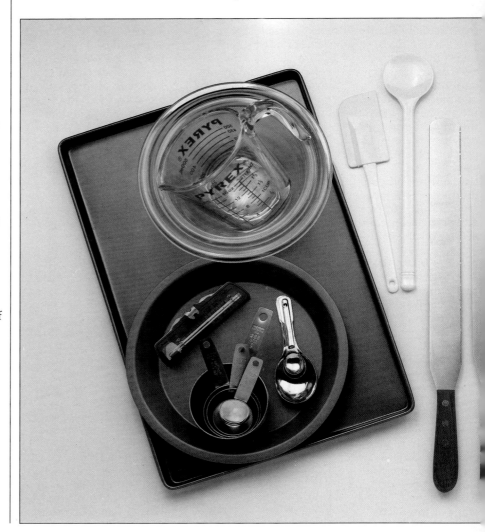

Basic Equipment

Whisk or wire whip: Available in several sizes. Use to beat egg whites and whipping cream, make custards and combine liquids.

Pastry brush: Available in several sizes. Avoid inexpensive brushes that are likely to shed. Use to glaze bread, tarts, pies and cakes, brush pastry, color marzipan shapes and grease pans.

Kitchen shears: Use to cut parchment or waxed paper to make piping bags, cut dried fruit, snip herbs, cut string and perform an almost endless list of other vital kitchen chores.

Rubber spatula: Available in several sizes with wooden or plastic handles. Use to fold, scrape bowls and pans and for gentle stirring.

Long handled wooden and plastic spoons: Available in several sizes. Use to stir hot liquids, to stir or mix in deep bowls and pans and with cooking equipment that has a non-stick surface.

Metal mixing bowls: Available in sets and in many sizes. Use over hot water as top of double boiler and to mix and store food.

Glass mixing bowls: Available in sets and in many sizes. Use to cook food in microwave oven and to mix and store food.

Pastry wheels, fluted and plain: Use to cut pastry and pizza dough. Fluted wheel will make fluted edge.

Zester: Use to remove zest or peel from citrus fruit.

Metal spatulas, long and short: Use to ice cakes, smooth icing, release cakes from springform pans and to lift or turn food.

Icing comb: Use to make decorative lines in icing on top and around side of cake.

Rubber dough scraper: Use to lift sticky dough, turn pastry, gather dough scraps and scrape bowls.

Wire rack: One rack is not enough for anyone who bakes a lot. Use to cool baked products, in or out of pan as recipe directs.

Pastry bag: Available in many sizes. Made of nylon, plastic-lined fabric or disposable paper. Use small bags to pipe delicate patterns. Use large bags to pipe whipped cream, buttercream, choux paste and other pastry.

Piping tips: Available in many sizes and shapes. Buy a set to provide good variety for different kinds of piping. Add individual tips to your collection for specific jobs.

Parchment paper: Use to make pastry bags and to line cake pans.

Mesh strainer or sieve: Available in many sizes. Mesh used in strainer can range from very fine to coarse. Use to drain food and sift powdered sugar over cakes and pastry.

Rolling pin: The most efficient rolling pins are well balanced, heavy and made of hardwood. They will do a better job of rolling out pastry than any other kind of rolling pin. Avoid rolling pins that are filled with ice cubes because they will make your pastry moist.

Liquid measuring cup: Available in many sizes. Use to measure liquid ingredients accurately. Don't use dry measuring cups as a substitute because you may spill some of the liquid and therefore will not get the necessary amount of liquid in your mixture.

Dry measuring cups: Sold in sets that usually include 1/4 cup, 1/3 cup, 1/2 cup and 1 cup. Also available in 1/8-cup and 2-cup sizes. Use to measure dry ingredients by filling correct size cup to the brim and leveling off with blunt edge of knife. Don't use liquid measuring cups as a substitute because you will not be able to get an accurate measure.

Measuring spoons: Buy at least 2 sets of thick metal measuring spoons. A standard set has 4 spoons held together by a ring at the top. The set includes: 1/4 teaspoon, 1/2 teaspoon, 1 teaspoon and 1 tablespoon. If a recipe calls for 1-1/2 tablespoons, to measure accurately, use 1 tablespoon, 1 teaspoon and 1/2 teaspoon (3 teaspoons equal 1 tablespoon).

Oven thermometer: Successful baking depends on an oven that has been preheated to the correct temperature. Many ovens are not accurate unless calibrated regularly. To overcome this problem, use an oven thermometer to check the temperature and adjust the temperature as necessary.

Pie weights: When pastry is baked before filling (baked blind), it must be covered with foil or parchment paper and dried beans or pie weights during baking to prevent the pastry from puffing up. Pie weights are handy to have and are, of course, reusable.

Pie plate: Standard size is 9 inch or 10 inch, although other sizes are also available. Pie plates are designed to go directly from the oven to the table.

Electric hand mixer: Use to beat egg whites and whipping cream and to mix light batters. Don't use a hand mixer to make a heavy dough.

Baking sheet: Use greased or ungreased, according to recipe, to bake cookies, free-form bread, rolls, and pastries not made in a specific-size pan with sides.

A Word of Caution

Baking recipes always specify the size and type of baking pan required. However, there are some cake batters and mixtures that can be baked in a variety of different shaped pans and, occasionally, in a different size pan. But, when the size of a pan is changed, all kinds of problems can result unless you are very careful about comparing the capacity of the pan called for in the recipe and the capacity of the pan you want to use as a substitute. Pan size directly effects the finished product. Obviously, if you use a pan that is too small, the cake will rise too high and overflow; if you use a pan that is too large, the cake will not rise high enough. Differences in the shape of a pan also must be considered. Although a batter baked in a standard cake pan, springform pan, tube pan or loaf pan usually also can be baked in a flat pan such as a jelly-roll pan or in a muffin tin, the reverse does not always work. When you change the size or shape of a cake pan, be sure to check your timing very carefully. Flat cakes and cupcakes usually take less time to bake than high, round cakes.

Special Pans—Big & Small

Some pans, such as a gugelhupf pan, are designed for a specific recipe; other pans, such as a loaf or springform pan, have many uses. If you buy good-quality pans and take good care of them, they will last a lifetime.

Preparing Pans for Baking

Be sure to follow recipe directions for greasing, flouring or lining cake pans even when using a pan with a non-stick surface. Use shortening, unsalted butter or margarine to grease pans. When a recipe directs you to grease and flour a pan, grease the pan first and then sprinkle flour over the greased surface. Turn the pan over and gently shake out the excess flour. Use parchment paper or waxed paper to line pans. If the recipe directs, grease the paper lightly.

It is important to note there are times when pans are not supposed to be greased. Pastry is never placed in a greased pan, cookies are sometimes baked on ungreased cookie sheets and certain kinds of sponge cakes are baked in ungreased tube pans.

Pans pictured above:

1. Fluted flan tin
2. Paper cupcake liners
3. Miniature tart pans
4. Loaf pan
5. Springform tube pan with decorative bottom
6. Chocolate rabbit mold (candy)
7. Heart-shaped cake pan
8. Fluted loaf pan
9. Springform pan
10. Gugelhupf pan or turk's head mold

Tips to Help Avoid Disaster

Cream Refuses to Whip:
This can happen if the room, cream, beaters or bowl are too warm, or if sugar or flavoring are added too soon. Flavoring should not be added until the cream has begun to thicken. To solve the temperature problem, stop beating immediately before the cream separates. Transfer the mixture to a chilled bowl or place it in the refrigerator until chilled. When chilled, beat slowly. If the cream separates, throw it out and start over or continue to beat and use as butter.

Egg Whites Refuse to Thicken:
This can happen if there is even a small drop of egg yolk in the egg whites or if the bowl or beaters are not completely clean and dry. The presence of any fat or water will prevent egg whites from thickening. There is no remedy except to start again with fresh egg whites. Volume will be increased if egg whites are brought to room temperature before beating.

Cake Is Too Dry:
The texture of cake will be too dry if it is baked at too high a temperature or is left in the oven too long. Soak the cake with fruit syrup, rum or brandy, or use the cake for crumbs or in a Trifle (see page 223).

Cake Is Too Heavy:
The texture of a cake will be too heavy if the batter is beaten too much, ingredients are not measured carefully or the oven temperature is too low. There is no remedy.

Cake Will Not Come Out of Pan:
Cake pans, even those with non-stick coating, should be thoroughly greased and floured. Exceptions to this rule are when angel food cakes and chiffon cakes are baked. Follow recipe instructions carefully on cooling cakes on racks before removing them from the pan. However, if a cake remains in the pan too long, it will be difficult to remove. If this happens, return the cake to a 340F (170C) oven for about 2 minutes. If necessary, run a spatula around the inside edge of the pan to loosen the cake. A parchment paper lining on the bottom of the pan will provide added assurance that the bottom will not stick.

Tricks of the Trade

Baking Blind
Prebaking a pastry case before filling helps prevent the pastry from blistering. Fit pastry into ungreased pan; line with foil or parchment paper. Fill with dried beans. Bake at 400F (205C) for 20 minutes. Remove beans and paper and bake 5 to 8 minutes more. Cool before filling.

Rolling Out Pastry
Flatten pastry ball with your hand. Roll out with lightly floured rolling pin in short and even strokes, from the center outwards.

Lifting Pastry
Fold pastry carefully over rolling pin, lift gently and drape over pan.

Decorating Edge of Cake with Slivered Almonds
Spread icing over top and around side of cake. Place 1 or 2 tablespoonfuls of toasted slivered almonds in the palm of your hand and press gently into the icing around the edge of the cake. Remove any nuts that fall off and reuse. If necessary, use a small spatula to press nuts firmly in place.

Lining Small Tart Pans

Lining several small tart pans with pastry can be time consuming. To save time, arrange the pans next to each other and place a large piece of pastry over them. Press the pastry gently into each pan and run a rolling pin firmly over the top to cut the edges of the pastry. Bake according to directions in recipe.

Cooking Pastry

Pipe small shapes of choux paste onto greased parchment paper. Invert paper over the hot oil. Heat will cause the pastry to drop into the pan.

Preventing Splashes When Whipping Cream

Hold a dish towel in front of beaters and bowl to prevent splashing when you whip cream.

Vanilla Sugar

Fill jar with powdered sugar and a vanilla bean cut in half lengthwise. Set jar aside for several days.

How to Use a Piping Bag

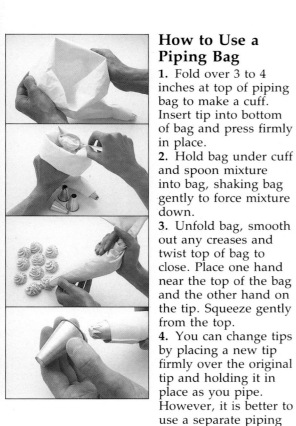

1. Fold over 3 to 4 inches at top of piping bag to make a cuff. Insert tip into bottom of bag and press firmly in place.
2. Hold bag under cuff and spoon mixture into bag, shaking bag gently to force mixture down.
3. Unfold bag, smooth out any creases and twist top of bag to close. Place one hand near the top of the bag and the other hand on the tip. Squeeze gently from the top.
4. You can change tips by placing a new tip firmly over the original tip and holding it in place as you pipe. However, it is better to use a separate piping bag with the proper tip or empty the bag and insert the new tip.

Covering Cake with Marzipan

Roll out marzipan about 2 inches larger than the cake to be covered. Fold marzipan gently over rolling pin and drape over top of cake.

Using an Icing Comb

It is easy to make a pattern around the side of a cake to provide a finished and professional look. Spread icing over the top and side of the cake and smooth the icing with a small spatula. Hold the edge of an icing comb against the side of the cake and draw it gently around the side as you turn the cake slowly with the other hand.

Using a Zester

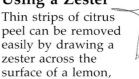

Thin strips of citrus peel can be removed easily by drawing a zester across the surface of a lemon, orange or grapefruit.

The Correct
Ingredients—Vital to
Successful Baking

Flours—Basic to Good Baking

Flour—from Wheat & Other Products

Most flour used in baking is made from wheat. However corn, buckwheat, rye and potatoes are also made into flour and used in baking, often combined with a wheat flour.

Wheat flour can be divided into three major categories: hard wheat, high in gluten, and ideal for yeast baking, is used to make all-purpose and bread flours; soft wheat, low in gluten, is used to make all-purpose, cake and pastry flours that are leavened with baking powder; and durum wheat, used to make semolina, the flour used to make pasta.

From Grains of Wheat to Flour

The process of milling wheat and turning it into flour is a major industry under rigid government regulation. The first step necessary to make flour is the removal of the outer covering, or bran, from the grain. But this process also removes most of the nutrients, which are often replaced in the finished product. When white flours are made, the wheat germ, which contains fat, is also removed. Flours, such as whole-wheat flour, that do not have the wheat germ removed, must be refrigerated because the fat that remains can cause the flour to turn rancid. Finally, the wheat is ground and sifted to varying degrees of fineness and nutrients are replaced and added.

Most Often Used Flours

All-purpose flour: This kind of flour is used for many kinds of cooking. It is usually made from a blend of wheats, sold bleached and unbleached, and can be used with yeast or baking powder.

Cake flour: Highly refined bleached flour made from soft wheat and used with baking powder rather than yeast. This flour is used in commercial cake mixes.

Self-rising flour: Bleached all-purpose or cake flour to which a leavening agent and salt have been added. This flour is never used with yeast.

Bread flour: Milled from blends of hard wheats and usually unbleached, it is used with yeast.

Pastry flour: Usually made from soft wheat, but not as finely milled as cake flour. Used to make pastry.

Instant-blending flour: Specially treated all-purpose flour that does not require sifting and blends quickly and easily with liquid.

Whole-wheat flour: Unrefined and unbleached brown flour made from hard or soft wheat. Usually combined with all-purpose or bread flour in baking.

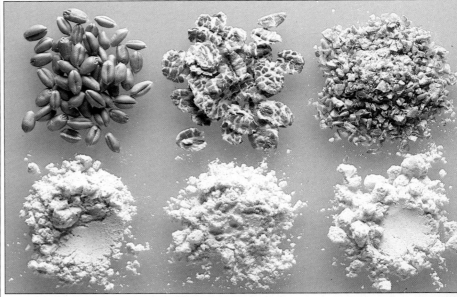

1. Wheat Berries (below)   2. Wheat Flakes (below)   3. Cracked Wheat (below)

7. Unbleached All-Purpose Flour (above)   8. Bleached All-Purpose Flour (above)   9. Bread Flour (above)

1. Rye and Medium Rye Flour   2. Oats and Oat Flour   3. Barley and Barley Flour

Although all-purpose flour is used more than any other type of flour, special kinds of baking often require the use of a different flour. Some may be familiar and some new. Be sure to use the kind of flour called for in a recipe. If you don't, you may be courting disaster.

4. Graham Flour (below)

5. Unprocessed Bran Flakes (below)

6. Semolina (below)

10. Self-Rising Flour (above)

11. Instant-Blending Flour (above)

12. Cake Flour (above)

4. Corn and Cornmeal

5. Millet Seeds and Millet Meal

6. Buckwheat and Buckwheat Flour

Special Kinds of Flour

In addition to the flours listed on the previous page, a wide range of other flours are sold in supermarkets and in health food stores for special kinds of baking. Ethnic cookbooks in particular may call for a flour with which you are not familiar. But if you look hard enough you probably can find it, sitting on the shelf next to the more familiar flours, or tucked on a shelf of ethnic foods. Some of these flours are:
Barley Flour
Bran Flour
Buckwheat Flour
Chick-Pea Flour
Corn Flour (Masa Harina)
Cornmeal
Cracked-Wheat Flour
Gluten Flour
Oat Flour
Potato Flour
Rice Flour
Rye Flour—Light, Medium, Dark and Rye Blend
Semolina
Soy Flour
Triticale Flour
Wheat Germ Flour

The Importance of Gluten

Gluten is the protein substance in flour that provides structure to baked products. In order to achieve the right texture in bread, a high amount of gluten is necessary. On the other hand, too much gluten can destroy the light tender texture desirable in cakes. Flour made from hard wheat has more gluten than flour made from soft wheat. Gluten is activated when wheat flour is combined with a liquid.

The Importance of Measuring Flour Correctly

Professional bakers, and cooks throughout most of the world, measure flour on scales in order to be certain they have exactly the right amount of flour. But few home cooks in America own scales, and American recipes rarely list flour or other similar ingredients by weight. Flour measurements in a recipe, whether by cup or by weight, are the measurements used when the recipe is tested. If you are casual about the amount of flour you use in a baking recipe, the ratio of flour to the other ingredients will not be correct and the results will, in all probability, be very unsatisfactory.

Flour must be measured in a dry measuring cup, never in a liquid measuring cup. If you use a liquid measuring cup there is no way you can measure accurately. Stir the flour gently and then spoon it lightly into the cup. Don't pack the flour down the way brown sugar is packed. Overfill the measure slightly and then run the edge of a knife across the top of the cup to level the flour off. If your recipe calls for "1 cup flour, sifted," measure the flour first and then sift. If a recipe calls for "1 cup sifted flour," sift the flour first and then measure.

The Importance of Sweeteners & Fats

Sweeteners

Sugar and other sweeteners play many roles in successful baking besides providing sweet flavor. One of the most important functions of sweeteners is to provide food for yeast. Sweeteners also give tenderness and structure to texture, help retain moisture in baked products, add color, function as a creaming agent when combined with fat and as a foaming agent when beaten with eggs.

There is no difference in the chemical makeup of cane sugar and beet sugar.

Therefore, they can be used interchangeably without detection.

Granulated Sugar

Pure white sugar used more than any other form of sugar for cooking.

Superfine Sugar

Finely ground granulated sugar that dissolves more easily than standard granulated sugar.

Powdered Sugar

Granulated sugar that has been crushed to a very fine powder. Cornstarch is added to the sugar to prevent it from caking. Used to make icing and dust over food, occasionally used in pastry dough, added to egg whites and whipped cream.

Brown Sugar (Light & Dark)

Can be made from the syrup that remains after white sugar has been made or by adding syrup to white sugar crystals. Brown sugar contains molasses, the more molasses present, the darker the sugar and the more intense the flavor. Brown sugar also contains moisture and, when there is not enough moisture present, the sugar hardens.

Molasses

A by-product of sugar refining. Used to color and flavor baked products and can be used as an acid to activate baking soda. Molasses is not quite as sweet as sugar. If substituted for sugar, use in a ratio of 1 cup of molasses to 3/4 cup of sugar.

Corn Syrup (Light & Dark)

Made by converting cornstarch into a glucose syrup. When corn syrup is used to replace sugar, twice as much corn syrup must be used.

Honey

The natural nectar of plants produced by bees. The flavor of honey depends on the plant which provided the nectar. Honey is sweeter than sugar. When used as a substitute, 1 cup of honey will replace 1-1/4 cups of sugar.

Caution: When substituting syrup for sugar, no more than half the amount of sugar called for in the recipe should be replaced with syrup. In addition, reduce the liquid in a recipe to compensate for the additional liquid content of the syrup.

Fats

Although fat is a vital and important ingredient in some kinds of baking such as the making of puff pastry, there are other baked products such as bread that can be baked without any fat at all. When fat is added, it can provide flavor and add to the tenderness of the finished product.

Butter

Butter graded by the USDA has a shield on the package indicating Grade AA (best quality), A or B. In accordance with government regulations, butter must have a fat content of 80%. Sweet or unsalted butter is made from pasteurized cream. Salt butter is sweet butter with salt added. Salt butter will keep fresh in the refrigerator slightly longer than sweet or unsalted butter. Both kinds of butter can be stored in the freezer. Some baking recipes call for unsalted butter, other simply call for butter. When in doubt, use unsalted butter in baking. You can always add a little salt if necessary.

Margarine

The fat in margarine is vegetable oil or a combination of vegetable oil and animal fat rather than cream. Margarine is available with or without salt added. It can be used in place of butter in most baking recipes but will affect the flavor and texture of the finished product. When a large amount of butter is included in a recipe, and butter is an integral part of the flavor of the finished product, margarine should not be substituted except for strict dietary reasons.

Shortening

White, tasteless shortening is solidified vegetable oil that does not require refrigeration. It is used to make flaky products such as pie crusts and biscuits and in some cakes, cookies, quick breads and other pastry. It is an ideal fat to use in deep-frying because it has a low smoking and burning point. Shortening is also ideal for greasing baking pans because it has no flavor.

Vegetable Oil

Vegetable oil is fat that is liquid at room temperature. Oils are not used as often in baking as are the solid fats. Vegetable oil is used in some quick breads, such as muffins, and chiffon cakes. Flavorless or mild-flavored oils that have a low smoking and burning point can be used successfully for deep-frying. Oil can also be used to grease baking pans. Olive oil is sometimes used in Mediterranean-type breads to add flavor.

It is vital to succesful baking that you use the
correct ingredients. Sugars and fats contribute
texture and flavor to baked products as well as performing
other important functions. Pictured are the
common types available in American grocery stores.

The Magic of Leavening

Many of the foods we bake—bread, cake and muffins, for example—must rise during baking in order to be edible. Therefore, we must add something to the dough or the batter in order to make them rise. There are three kinds of rising agents:

Carbon dioxide: Provided chemically by the use of yeast, baking powder or baking soda.

Air: Beaten or folded into a batter, often in the form of beaten egg whites.

Steam: Created when water in batter is heated to a high temperature during baking.

Most of the time only one rising agent is used, but occasionally some of the agents are combined.

Chemical rising agents have very specific characteristics. Baking powder and baking soda, in spite of their chemical differences, are added to batters in the same way, but for different reasons (see Baking Powder and Baking Soda). Yeast, however, requires special handling that must be understood in order to make it perform properly.

Yeast

Yeast is the leavening agent used for bread and some kinds of cakes. In addition to the fact that it will cause the dough to rise, it adds both flavor and aroma. Information about yeast and how it works can be found on page 116.

Although yeast can be used in several ways, there are two major methods used most often; the conventional method used in the recipes in this book, and the rapid-mix method.

Conventional Method: Yeast is sprinkled over a small amount of warm water (105-115F/40-45C) and a little sugar is added. The mixture is stirred and allowed to stand at room temperature 5 to 10 minutes until it begins to foam. This procedure is called "proofing." If the yeast does not foam, it means it is not alive and must be discarded.

Rapid-Mix Method: Undissolved yeast is combined with some of the dry ingredients. Liquid is heated to 120-130F (50-55C) and stirred into the dry ingredients. The dough is then beaten with an electric mixer. In this method there is no way to "proof" yeast, so it is of particular importance to check the expiration date on the package.

Once the dough has been made, it must be kneaded in order to distribute the yeast. Form the dough into a ball and place it on a lightly floured flat work surface. Flour your hands lightly and place the heels of your hands at the front of the dough with your fingers curved over the top. Push the heels of your hands down on the dough and push the dough away from your body. Make a quarter turn with the dough, fold the dough over and repeat the pushing process. Continue kneading 8 to 10 minutes or for as long as directed in the recipe. The dough should feel smooth and elastic.

Once the dough has been kneaded it must be allowed to rise. Grease a large mixing bowl, place the kneaded ball of dough in it and turn the dough to coat the entire surface. Cover the bowl with a clean dish towel and set it aside in a warm, draft-free place to rise until it has doubled in bulk. This should take 1 to 2 hours, and the time usually is indicated in the recipe. In order to determine if the dough has actually doubled, press two fingers into the risen dough. If the dough springs back, it has not finished rising. If the indentations remain, the dough is ready for the next step.

Punch the dough down with your fist and place it on the floured work surface. Shape the dough as desired and place it in a greased pan or on a greased baking sheet. Cover and place it in a warm, draft-free place to rise for the second time until it has doubled in bulk again, about 45 minutes to 1 hour. At this point the dough is finally ready to be baked in a preheated oven.

Baking Powder

Most of the baking powder sold today is "double-acting," and this is the kind of baking powder to use when a recipe simply calls for baking powder. Double-acting means the baking powder acts in two separate stages. Chemical action begins when the baking powder is added to a cold batter. It continues when the batter is placed in a hot oven. Baking powder is made from a combination of ingredients that include an alkaline and an acid. When liquid is added to the batter, the alkaline and acid interact with each other and form tiny bubbles of gas that, in turn, cause the batter to rise.

Keep baking powder in a tightly closed container to keep moisture out. It is a good idea to check baking powder for freshness if you have had it for a long time. Add 1 teaspoon of baking powder to 1/3 cup of hot water. If nothing happens, you need fresh baking powder. If bubbles form, your baking powder is fine.

In the event you don't have any baking powder on hand, you can make some. Combine 1/3 teaspoon baking soda with 1/2 teaspoon cream of tartar and 1/8 teaspoon salt for each teaspoon of baking powder needed. Use it immediately; don't make a batch of homemade baking powder to keep on hand.

Baking Soda

Baking soda, which is really sodium bicarbonate, is an alkaline substance that has no leavening ability when used by itself. It is used when it is necessary to neutralize an acid ingredient and must be combined with an ingredient that contains an acid such as buttermilk, molasses, brown sugar or even some kinds of cocoa in order to work. However, if the acid ingredient is not strongly acidic, the recipe may call for the addition of some baking powder too. Baking soda is added to dry ingredients in the same way baking powder is added. Action begins when liquid is added.

The amount of baking powder or baking soda called for in a recipe should never be arbitrarily increased. This will not make the batter rise higher, it will simply add an unfortunate flavor to the finished product. If too much leavening agent is added to batter, it can cause the batter to expand too much during baking. When this happens, the finished product will collapse and you will end up with a major baking disaster.

Air

Air can be incorporated into a batter through the process of foaming or creaming. Beaten egg white folded into a batter is one of the most often used foaming methods. In some cases, beaten whole eggs are added to a batter to provide the air needed for leavening. When fat, usually butter, and sugar are beaten together, or creamed, the process can also provide air for leavening. Although it is important to beat ingredients thoroughly, it also is important to avoid overbeating. This is particularly true for egg whites that will begin to deflate when overbeaten.

Steam

When water is heated it turns into steam which, believe it or not, expands to over 1000 times its original volume. This process serves as the leavening agent for cream puffs, popovers and pastry when they are baked at a high temperature.

Flavorings for Taste, Aroma & Color

In many cases it is the special flavor of a spice,
added to dough, batter, filling or icing, that
makes the finished product unique. Butter and sugar add
basic flavor, but spices are used to provide
individual and sometimes exotic flavor.

1. Vanilla Pod

Pod of an orchid, native to Central America. Vanilla extract is made from the pod, but pods provide stronger flavor. If you immerse a pod in sugar, cover and set aside, the sugar will develop a strong vanilla flavor that can be used successfully in baking. The pith from vanilla pods is used to flavor batter, custard, whipped cream, icing, ice cream and many desserts.

2. Fennel Seed

Seed of a member of the parsley family. Mildly licorice in flavor. Used in cookies, cakes, bread and rolls.

3. Allspice

Also known as Jamaica pepper, native to the Western Hemisphere. Flavor resembles a blend of cinnamon, cloves and nutmeg. Used ground in cakes, cookies, icings and many desserts. Particularly good with fruit.

4. Nutmeg

Aromatic dried seed of evergreen tree. Very spicy. Available whole or ground. Flavor is best when freshly ground from whole seed. Used in cakes, cookies, pies and pastry.

5. Mace

Bright red skin that covers the nutmeg shell. Flavor similar to nutmeg, but more delicate. Used in cakes, icing and many desserts. May be substituted for nutmeg in recipes.

6. Star Anise

Star-shaped fruit of evergreen tree in the magnolia family. Licorice flavor similar to aniseed and sometimes used as substitute. May be used in fruit cake.

7. Aniseed

Seed of a member of the parsley family. Strong licorice flavor. Used crushed or whole in cake, bread, cookies and pies. Good with fruit desserts.

8. Cardamom

Seed of a plant of the ginger family. Strong sweet flavor. Very aromatic. Available whole or ground. Used in coffee cakes and ethnic breads. Excellent with fruit.

9. Stick Cinnamon

Dried inner bark of evergreen tree of the laurel family. Spicy, sweet flavor, highly aromatic. Sold in sticks and ground. Used in almost all kinds of baking and with fruit.

10. Saffron

Dried stigma of the saffron crocus. Considered the most expensive spice in the world. Slightly bitter and used very sparingly for flavor and color. Used to make biscuits and challah bread.

11. Ginger

Root of the ginger plant. Sweet, hot, spicy flavor. Sold whole, ground, in syrup and candied. Used in cakes and cookies and to flavor ice cream and other desserts.

12. Caraway Seed

Seed of biennial plant Carum carvi. Slightly sweet flavor. Used with bread, particularly rye bread, and rolls.

Extracts

Extracts are sold in a wide range of flavors. The most often used extract is vanilla, but other flavors, such as almond or peppermint, can be used very successfully to flavor batters, fillings and icings. When lemon or orange flavor is wanted, fresh juice will provide better flavor than an extract. It should also be noted that the only benefit from the use of a liqueur extract is when flavor is needed in an icing but the alcohol is not wanted. Alcohol in a liqueur will burn off during baking when added to a batter. When substituting a liqueur for an extract, use twice as much liqueur in order to achieve good flavor.

Chocolate—The Most Popular Flavor in the World

All chocolate sold for baking starts out as unsweetened chocolate. The only difference between brands of unsweetened chocolate is the quality of the chocolate. Once additional flavoring is added to the chocolate you will find bitter, extra bittersweet, bittersweet, semisweet and sweet chocolate. The difference between one chocolate and another is related to the amount of cocoa butter or shortening used to make the chocolate as well as the amount of sugar added. Experiment with various brands until you find the chocolate with the most appealing flavor.

Nuts, Dried Fruit & Other Products to Use in Baking

Nuts

Nuts are sold loose, vacuum-packed and in sealed bags. They can be bought in the shell or shelled; whole, halved, sliced, slivered, chopped or ground; roasted or unroasted; with or without salt added. Buying nuts can be very confusing because of these many options. And each of these differences is reflected in the cost of the nuts. Obviously the most inexpensive way to buy nuts is loose and still in the shell, the perfect solution if you have the time to shell and prepare the nuts yourself. However, some nuts are much easier to remove from their shells than others. Although you can shell English walnuts or peanuts fairly quickly, it can take a very long time to shell Brazil nuts. Before you buy nuts, it is important to determine exactly how you are going to use them and how much time you have to prepare them.

Nuts with skin that is difficult to remove should be blanched. Cover the nuts with boiling water and let them stand 3 to 6 minutes. Drain, pat dry and slip off the skin.

Brazil Nuts

Difficult to shell but also difficult to buy shelled. Freeze or blanch before shelling. Estimate 1 pound unshelled to equal about 8 ounces shelled or about 1-1/2 cups whole shelled nuts.

Whole Almonds & Pine Nuts

Almonds can be bought in the shell, but pine nuts are usually sold shelled and blanched, often in small jars.

Walnuts

Persian or English walnuts are easy to shell or can be bought shelled, halved or chopped. Estimate 1 pound unshelled to equal about 6 ounces shelled or about 1-1/2 cups walnut halves.

Pecans & Peanuts

One pound unshelled pecans equals about 1/2 pound shelled or 2 cups pecan halves. One pound unshelled peanuts equals about 3/4 pound shelled or about 2-3/4 cups whole nuts.

Almonds, processed

Sold whole, sliced, slivered, chopped and ground. One pound unshelled equals about 5-1/2 ounces shelled or about 1 cup whole shelled nuts.

Hazelnuts

Hazelnuts, or filberts, are usually sold in the shell. Estimate 1 pound unshelled to equal about 6-1/2 ounces shelled or about 1-1/2 cups shelled nuts.

Pistachio Nuts

Usually sold unshelled in red dyed or natural color shells. If the nuts are not partially open, roast 5 to 10 minutes in a 350F (175C) oven.

Coconut

Coconut can be bough in cans or packages already shredded or flaked, ready to be used fresh or toasted.

Chopped nuts and dried fruit can be added to plain cakes, quick breads and yeast breads. Nuts and dried, candied fruit of all kinds can be used to decorate cakes as well.

Apricots & Prunes

Snip with floured kitchen scissors when small pieces are needed. Buy prunes with or without pits.

Candied Flowers

Rose petals and violets, as well as mint leaves, can be bought in specialty stores and used to decorate special occasion cakes. They are not used in baking.

Candied Fruit

Candied fruit is easiest to find during the holidays. Since it keeps well, buy enough to use throughout the year.

Muscats & Golden Seedless Raisins

Large, dark muscat raisins are often difficult to find. Use golden raisins interchangeably with dark raisins as desired.

Dried Fruit in Baking

When dried fruit is mixed into a cake batter, or added to a tart or pie filling, the fruit will not soften during baking. Therefore most dried fruit should be soaked in a warm liquid before it is added to the batter or filling. Dried fruit can be soaked in water simply to soften it, or it can be soaked in a juice or liqueur that has a flavor appropriate to the flavor of the cake or filling. If the fruit is very hard, it can be simmered gently in liquid for about 10 minutes to soften it further.

Dredge dried fruit lightly in flour before adding it to any kind of batter. This will prevent the fruit from sinking to the bottom.

Many kinds of dried fruit can also be poached in a sweetened liquid and served warm or cold for a light and refreshing dessert.

Dried Figs & Stem Ginger

Many varieties of figs are available. Ginger is sold in many forms—as a spice, a root, dried, preserved or candied.

Banana Chips & Dates

Use as other dried fruit is used. Buy dates with or without pits, plain or sugared.

Angelica & Glacé Cherries

These candied fruits are usually available all year and are used in fruit cakes as well as to decorate cakes and other desserts.

Dark Seedless Raisins & Currants

Dark raisins, unlike golden raisins, have not been treated with sulfur dioxide. Currants are smaller than raisins.

Storage—The Ingredients You Buy & the Food You Bake

Dairy Products

Perishable dairy products—milk, cream, butter, sour cream, yogurt, cheese and eggs—must be bought with care and properly refrigerated. Be sure to check the "sell by" dates on packages and buy only the freshest dairy products possible. Don't leave them in a hot car while you do errands on the way home from the market, and always refrigerate them promptly when you get home. Butter and some kinds of cheese can be kept in the freezer.

Fresh Fruit

Pick over berries carefully and remove any that are overripe, underripe or slightly moldy. Store them in the refrigerator, unwashed, in a single layer and use them promptly. All other fresh fruit, including bananas, should be allowed to ripen at room temperature when necessary and then stored in the refrigerator. Citrus fruit and apples do not have to be used immediately, but other fruit should be used within a few days.

Dried Fruit

Most kinds of dried fruit should be stored in unopened packages in a cool dry place and used within a few months of purchase. Once the packages have been opened, dried fruit should be transferred to tightly covered containers.

Nuts

Nuts will turn stale and rancid if not properly stored. Vacuum-packed nuts can be kept on the shelf. All other nuts should be stored in the refrigerator or, better still, in the freezer.

Flavoring Ingredients—Spices, Extracts and Seeds

Keep flavoring ingredients in tightly covered containers away from light and heat. Use them within a few months of purchase to get the benefit of full flavor.

Chocolate & Cocoa

Both chocolate and cocoa should be stored in a cool place, 60-70F/15-20C is ideal. Keep chocolate well wrapped and keep the container of cocoa firmly closed to keep out humidity.

Leavening Agents

Dry yeast should be kept in a cool dry place and used before the expiration date on the package. Cake yeast must be kept in the refrigerator and used within 2 weeks of purchase.

Baking powder and baking soda should be kept in tightly closed containers in a cool dry place. Since baking powder will not remain effective indefinitely, buy it in small quantities if you don't use it often.

Flour

Place flour in a dry airtight container to keep out moisture and unwelcome bugs. All-purpose flour and cake flour may be stored in a cool dry place or in the refrigerator. All other flour should be refrigerated.

Sugar

Although granulated sugar may be kept in a canister, other kinds of sugar should be kept in airtight containers. If brown sugar hardens, soften it at low power in a microwave oven or with a little water sprinkled over it in a radiant oven at very low temperature.

Success in baking depends not only on the quality of ingredients bought, but also on the quality maintained by proper storage. Even the best and most expensive ingredients will loose their quality, and detract from the success of the finished product, if they are not stored correctly. And since the food you bake cannot always be eaten immediately, it is also important to store finished baked goods with loving care.

Bread and Rolls

Homemade bread and rolls don't have chemical preservatives and therefore won't keep fresh as long as commercially made bread or rolls. Once they have cooled completely, wrap them in foil or plastic wrap and store them in the refrigerator for a few days, or the freezer for as long as 3 to 4 months. Defrost at room temperature and, if desired, warm before serving.

Cookies

There are so many kinds of cookies, it is obvious they cannot all be stored in exactly the same way. However, most cookies will keep fresh if they are cooled completely and then stored in airtight containers. Most of them also freeze well. Freeze cooled cookies unwrapped; place in freezer bags or containers after freezing. Unwrap and thaw at room temperature, or heat briefly in a low oven to restore crispness.

Cakes

Cake layers that have not been filled or frosted can be wrapped in foil or plastic wrap and kept at room temperature for a brief time, in the refrigerator for 2 to 3 days or in the freezer for a few months. Once a cake has been filled and frosted it should be placed in a covered cake keeper. If whipped cream or custard have been used for filling or frosting, store the cake in the refrigerator. Cakes with ice cream filling must be stored in the freezer. Completely perishable cakes, such as cheesecakes, must be refrigerated. Some, but not all, can be frozen. If in doubt, don't freeze.

Pastry

The category of pastry covers everything from pie crust to puff pastry. Although baked choux paste can be stored, unfilled, in airtight containers at room temperature for about 24 hours, most pastry must be refrigerated or frozen. Unbaked pastry can be kept in the refrigerator for 1 or 2 days or in the freezer for 3 to 4 months if well wrapped. Most baked pastry can be stored in the same way, provided it has not been filled. Once filled, the pastry tends to get soggy if kept for too long.

Additional Storage Tips

Don't freeze gelatin dishes, custards or meringues.

Frozen food must be very well wrapped. Double wrapping is recommended to keep out moisture.

Be sure to date and label any food placed in the freezer. You may think you will be able to remember what is stored inside a foil-wrapped package, but after a month or so, you may have more difficulty remembering what you have frozen than you may think.

Convenience Products

Although just about everyone agrees that homemade is best, there are an ever increasing number of convenience products on the market that are very good. Some of them, such as filo dough and puff pastry, are particularly helpful products that make it possible for the home baker to create elegant desserts, even when time is limited. Other products, like frozen or refrigerated pie crusts, cake mixes and frozen bread dough, provide wonderful solutions for emergency situations or simply help fulfill the desire to bake something in a hurry. When the need arises, take advantage of the many products available in your local supermarket. After baking, you can combine the pastries or cakes with fresh fruit or whipped cream, or make a quick chocolate frosting, and serve something almost as good as if you had made it completely from scratch.

Puff Pastry

Keep frozen puff pastry in your freezer, ready to use at any time. Check the date on the package before you buy it, thaw it in the refrigerator or at room temperature and follow the directions on the package.

Filo Dough

Very few bakers have either the time or skill to make filo dough. Keep some in your freezer if you like strudel or baklava. Follow the instructions on page 190 for proper use.

Pie Crusts (Frozen and Refrigerated)

Frozen pie crusts in foil pie plates are familiar to just about everyone and make it possible to put a pie together in a hurry. A newer, ready-made pie crust can be found in the dairy case. The package contains two pieces of flat pastry, folded in quarters. One piece can be fitted into your own pie plate, the second piece of pastry dough can be used to make a top crust or a second pie. Crumb crusts for pies can be found in foil pans on grocery shelves.

Tart Shells

Look for frozen pastry tart shells in the freezer case and graham cracker crumb tart shells on grocery shelves.

Frozen Bread/ Pizza Dough

Use frozen bread dough to make bread, rolls, pizza, coffee cake and sweet yeast dough recipes.

Refrigerator Dough

The dairy case in your supermarket is filled with tubes of dough for biscuits, crescents, dinner rolls, bread sticks, small loaves of bread and other items that can be baked quickly and will have a fresh-baked flavor. Be sure to check the expiration date on the package before you buy. Nearby you will find long rolls of cookie dough, ready to slice and bake in a flash.

Sponge Bases

Packaged sponge bases, large and small, as well as individual dessert sponge shells can be found in the packaged cake section of many stores. You'll also find them in the vegetable section when fresh berries are in season. Fill them with fresh fruit and top them with sweetened whipped cream for a really speedy dessert you can serve to company.

Packaged Mixes

There are mixes available for cakes of all kinds, brownies, quick breads, yeast breads, popovers, muffins, pancakes and waffles. Some mixes are better than others. But just about all of them are a blessing in an emergency. You can use them in many ways and make them unique by adding your own fillings and frostings or other ingredients such as spices, nuts or dried fruit.

Pie Fillings

Some pie fillings, such as pumpkin pie mix, are really excellent. Others range from very good to adequate. You can use them when fresh berries are not in season or when you simply don't have the necessary ingredients on hand to make your own pie filling.

Jams and Jellies

Although you may never have thought of jam or jelly as convenience foods for baking, they can be of tremendous help to a busy baker. Jam can be used to make a delicious cake filling and jelly can be heated until it melts and then used to make a perfect glaze.

Nut Toppings

Keep a jar or can of nut topping on hand to use for a quick finish on plain cakes and coffee cakes.

Baking for Every
Occasion

To Begin the Day

Professional bakers may begin their
day in the wee hours of the
morning, but for the rest of us who
prefer to sleep longer, the solution to
a special breakfast or brunch
is baking that can be done ahead of
time. Home-baked treats
for breakfast are a satisfying
and nutritious way to start the day.

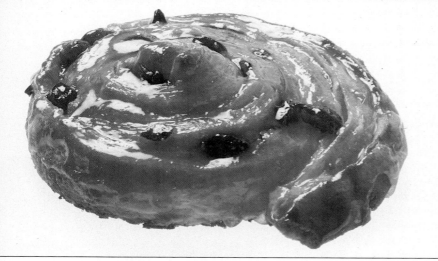

Breakfast & Brunch

Serve homemade rolls or toast from
homemade bread for a weekday breakfast.
Try some of the other
breakfast treats on weekends or when
serving brunch to company.

Croissants

(Illustrated opposite
page—top)
Recipe appears on
page 181. See page 182
for filling variations.
Serve warm with
butter, honey or jam.

Butter Cake

(Illustrated opposite
page—2nd from top)
Recipe appears on
page 87. Serve plain or
with fresh or stewed
fruit.

Churros

(Illustrated opposite
page—3rd from top)
Recipe appears on
page 200. Serve warm
dredged in sugar and
cinnamon.

Poppy Seed Rolls

(Illustrated opposite
page—bottom)
Recipe appears on
page 148. Sprinkle
with poppy seed and
serve warm with
butter, honey or jam.

Snail Buns

(Illustrated this
page—top)
Recipe appears on
page 119. Brush with
Apricot Glaze, page
244 for an extra
finishing touch.

Toasted White Bread

(Illustrated this
page—2nd from top)
Recipe for White Bread
appears on page 144.
See toast variations.
Serve with scrambled
eggs.

Danish Pastry

(Illustrated this
page—3rd from top)
Recipe appears on
page 185. Top
cheese-filled Danish
with cherries.

Panettone

(Illustrated this
page—bottom)
Recipe appears on
page 155. Serve
toasted, with lots of
butter, on Christmas
morning.

Snacks & Other Special Treats

A quick bite for lunch or supper, an appetizer before dinner, or just a snack with coffee—good ideas for light eating.

Sausage Rolls

(Illustrated this page—top)
Wrap frankfurter or other cooked sausages in Puff Pastry, see page 165. Brush with egg wash and sprinkle with cheese, if desired, before baking.

Hawaiian Toast

(Illustrated this page—center)
Recipe appears on page 144. See bread recipe on same page. Serve hot.

Raisin Beignets

(Illustrated this page—bottom)
Recipe appears on page 200. Dust Beignets with powdered sugar just before serving.

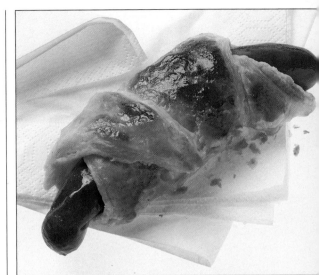

Canapes

(Illustrated this page—top left)
Cut out small rounds of White Bread (see page 144) and toast them in hot oven. Mash hard-cooked egg yolks and mayonnaise and pipe onto toast rounds. Garnish with capers, red caviar, fresh herbs and pimiento strips.

Puff Pastry Cases

(Illustrated this page—center left)
Puff Pastry appears on page 165. Filling suggestions appear on page 170. Serve warm.

Zuppa Pavese

(Illustrated this page—bottom left)
Recipe appears on page 144. Serve piping hot.

Sandwich

(Illustrated this page—top right)
Bread recipe appears on page 144. Filling suggestions appear on pages 160 - 161.

Currant Bread Pudding

(Illustrated this page—center right)
Recipe appears on page 144.

Individual Tarts

(Illustrated this page—bottom right)
Pastry recipe for Tarts appears on page 108. Fill Tarts with egg custard and sprinkle with cheese and fresh herbs before baking.

Tantalizing Desserts . . .

Babas au Raisins

Recipe appears on page 131. Serve with
rhubarb sauce, dust with powdered
sugar and decorate with sprigs of lemon
balm or fresh mint.

Strawberry Mousse Cake

Recipe appears on page 212. Decorate with
piped whipped cream, finely ground
pistachio nuts and fresh strawberries.

Pineapple Tart Tatin

Prepare recipe for Tart Tatin, page 111.
Substitute thick slices of
fresh pineapple for apples. Serve warm.

Puff Pastry Tarts

Prepare tart shells as directed on page
174 for Apple Tarts. Bake blind
(page 24). Top with raspberries and
blackberries. Brush fruit with Red Currant
Glaze, page 244, and serve with
raspberry sauce.

Meringue Kisses with Raspberry Buttercream

Prepare recipe for Hazelnut Kisses on
page 218, omitting ground
hazelnuts. Sandwich Kisses together with
Raspberry Buttercream, page 229.

Filled Almond Cups

Recipe appears on page 220. Fill cups
with vanilla ice cream, fresh
raspberries and toasted sliced almonds.
Sprinkle with crystal sugar.

Miniature Savarins with Red Currants

Prepare recipe, page 130, using
individual savarin molds. Fill
Savarins with fresh red currants and serve
with sweetened whipped cream.

Apple Charlotte

Recipe appears on page 144. Serve
well chilled.

Open Sandwich

(Illustrated this page—top left)
Use slices of a sourdough Multi-Grain Bread, from the recipe on pages 158-159. For topping suggestions, see page 160.

Pizza

(Illustrated this page—center left)
Homemade pizza, sauce and topping suggestions appear on pages 134-135.

Filled Puff Pastry Cases

(Illustrated this page—bottom left)
Recipe for Puff Pastry appears on page 165. Filling suggestions appear on page 170-171.

Deep-Dish Pizza

(Illustrated center top)
Recipe appears on page 137. Substitute quiche filling for variety.

Pita Bread

(Illustrated center)
Recipe appears on page 155. Pita pockets can be filled in almost any way desired.

Savory Baking . . .

Sauceless Pizza

(Illustrated center
bottom)
Recipes appear on
pages 138-139.

Garlic Bread

(Illustrated this
page—top right)
Prepare bread recipe,
page 144, and shape
dough into Baguette,
page 147. Cut bread in
diagonal slices, spread
with softened butter
and top with thin
slices of garlic and
freshly chopped
parsley. Place in hot
oven until crisp.

Surprise Loaf

(Illustrated this
page—center right)
Wrap cooked, smoked
meat in yeast dough,
page 144, and bake.

Pot Pie

(Illustrated this
page—bottom right)
Prepare any beef,
chicken or turkey pot
pie recipe. Top with
Shortcrust Pastry, page
101 or Puff Pastry,
page 165.

. . . for Casual Eating

Light Fruit Cake

(Illustrated this page—top left) Prepare recipe, page 95 and add 1/2 cup chopped pistachio nuts. Increase candied cherries to 1 cup.

Raisin Cupcakes

(Illustrated this page—top right) Prepare recipe for Raisin Cake, page 90, and bake in muffin pans lined with paper cupcake liners. Top with diced candied lemon or orange peel before baking.

Oatmeal & Date Cookies

(Illustrated this page—bottom left) Prepare recipe for Oatmeal Raisin Cookies, page 104, and substitute 1 cup snipped dates for raisins.

Marble Cake

(Illustrated this page—bottom right) Prepare recipe, page 90, and bake in 11"x 4" loaf pan.

A Medley of Treats . . .

. . . to Serve at Any Time

Palmiers
(Illustrated this page—top left) Double recipe on page 168. Roll out pastry to 24"x 20" rectangle and proceed as directed.

Filled Almond Horns
(Illustrated this page—top right) Prepare recipe, page 220, and fill horns with sweetened whipped cream. Decorate with shaved or grated chocolate. Serve immediately.

Fancy Cookies
(Illustrated this page—bottom left) Prepare Spritz Cookies, page 106. Pipe into desired shapes. See pages 250-251 and 254-255 for decorating ideas.

Almond Toast
(Illustrated this page—bottom right) Prepare recipe, page 144, and sprinkle with sugar before baking. Cut into slices, spread with butter and sprinkle with almonds and sugar. Broil until browned and bubbly. Serve warm.

From Plain to Fancy

Entertaining need not automatically mean dinner guests. Whether it's an evening of company for dessert and coffee, or the appropriate food to serve after a hectic meeting, these desserts will make the occasion festive.

Frankfurt Ring

(Illustrated opposite page—top)
Recipe appears on page 87. Fill and frost with Rich Buttercream, page 226-227.

Lemon Cake

(Illustrated this page—top)
Prepare recipe for Butter Cake, page 87. Omit vanilla extract and add 1 to 2 teaspoons grated lemon peel.

Strawberry-Orange Sponge Cake

(Illustrated opposite page—center left)
Fill ready-made sponge shell with fresh strawberries. Arrange peeled orange slices around edge. Brush fruit with Apricot or Red Currant Glaze, page 244. Serve with whipped cream.

Pastry Cream Slice

(Illustrated opposite page—center right)
Recipe appears on page 175. Dust with powdered sugar.

Sunken Apple Cake

(Illustrated this page—center left)
Prepare Pear Cake, page 92. Substitute peeled, quartered apples for pears. Omit pistachio nuts and sprinkle raisins and crystal sugar over apples.

Cherry-Buttercream Slice

(Illustrated this page—center right)
Prepare Swiss Roll, page 82. Cut in half lengthwise. Fill and frost with Quick Cherry Buttercream, page 236. Decorate with red candied cherries.

Almond Meltaway

(Illustrated opposite page—bottom left)
Recipe appears on page 119. Split cake and fill with Vanilla Cream, see variation.

Apricot Mousse Cake

(Illustrated opposite page—bottom right)
Prepare Frozen Mousse Cake, page 211. Arrange 1 (16-oz.) can drained apricot halves on bottom layer of cake.

Red Currant Refrigerator Cheesecake

(Illustrated this page—bottom left)
Prepare Berry-Topped Refrigerator Cheesecake (page 222). Omit berries and decorate cake with Red Currant Glaze, page 244 and fresh red currants.

Snail Buns

(Illustrated this page—bottom right)
Prepare recipe, page 119, in two 8-inch-round cake pans. Brush with Apricot Glaze, page 244, while still warm.

Chocolate Almond Loaf

(Illustrated this page—top left) Prepare Butter Cake, page 87, decreasing flour to 2 cups. Add 1/4 cup cocoa powder and 1/2 cup finely ground blanched almonds. Bake in fluted loaf pan. Cover with Dark Chocolate Glaze, page 88, and stud cake with slivered almonds.

Mini St. Honoré

(Illustrated this page—bottom left) Prepare 1/2 recipe Gâteau St. Honoré, page 202. Roll out pastry to 7-inch circle and use 8 small choux balls. Decorate with whipped cream, candied orange peel and red candied cherry.

Mocha Cream Gâteau

(Illustrated center top) Prepare Chocolate Sponge, page 74, and split cake into 3 layers. Fill and frost with Coffee Buttercream, page 229. Decorate with swirls of buttercream and finely grated chocolate.

Cakes for Special Occasions

Chocolate & Orange Gâteau

(Illustrated center bottom)
Prepare Orange Sponge, page 74, and split cake into 2 layers. Fill and frost with Chocolate Buttercream, page 229. Decorate with piped swirls of Chocolate Buttercream, red candied cherries and finely shredded orange peel.

Chocolate Log

(Illustrated this page—top right)
Prepare Swiss Roll, page 82. Decrease flour to 3/4 cup and add 1/4 cup cocoa powder. Spread Chocolate Buttercream, page 229, over cake and roll up, jelly-roll style. Frost with thin layer of Chocolate Buttercream and decorate with chocolate curls, page 246.

Valentine Heart

(Illustrated this page—bottom right)
Prepare Butter Cake, page 87, and bake in deep heart-shaped pan. Add a few drops of red food coloring to the Raspberry Buttercream, page 229. Use to fill and frost cake.

Birthdays, weddings, anniversaries, graduations and other special celebrations provide wonderful opportunities to serve elegant cakes. Take the time to make sure they look as good as they taste.

The Wedding Cake

If you are ambitious enough to make a wedding cake, it is important to plan well in advance allowing time to make the cake, make the marzipan decorations and perfect the art of piping.

The Cake

The base of a wedding cake must be very firm in order to support the weight of the tiers above it. Since a wedding cake is not likely to be made at the last moment, choose the type of cake that will keep well for several days or longer. A fruit cake is the best choice, but a butter cake can be used too. If you want to make a traditional English wedding cake, make the Rich Holiday Fruit Cake, page 95. Reduce the ingredients by 1/3 and bake one 9-inch cake and one 6-inch cake. Wrap the cakes in brandy or rum-soaked cheesecloth and store them in a cool, dark place for at least 2 weeks.

Assembling, Icing and Decorating the Cake

The cake should be assembled and decorated the day before the wedding. Trim the tops of the layers absolutely flat. Place the large cake on a decorative cardboard disc, 1 inch larger than the circumference of the cake. Brush the top of the cake with Apricot Glaze, page 244, and place the smaller cake on top.

To make icing and decorating as easy as possible, place the tiered cake on a rotating cake stand.

Prepare Pink Marzipan Roses and Green Marzipan Leaves, page 243, and set them aside to dry.

Prepare Royal Icing, page 244, and keep the bowl covered with a damp towel to prevent the icing from drying out. Cover the entire cake with a thin layer of icing and let the cake stand several hours or until the icing is firm and dry. Repeat the process 2 or 3 times. Spoon some icing into a pastry bag fitted with a medium size open-star tip and pipe the icing in decorative scrolls around the edge of the cake and on the side of each layer. When the icing is completely dry, decorate the cake with Marzipan Roses, Leaves and silver dragées. Use a dab of icing to attach the decorations.

Holiday Treats

Holidays, particularly Christmas, mean company and festive eating. It also means too many things to do, and never enough time. Most of these recipes can be baked in advance and stored in airtight containers, ready to serve whenever you like.

Fruit Cake

(Illustrated top) Prepare recipe for Light Fruit Cake, page 95, and bake in 9″ x 5″ or 11″ x 4″ loaf pan. Wrap in plastic wrap and overwrap with foil. Store in airtight container.

Lebkuchen

(Illustrated center) Prepare recipe, page 189, and cut into bars. Store in airtight containers with a piece of apple to allow cookies to soften.

Spice Swirls

(Illustrated bottom) Recipe appears on page 189. Brush with Apricot Glaze, page 244.

Speculaas

(Illustrated opposite—top) Prepare recipe, page 104, and bake cookies in wooden molds.

Sugared Fruit Hearts

(Illustrated opposite—center left) Prepare Fruited Braid, page 133. Divide dough into 4 equal-size pieces. Shape into four 16-inch ropes. Twist 2 ropes together, and place on greased baking sheet. Pinch ends together and shape into heart. Repeat with remaining 2 ropes. Brush with egg wash and sprinkle with crystal sugar. Bake as directed.

Dundee Cake

(Illustrated center right)
Recipe appears on page 95. Wrap in plastic wrap and overwrap in foil. Store in airtight container. Dust with cocoa powder and powdered sugar before serving.

Honey Cake

(Illustrated bottom left)
Prepare recipe, page 189, and cut into bars. Store in airtight containers.

Spice Cake

(Illustrated bottom right)
Prepare Light Fruit Cake, page 95, but omit fruit. Substitute dark brown sugar for granulated sugar, increase cinnamon to 2 teaspoons and add 1/4 teaspoon ground cloves. Bake in greased 8'' x 4'' loaf pan. Cool and brush with Apricot Glaze, page 244, and sprinkle with sliced almonds. Serve with whipped cream, if desired.

Christmas Cookies

Colorful Christmas cookies make wonderful
gifts and delightful ornaments,
to say nothing of festive eating. Don't forget
to make a hole in the top of the cookies
with a plastic straw before baking if you want
to hang them on a tree.

Use the recipe for Shortcrust Cookies, page 101, or Gingerbread Cookies, page 189, to make these beautiful Christmas cookies. Roll out dough and cut into desired shapes. If you use metal cookie cutters be sure to dip cutters in flour before cutting shapes. You can also use patterns made from stiff cardboard. Trace around a cardboard pattern with a pastry wheel or the tip of a sharp knife.

Decorating cookies is lots of fun, but it can be very time consuming. Use Glacé Icing or Royal Icing, page 244. Tint small amounts of icing in a variety of colors with food coloring. Decorate iced cookies with small colorful candies (see pages 254-255 for decorating ideas). Allow icing to set completely before storing cookies in airtight containers.

Holiday & Party Ideas . . .

1. Raspberry Charlotte for Easter Dessert

Prepare recipe, page 83, and refrigerate
Charlotte until ready to serve.
Invert onto serving plate, top with fresh
raspberries and decorate with sprigs
of lemon balm.

2. Fanciful Animal Bread for Children's Party

Prepare Basic Yeast Dough, page 117.
Divide dough into several pieces
and shape into balls and ropes to create
desired shape. Brush with beaten
egg wash. Use raisins or currants for eyes.

3. Filled Easter Egg

Use fancy pottery, porcelain or
cardboard egg as dish. Fill with
Petits Fours, page 266-267 and assorted
candies, pages 262-263.

4. Orange Cream Cake

Prepare Orange Sponge Cake, page 74,
and bake in 10-inch-square pan. Split
cake into 2 layers and fill with orange
marmalade. Frost cake with sweetened whipped
cream and decorate with julienned
strips of orange peel.

. . . for Young & Old

5. Quick Fruit Tarts
Fill homemade or ready-made individual sponge shells with assorted fresh fruit. Brush fruit with Apricot Glaze, page 244.

6. Strawberry Mousse Gâteau
Prepare Shortcrust Pastry, page 101, and divide pastry into 5 equal-size pieces. Roll out to five 8-inch circles and bake. Sandwich pastry rounds with Strawberry Mousse, page 234. Dust with powdered sugar and decorate with strawberries.

7. Easter Lamb
Prepare Butter Cake, page 87, and bake in lamb mold. Dust with powdered sugar before serving.

8. White Chocolate Gâteau
Prepare Genoise Sponge, page 71, and split cake into 2 layers. Fill and frost with Quick Buttercream, page 236. Decorate with large leaves of white chocolate, page 247. Pipe melted chocolate over top of cake in zigzag lines.

Special Gifts

The gifts we make for those we love are always
the most special gifts. Use paper
bonbon cases and a pretty box to package your gift.

1. Truffles

Recipe appears on page 258. Shape truffle mixture into small rough logs. Dip in melted chocolate and roll in Cocoa Powder Coating, page 262.

2. Cognac Truffles

Recipe appears on page 258. Flavor truffle mixture with cognac and dip Truffles in White Chocolate & Sugar Coating, page 262.

3. Petits Fours

Recipe appears on page 266. See page 267 for frosting and decorating ideas.

4. Pear Truffles

Recipe appears on page 264. Dip Truffles in melted chocolate and roll in Powdered Sugar Coating, page 262.

5. Chocolate Almond Bars

Prepare Cherry Almond Bars, page 105, omitting red candied cherries. Dip bottom of bars in melted chocolate and let stand until set.

6. Caramelized Profiteroles

See page 207 for Profiteroles in Croquembouche. Dip tops in Caramel Syrup (pages 204-205).

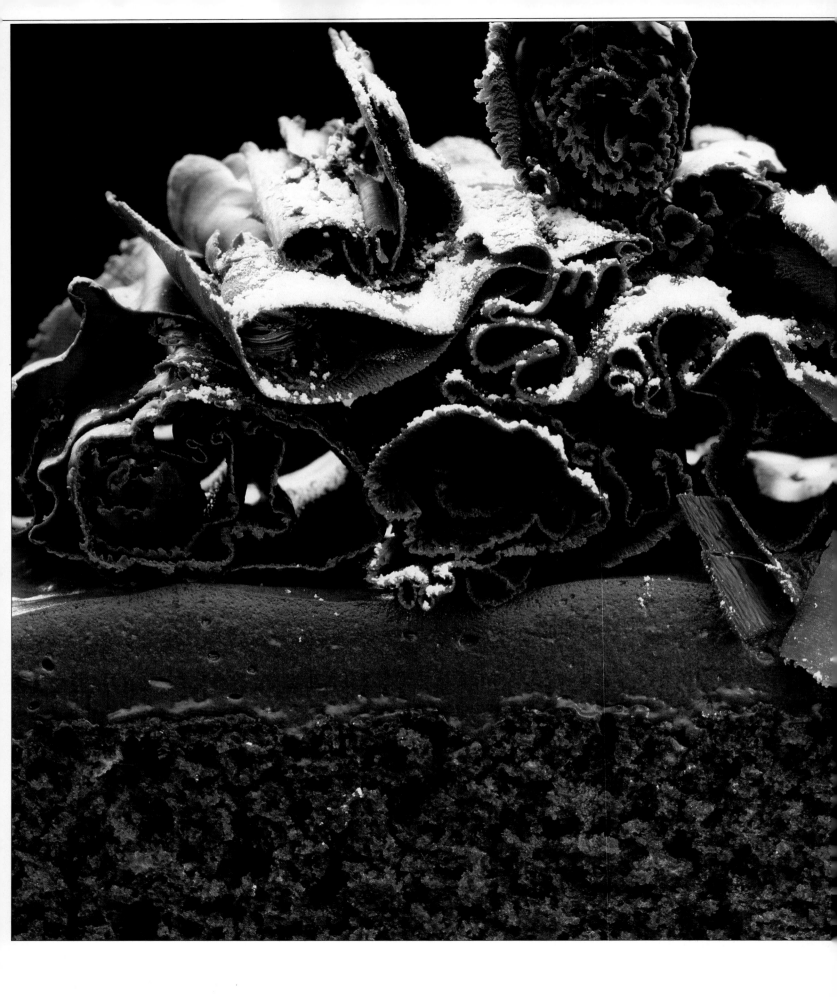

Sponge
Cakes—Light, Airy
& Delicious

The Cake Mixture That Rises on Air

When the ingredients used to prepare a cake include baking powder or baking soda to make the cake rise, we refer to the combined ingredients as "batter." When yeast is used instead, the combined ingredients are called "dough." However, when no chemical rising agent is used, air must be beaten into eggs, the eggs are then "mixed" with the other ingredients, and the combined ingredients are called a "mixture."

Beating Air Into Sponge Mixtures

Sponge cakes, by definition, don't have any chemical leavening agent in the mixture. But all cakes need something to make them rise. The rising or leavening agent in a sponge cake is air that must be beaten into the eggs. Eggs are beaten until they are foamy, which is why sponge cakes are sometimes called "foam" cakes. The air expands in the hot oven, causing the mixture to expand to about three times its original size. Sponge cakes are used to make simple or elegant round cakes, Swiss rolls, petits fours, lady fingers and other fancy small cakes.

Tips for Making a Sponge Mixture

If you beat eggs in the top of a double boiler, or in a bowl over a pan of warm water, they will get fluffy and will bind well with the other ingredients. A mixture made with warm eggs rather than cold eggs, will expand better and be nice and firm. However, it is important to remember the bowl must be warm, but never hot. If the bowl is hot, the eggs will cook and you will have to discard them and start over.

Use superfine sugar rather than granulated sugar in the mixture and beat it with the eggs until it has dissolved completely and volume has tripled. If the sugar is not completely dissolved, the texture of the finished cake will be "gritty."

The best way to add flour to the egg mixture is to place the flour in a sieve and sift it over the mixture before folding. This method will eliminate the danger of lumps.

To add flavoring to a sponge mixture, add 1 teaspoon vanilla or almond extract, or the grated peel of one orange or lemon.

Baking Tips

Grease and flour the cake pan, even if it has a nonstick coating, to be sure the cake will come out of the pan easily. For added assurance, line the bottom of the greased and floured pan with parchment paper or waxed paper.

Be sure to preheat the oven to 350F (175C) and place the sponge mixture in the preheated oven immediately. If a sponge mixture is allowed to stand before being placed in the oven, air will escape and the volume will decrease.

To determine whether or not a sponge cake is fully baked, insert a cake tester or wooden pick into the center of the cake. If it comes out clean, the cake is done. Additional indications that the cake is done include a golden brown top and slight shrinkage away from the side of the pan.

When the cake is baked, remove it from the pan immediately and cool it completely on a wire rack. Peel off parchment paper while cake is still warm.

3 Tblsp.
5 oz semi-sweet choc

Classic Genoise Sponge

Equipment:
10-inch springform pan
Large saucepan and heatproof bowl to fit over pan

Ingredients:
7 tablespoons sweet butter
6 eggs
3/4 cup superfine sugar
1-1/4 cups cake flour
1 teaspoon grated lemon peel or 1 teaspoon vanilla extract (optional)

Oven Temperature:
350 (175C)

Baking Time:
35 minutes

Cooling Time:
1 to 2 hours

Servings:
8 to 10

Storage:
Let cake cool completely. Wrap in aluminum foil and freeze up to three months. Thaw, wrapped, at room temperature.

Preparation

1. Allow eggs to come to room temperature. Measure ingredients.

2. Grease bottom and side of pan. Dust with flour.

3. Melt butter in small saucepan over low heat. Set aside to cool.

4. Break eggs into large heatproof bowl.

5. Add sugar to eggs.

6. Set bowl over pan of barely simmering water and beat eggs and sugar.

7. Beat 3 minutes or until mixture is lemon colored and thickens.

8. Remove bowl from pan. Gradually sift flour over mixture and fold in.

9. Add melted butter and lemon peel, if using. Fold in.

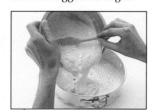
10. Pour batter into prepared pan and smooth top.

11. Place cake in preheated 350F (175C) oven.

12. Bake 35 minutes or until cake springs back when lightly pressed.

13. Run tip of sharp knife around inside edge of pan.

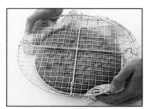
14. Remove side of pan. Place cake rack on top of cake and invert.

15. Remove bottom of pan from cake.

16. Let cake cool completely. Fill and frost if desired.

Turning a Sponge Into a Gâteau

1. Cut cake horizontally in 3 even-size layers.

2. Spread jam evenly over bottom layer. Top with second layer.

3. Arrange half the strawberries on top. Cover with 1/2 of whipped cream.

A Genoise sponge can easily be used as the base for a fruit gâteau. In this case we have turned a plain sponge into a magnificent strawberry gâteau, a close cousin of the strawberry shortcake. If desired, you can substitute almost any kind of fruit for the strawberries. To make a fruit gâteau you will need: fresh or canned fruit, jam that is compatible with the fruit, whipped cream or buttercream and, of course, a sponge base (see page 71). In an emergency, you can even use a ready-made sponge base instead of one that is homemade. Once the sponge has been made, it should take only a very short time to assemble a fruit gâteau. Make the cake ahead of time and place it in the refrigerator until you are ready to serve.

Strawberry Cream Gâteau

10-inch Classic Genoise Sponge, page 71.
4 to 5 tablespoons strawberry jam
1 qt. or 1-3/4 lbs. strawberries, rinsed and hulled
1-1/2 cups whipping cream, sweetened and whipped
1 tablespoon finely chopped pistachios

Cutting Layers

A Genoise sponge is usually baked in a single layer that is then split, rather than baked in separate layers. The important thing to learn about splitting a cake is how to cut layers of equal thickness. Begin by placing the cake on a level surface. The best cutting implement to use is a cake leveler. The thin serrated blade is attached to legs at each end and can be drawn evenly through the cake quickly and easily. If you don't own a cake leveler, place one hand firmly but gently on top of the cake and cut horizontally through the center of the cake with a long, thin serrated knife.

Gâteaux Made Easy

4. Cut a wedge in the third cake layer and place on top of whipped cream.

5. Cover cake with remaining whipped cream.

6. Decorate cake with remaining strawberries and sprinkle with pistachios.

A sponge cake is a plain cake, made elegant by the addition of other ingredients such as fruit and whipped cream.

Filling Tips & Finishing Touches

Filling should be firm enough to prevent it from oozing out when the cake is cut.

To stabilize 1 cup of whipping cream, dissolve 1/2 teaspoon of unflavored gelatin in 2 teaspoons of cold water. Scald 1/4 cup whipping cream and stir in gelatin mixture. Refrigerate until thoroughly chilled. Partially whip 3/4 cup whipping cream. Before it is firm, add chilled gelatin mixture and any flavoring desired. This will make firm whipped cream.

Spread filling evenly between layers. Remove excess filling around the edge of the cake when a cake layer is placed over the filling.

Use a long, thin spatula to spread the filling evenly.

Cover the top and side of the cake with buttercream or whipped cream. Smooth frosting or make a ripple effect with an icing comb. Decorate with nuts, fruit, chopped praline or chocolate curls. If desired, use a pastry bag to pipe rosettes of frosting around the cake.

Genoise Sponge

Sponge cake can be changed to provide a different
texture and flavor just by adding bits of
chocolate, grated nuts, more butter or ground poppy seed
to the mixture. These ingredients add fat to the
mixture and the cake therefore is more moist and rich. It
is also firmer and can therefore be used to make a
multi-layered gâteau without worrying about whether or
not the bottom layer will collapse.

Viennese Sponge to Chocolate Sponge

These are classic sponge variations,
made the same way the basic recipe is made
(see page 71). Most of the additional
ingredients are added before the melted butter
is stirred into the mixture.

Nut Sponge

(Illustrated opposite—
top)
The fat content of the
nuts will add firmness
and a lovely nutty
flavor to the sponge.
Finely grind the nuts
but, if using a food
processor, be careful
not to overprocess.
The result will be nut
paste. Use the basic
recipe (see page 71)
but decrease cake flour
to 1 cup. Add 3/4 cup
finely ground nuts
(walnuts, hazelnuts,
almonds, pecans, etc.).

Viennese Sponge

(Illustrated opposite—
second from top)
This rich sponge has a
delicate taste. Extra
butter gives it a rich,
moist consistency.
Increase sweet butter
in recipe (see page 71)
from 7 tablespoons to
10 tablespoons (1/2 cup
plus 2 tablespoons).
Melt and cool butter
before adding it to the
mixture.

Chocolate Chip Sponge

(Illustrated opposite—
third from top)
Add 4 ounces
semisweet chocolate to
the basic recipe (see
page 71). Coarsely
grate or chop the
chocolate, then stir
together with cake
flour before adding to
the egg-sugar mixture.

Orange Sponge

(Illustrated opposite—
fourth from top)
Add the finely grated
peel of two oranges to
the basic recipe (see
page 71) before the
melted butter is stirred
into the mixture.

Chocolate Sponge

(Illustrated opposite—
bottom)
Use good-quality
semisweet chocolate;
the cake will be rich
and moist. Decrease
the amount of butter
called for in the basic
recipe to 3 tablespoons
(see page 71). Melt and
cool 5 ounces
semisweet chocolate
and add it to the basic
mixture.

Assembling the Cake . . .

The Sponge Cake

Bake the cake at least one day before you plan to cut it into layers. If the cake is cut while it is too fresh, it will crumble when cut. If a dome has formed on the center of the cake during baking, cut it off with a serrated knife when the cake has completely cooled.

Jam for Filling

Spreading jam between the layers of a cake is one of the easiest ways to fill a cake. Place the jam in a small, deep bowl and stir in a small amount of liqueur, if desired. You can add a little fresh fruit to jam to improve its flavor and make it less sweet. Add 1/2 cup lightly crushed berries to 1 cup of berry jam.

Nut Sponge Gâteau

1 recipe 10-inch Nut Sponge, page 74
1 recipe French Buttercream or Rich
  Buttercream, page 226-227
1 cup prepared Praline Nut Topping

Cut cake into 3 layers. Reserve 1 cup buttercream. Fold nut topping into remaining buttercream. Place one layer on plate and spread with buttercream mixture. Add next layer; spread with mixture. Top with third layer and spread buttercream mixture around side of cake. Spread plain buttercream over top of cake; sprinkle with additional nut topping.

Apricot Cream Gâteau

1 (10-inch) Viennese Sponge, page 74
1 lb. fresh apricots, poached, peeled
  and pitted or 1 (30-oz.) can peeled apricot
  halves, drained
2 cups whipping cream, sweetened and whipped
3 tablespoons apricot jam
Finely chopped pistachio nuts for decoration

Cut cake into 2 layers. Cut 1/3 of apricots into small chunks; fold into 1-1/2 cups whipped cream. Place one layer on plate and spread with apricot-cream mixture. Top with next layer. Spread remaining cream around side of cake. Spread apricot jam over top. Decorate with apricots and nuts; chill.

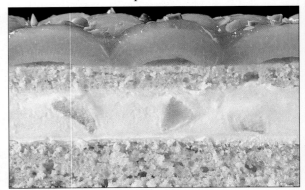

Red Cherry Gâteau

1/4 cup cold water
1 envelope unflavored gelatin
1 (12-oz.) jar red cherry jam or preserves
2 cups whipping cream, sweetened and whipped
1 recipe 10-inch Viennese Sponge, page 74
2 tablespoons rum

Place water in small saucepan, sprinkle gelatin over and let stand 5 minutes. Cook over low heat until gelatin is dissolved. Let cool. Stir gelatin into half the cherry jam until well blended. Fold gelatin mixture into half the whipped cream. Cut cake into 2 layers. Place one layer on plate and spread with cherry-cream mixture. Top with next layer. Spread remaining whipped cream around side of cake. Stir rum into remaining jam. Spread over top of cake. Refrigerate.

Mocha Gâteau

1 recipe 10-inch Genoise Sponge, page 71
1 recipe Quick Mocha Buttercream, page 236
1/2 cup toasted slivered almonds

Cut cake into 3 layers. Fill and frost cake with Mocha Buttercream. Sprinkle toasted almonds over top.

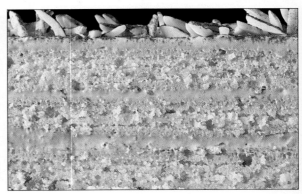

. . . Filling & Frosting

Chocolate Ganache Gâteau

1 recipe 10-inch Chocolate Sponge, page 74
2 tablespoons raspberry-flavored liqueur
3/4 cup black raspberry jam
1 recipe Chocolate Ganache Cream, page 232
Shaved chocolate for decoration

Cut cake into 3 layers. Stir liqueur into
jam. Spread jam between layers.
Spread Ganache Cream around side and over top
of cake. Decorate with
chocolate shavings.

Raspberry Gâteau

1 recipe 10-inch Chocolate Sponge, page 74
1/4 cup raspberry-flavored liqueur
1 recipe French Buttercream or Rich Buttercream,
pages 226-227
1 pint fresh raspberries

Cut cake into 2 layers. Sprinkle layers
with liqueur. Fill and frost cake
with buttercream. Arrange raspberries over
top of cake in concentric circles.

Hints and Tips

See page 72 for
information on how to
cut a cake into several
even layers.

If a buttercream
mixture is not of
spreadable
consistency, allow it to
stand at room
temperature to soften.

If you are filling a
3-layer cake with jam,
use a different kind of
jam to cover each
layer.

It is all but impossible
to move a cake that
has been filled and
frosted. Therefore it is
important to protect
the serving plate on
which a cake has been
placed for filling and
frosting so the edges
of the plate will not be
covered with cake
crumbs, drops of
filling or unsightly
drippings from the
frosting. Before the
bottom layer of the
cake is placed on the
plate, line the outer
edge of the plate with
4 strips of waxed
paper. Position the
strips so only the edge
of the bottom cake
layer will be on the
paper, but the entire
edge of the plate will
be covered. When the
cake has been filled,
frosted and decorated,
pull the strips of paper
out carefully before the
frosting sets.

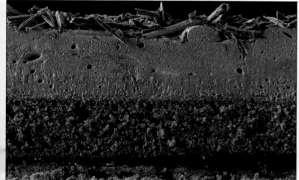

Dobos Torte

1 recipe 10-inch Genoise Sponge, page 71
1/2 cup sugar
1 tablespoon butter
1 recipe Nougat Buttercream, page 228 or
1 recipe Quick Mocha Buttercream, page 236

Cut cake into 6 layers. Set top layer
aside. Heat sugar in small
skillet over moderate heat until golden.
Stir in butter until melted and
mixture is caramel colored. Grease blade
of a thin icing spatula. Spread, hot
caramel over reserved top layer. Score into
serving portions with blade before caramel
is completely set. Let stand until set.
Fill cake layers with 2/3 of buttercream.
Top with caramel-covered layer.
Spread remaining buttercream around
side of cake.

Chocolate Chip-Strawberry Gâteau

1 recipe 10-inch Chocolate Chip Sponge, page 74
2 tablespoons kirsch
1 (12-oz.) jar strawberry jam or preserves
1 cup sifted powdered sugar

Cut cake into 3 layers. Stir kirsch
into strawberry jam. Spread jam between
layers. Dust top of cake with
powdered sugar.

Finishing a Cake

Even after a cake has been filled and frosted, it can be improved by the addition of decorative touches on top of the cake.

Fresh Currants & Fruit Glaze

(Top Slice)
1. Spread a thin layer of whipped cream over top of baked and chilled cheesecake. Scatter fresh red currants or berries on top of whipped cream and refrigerate 1 hour.
2. Prepare Apple Jelly Glaze (see page 252) and cool slightly. Spoon over top of cheesecake and refrigerate until glaze is set.

Whipped Cream & Cake Crumbs

(Second Slice)
1. Spread a thin layer of whipped cream over top of Frozen Mousse Cake (see page 211).
2. Spread sponge cake crumbs on a baking sheet and place in preheated 225F (105C) oven 10 to 15 minutes.
3. Press dried cake crumbs through a coarse sieve and scatter over top of cake. Return cake to freezer until ready to serve.
4. To serve, decorate top of cake with piped swirls of whipped cream and walnut halves.

Cocoa Powder

(Third Slice)
1. Frost cake with Chocolate Buttercream (see page 228) or chocolate-flavored whipped cream.
2. Combine cocoa powder with a little powdered sugar and sift over top of cake.

Grated Chocolate

(Fourth Slice)
1. Scatter a thick layer of grated or shaved chocolate over top of frosted cake and dust chocolate with sifted powdered sugar.

Kiwifruit

(Fifth Slice)
1. Frost cake with whipped cream. Arrange peeled, thinly sliced kiwifruit on top of cake.
2. Prepare Apple Jelly Glaze (see page 252) and cool slightly. Brush glaze over kiwifruit. Refrigerate until glaze is set.
3. To serve, pipe whipped cream in swirls around top edge of cake.

Chocolate Cloud

(Sixth Slice)
1. Frost cake with Chocolate Buttercream (see page 228). Swirl buttercream into peaks with the back of a metal spoon to create cloud effect.
2. Dust buttercream with sweetened cocoa powder.

Strawberries & Whipped Cream

(Seventh Slice)
1. Frost cake with whipped cream. Decorate top edge of cake with piped swirls of whipped cream. Sprinkle nut topping on whipped cream. Arrange whole strawberries on top of cake. Brush melted and slightly cooled red currant jelly over strawberries. Refrigerate until ready to serve.

Lemon Glacé Icing

(Eighth Slice)
1. Cover top and side of cake with a thin layer of marzipan, if desired.
2. Prepare Lemon Glacé Icing (see page 244) and add a few drops of yellow food coloring to icing. Spoon or pour icing over cake and spread evenly. Sprinkle with finely chopped pistachio nuts. Let stand until icing is set.

Chocolate Glaze

(Ninth Slice)
1. Cover cake with a thin layer of marzipan, if desired.
2. Melt 12 to 14 ounces semisweet chocolate. Cool slightly and pour over cake. Spread with icing spatula and let stand until chocolate is set.
3. Decorate top of cake with piped swirls of Mocha Buttercream (see page 236), small chocolate cookies and whole blanched almonds.

Streusel Topping

(Bottom Slice)
1. Frost cake with thin a layer of Rich Buttercream (see page 227).
2. Prepare Streusel Topping (see page 106). Scatter over top and around side of cake, lightly pressing crumbs onto side of cake.
3. Dust with powdered sugar.

A Classic Favorite

This special and famous cake looks fantastic
and is sure to win genuine admiration from all. And yet
it is not really very difficult to make.
You may need a bit of time to make it, but the results
will more than pay off in the long run.

Black Forest Gâteau

10-inch Chocolate
   Sponge (see page 74)

Filling:
2 (16-1/2 oz.) jars dark
   sweet pitted cherries
2-1/2 tablespoons
   cornstarch
1/2 teaspoon ground
   cinnamon
3 tablespoons kirsch
5 to 6 tablespoons
   cherry jam
2 cups whipping
   cream
1/4 cup sifted
   powdered sugar
Grated chocolate to
   decorate

1. Prepare Chocolate Sponge according to directions on pages 71 and 74. When cake is completely cooled, cut in 4 even layers.
2. Drain cherries, reserving 1 cup syrup. Set 10 to 12 cherries aside for decoration. Cut remaining cherries in half. Blend reserved cherry syrup, cornstarch and cinnamon until smooth. Pour mixture into saucepan and place over low heat. Cook, stirring, until mixture thickens and comes to a boil. Add halved cherries and stir well. Cook 2 minutes. Remove from heat and set aside to cool.
3. Add kirsch to jam and stir until blended. Place 1 cake layer on serving plate and spread with jam mixture. Top with second layer. Spread reserved cherry filling over second layer. Top with third layer and press down lightly. Refrigerate 30 minutes.
4. Beat cream until soft peaks form. Add powdered sugar and beat until firm. Spread 1 cup whipped cream over third layer. Top with remaining layer. Spoon 1 cup whipped cream into pastry bag fitted with open-star tip and set aside. Spread remaining whipped cream around side and over top of cake.
5. Pipe reserved whipped cream in swirls around outer edge of cake. Decorate with reserved cherries and grated chocolate. Refrigerate until ready to serve.
Makes 8 to 10 servings.

Cake Made on a Baking Sheet

A sponge cake made on a baking sheet is often used to make a cream-filled Swiss roll or jelly roll. You can also use it to make a variety of different shaped small cakes. Cut the cake in any shapes desired:
1. Diamonds
2. Rectangles
3. Squares
4. Circles
5. Triangles
6. Hearts
Spread jam or flavored whipped cream over the cakes and sandwich them together. You can also sprinkle powdered sugar over the top of the cakes or coat them with an icing made from 2 egg whites combined with 2 cups of powdered sugar (see Decorating Cakes, pages 254-255 and Petit Fours, pages 266-267).

Swiss Roll

6 eggs, separated
3/4 cup superfine sugar
1 teaspoon vanilla extract
1 cup cake flour
1/4 teaspoon salt
3 tablespoons butter, melted

Filling:
1 jar (12-oz.) apricot jam
1-1/2 cups whipping cream, sweetened and whipped
Powdered sugar for dusting

Flat Sponge Cakes

When a sponge cake mixture is spread on a lined baking sheet and baked flat, it can be used to make a Swiss roll or a variety of small cakes. Swiss rolls are spread with a flavored cream filling, carefully rolled and then sliced.

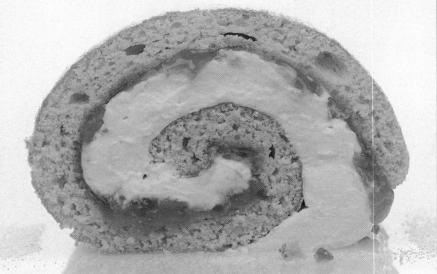

Beat egg yolks in large bowl until foamy. Add superfine sugar and beat until thick and pale yellow in color. Beat in vanilla. Sift flour and salt over egg yolk mixture and fold in thoroughly. Fold in melted butter. Beat egg whites in separate bowl until stiff peaks form. Fold beaten egg whites into egg yolk mixture.

(See step-by-step photographs from left to right)

1. Lightly grease 15″ x 10″ jelly-roll pan. Line pan with parchment or waxed paper. Grease paper.
2. Spread cake mixture as evenly as possible in prepared pan with long, thin spatula.
3. Place in preheated 350F (175C) oven and bake 12 to 15 minutes or until top springs back when lightly pressed.
4. Sprinkle powdered sugar over dish towel. Invert cake onto towel. Remove pan.
5. Lightly brush paper all over with cold water to prevent paper from sticking to cake.
6. Gently peel paper off of cake. Trim any crusty edges.
7. While cake is still warm, lift end of towel so cake starts to roll up on its own. Continue to lift towel to roll remainder of cake.
8. Unroll cake carefully and spread with jam. Spread whipped cream over jam.
9. Carefully roll filled cake and place, seam side down, on serving plate. Dust with powdered sugar and slice. Makes about 8 servings.

Lady Fingers

5 eggs, separated
3/4 cup superfine
  sugar
1-1/4 cups sifted cake
  flour
1 teaspoon vanilla
  extract
Powdered sugar

(See step by step photos from left to right)
1. Place egg yolks in medium bowl. Add 1/2 cup superfine sugar and beat with mixer.
2. Continue beating until thick and pale yellow in color, 6 to 8 minutes.
3. Beat egg whites in separate bowl until soft peaks form.
4. Add remaining 1/4 cup superfine sugar and continue beating until stiff peaks form.
5. Stir 1/3 of beaten egg whites, flour and vanilla into egg yolk mixture until blended.
6. Fold in remaining beaten egg whites.
7. Spoon mixture into pastry bag fitted with 1/2-inch-plain tip.
8. Pipe mixture onto greased baking sheets, making each finger about 3-1/2 inches long. Bake in preheated 400F (205C) oven 6 to 8 minutes or until golden.
9. Sprinkle with powdered sugar and remove to wire racks; cool. Makes about 4 dozen.

Ideas for Using Lady Fingers

Use lady fingers to make trifle. Spread with flavored whipped cream or jam and sandwich 2 lady fingers together. Use to line a mold for a charlotte or other refrigerated dessert.

Lady Fingers

Lady fingers are delicious served plain, sprinkled with powdered sugar, served with ice cream, or served with fruit and coffee. You can also use them as part of a special dessert.

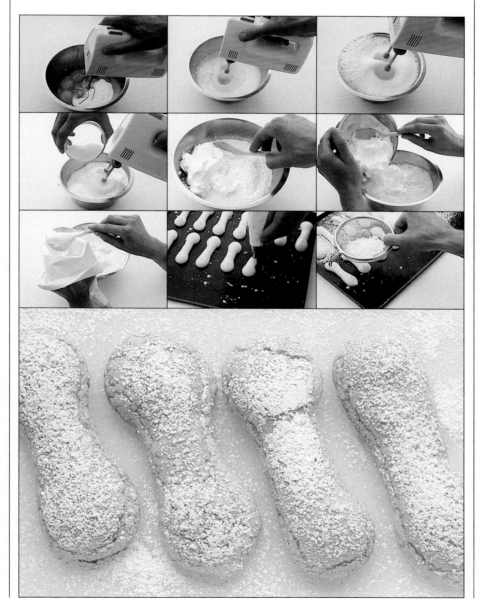

Raspberry Charlotte

1/2 cup granulated
  sugar
1 envelope unflavored
  gelatin
1 cup milk
2 cups whipping
  cream
4 egg yolks, beaten
2 teaspoons vanilla
  extract
12 to 15 Lady Fingers
  (see Column 1)
1/2 pint raspberries
Powdered sugar

1. Stir granulated sugar, gelatin, milk and 1 cup cream in top of double boiler.
2. Place over pan of simmering water and cook, stirring constantly, until mixture coats back of wooden spoon.
3. Stir 4 tablespoons hot milk mixture into beaten egg yolks. Add to double boiler and cook, stirring, until mixture thickens.
4. Pour into large bowl and stir in vanilla. Cover surface of custard with waxed paper. Refrigerate until mixture mounds when dropped from spoon.
5. Whip remaining 1 cup cream until firm. Fold into custard.
6. Butter a 6-cup charlotte mold. Line bottom with circle of waxed paper. Arrange Lady Fingers upright around inside edge and trim to fit.
7. Spoon half of custard into mold. Arrange half of raspberries over custard. Top with remaining custard. Cover with waxed paper and chill 3 hours or until set.
8. Unmold onto plate. Peel off paper and decorate with raspberries and powdered sugar. Makes about 4 servings.

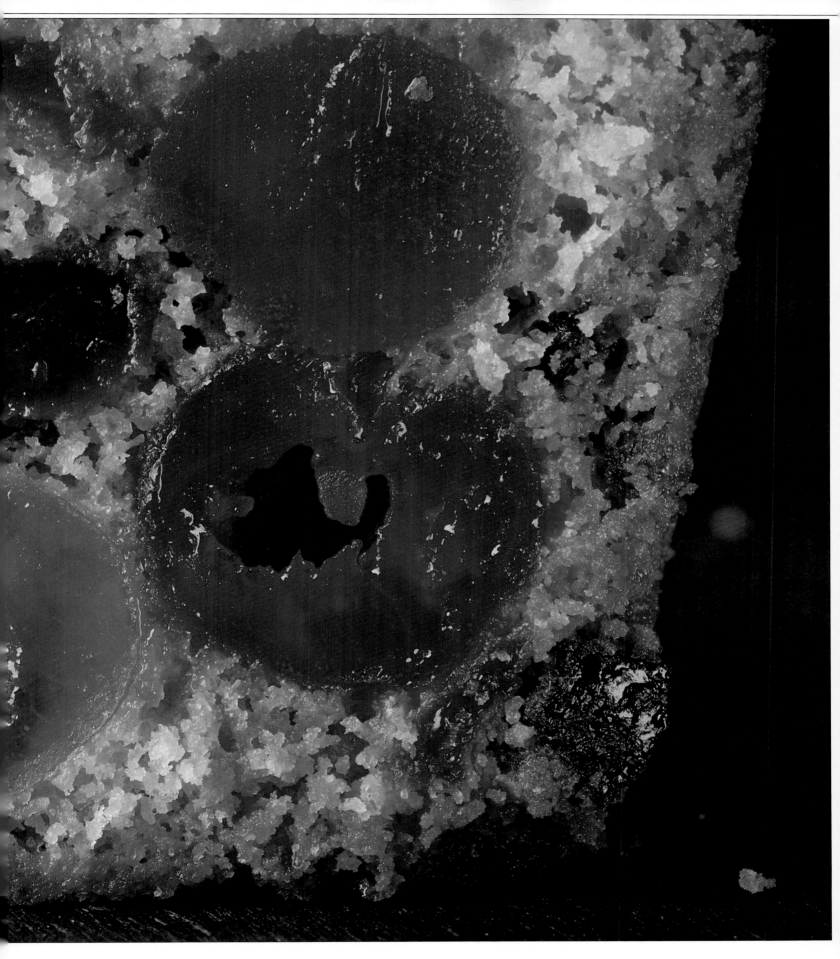

Butter Cakes—Plain & Fancy

Butter Cake — Another Cake That Needs Lots of Beating

Bring all ingredients, particularly eggs, to room temperature. If you are in a hurry, place the eggs in warm water briefly, and cut the butter into cubes and place in a warm spot near the stove or oven.

Beat egg whites in a clean bowl until stiff peaks form. Don't beat the egg whites until you are ready to use them. They will lose volume if they are allowed to stand. Remember, it is the air that is beaten into the egg whites that will make the cake rise.

To make a cake with a fine grain, beat butter and sugar first, then add egg yolks. Add flour and beat lightly. Don't overbeat.

If the batter is too thick to stir, add 2 to 3 tablespoons milk and stir in until well blended.

Tips on Baking

Grease and flour the cake pan, even if it has a non-stick coating. Line the bottom of the pan with parchment paper or waxed paper for added protection against the possibility of the cake sticking to the bottom of the pan.

Preheat the oven to 350F (175C). Place the cake in the center of a preheated oven.

To determine whether or not the cake is done, insert a cake tester or wooden pick into the center of the cake. If the cake is done, it will come out clean.

Cool cake in pan on wire rack 10 minutes. Invert from pan and cool completely on wire rack.

Butter cakes are similar to classic Genoise sponge cakes. Air is used as the leavening agent, but the air is beaten into egg whites instead of whole eggs. The batter contains an increased amount of butter and the butter is not melted, it is brought to room temperature and creamed with the sugar.

Old-fashioned traditional recipes for pound cake were based on weight: 1 pound (8 large) eggs, 1 pound butter, 1 pound sugar and 1 pound flour. The only thing that had to be added to these ingredients was flavoring. Cakes with these proportions are rarely made today because of their unusually high cholesterol content.

Butter Cake

Equipment:
11" x 4" loaf pan

Ingredients:
1 cup butter, room
  temperature
1-1/2 cups sugar
5 eggs
1 teaspoon vanilla
  extract
2-1/4 cups sifted
  all-purpose flour
1/2 teaspoon salt

Oven Temperature:
350F (175C)

Baking Time:
50 to 60 minutes

Cooling Time:
About 1 hour

Servings:
16 to 18

Madeira Cake

A fine-grained cake
that almost melts in
the mouth. It is made
with a mixture of
cornstarch and flour
that gives the cake
something of the
consistency (but not
grittiness) of sand. To
make, replace about
1/3 of the flour in
recipe above with
cornstarch.

Frankfurt Ring

This is Madeira Cake
baked in an 11-cup
ring mold. It is cut into
3 layers and the layers
are sandwiched
together with
buttercream (pages
226-229) and decorated
with nut topping,
swirls of whipped
cream and maraschino
cherries.

Preparation

1. Assemble all ingredients and bring to room temperature.

2. Generously grease 11" x 4" loaf pan.

3. Dust inside of pan with flour. Tap out excess flour.

4. Place softened butter in large mixing bowl.

5. Beat butter with electric mixer until very fluffy.

6. Add sugar and beat until well creamed, 6 to 8 minutes.

7. Separate eggs.

8. Add egg yolks to butter mixture.

9. Beat mixture until thoroughly blended. Beat in vanilla.

10. Sift flour and salt over butter mixture.

11. Beat in flour at low speed until incorporated.

12. Beat egg whites in separate bowl until stiff peaks form.

13. Stir 1/3 of beaten egg whites into butter mixture to lighten.

14. Gently fold in remaining beaten egg whites.

15. Spoon mixture into prepared pan and smooth top.

16. Bake in preheated 350F (175C) oven.

17. Test cake for doneness with wooden pick.

18. Return cake to oven if not completely baked.

19. Cool in pan on wire rack 10 minutes. Remove from pan.

20. Cool completely on wire rack.

Decorative Ways to Dress Up a Bundt Cake

Although the finished cake will be a lovely deep golden brown, you can decorate it in many different ways to make it even more tempting. The simplest way to dress it up is to dust it with powdered sugar. A coating of melted chocolate, icing or jam will help keep the cake moist so it will stay fresh longer. Here are a few ideas you might like to try.

1. Dark Chocolate Glaze

You will need about 8 to 10 ounces semisweet chocolate to cover a cake baked in a 12-cup Bundt pan (page 90). Coarsely chop chocolate and set 1/3 of chopped chocolate aside. Place remaining 2/3 of chopped chocolate in top of double boiler (or small bowl) set over a pan of barely simmering water. Cook over low heat, stirring, until chocolate is melted and smooth. Remove top of double boiler from heat. Add remaining 1/3 of chopped chocolate and stir until smooth. Melted chocolate should be just lukewarm. For a smooth finish, pour or spoon melted chocolate over cake. Place cake on wire rack set over a jelly-roll pan to catch dripping chocolate. Scrape up excess chocolate and, if necessary, remelt until smooth. Spoon over cake, covering cake completely. Let cake stand until chocolate is set.

If desired, scatter decoration over chocolate-glazed cake before chocolate sets. Try whole or chopped almonds, pistachio nuts, walnuts, silver balls or chocolate sprinkles.

minutes or until syrupy. Remove from heat and let cool 1 minute. Brush apricot mixture over cake, covering cake completely. Let cake stand until glaze is completely set. Decorate with slices of candied orange peel, if desired.

2. Apricot Glaze

Press 1 cup (12-oz. jar) apricot jam through a mesh strainer into a small heavy saucepan. Add 2 tablespoons water and 1 tablespoon sugar. Bring mixture to a boil over moderate heat, stirring occasionally. Lower heat and cook 3 to 4

3. Powdered Sugar

For a quick and easy finishing touch, dust cooled cake with 1/2 cup sifted powdered sugar.

4. Icing Glaze

Beat 1 egg white and 2 cups sifted powdered sugar in medium bowl until very stiff. Spread icing over cake, covering cake completely. Decorate with red or green glacé cherries, nuts or crystallized violets.

Variations

Omit egg white and substitute 2 tablespoons lemon or orange juice, water, milk, rum or other flavored liqueur. Stir until icing is smooth and of good drizzling consistency. Icing can be tinted with a few drops of edible food coloring.

5. Milk Chocolate Glaze

Use 8 to 10 ounces good quality milk chocolate. Coarsely chop and melt chocolate, and coat cake according to directions for Dark Chocolate Glaze (see opposite page). Let cake stand until chocolate is almost set. Decorate with finely chopped nuts or crushed praline.

Butter Cakes with a Difference

There is hardly any other type of cake batter that can be used to make so many different kinds of cake simply by adding something extra to the batter — cocoa powder, nuts, dried fruit and chocolate are good examples. (See previous pages for decorating ideas.)

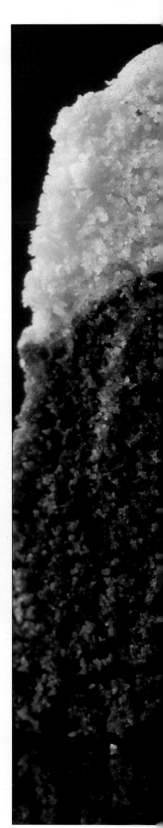

Marble Cake

1 cup butter, room
  temperature
1-1/2 cups sugar
5 eggs
1 teaspoon vanilla
  extract
2-1/4 cups sifted
  all-purpose flour
1/2 teaspoon salt
3 oz. semisweet
  chocolate, melted
  and cooled

1. Preheat oven to 350F (175C). Grease and flour 12-cup Bundt pan or 10-inch tube pan.
2. Prepare Butter Cake using ingredients listed above according to directions on page 87.
3. Spoon half the batter into second bowl. Stir in melted chocolate until blended.
4. Spoon plain cake batter into prepared pan. Spoon chocolate batter over. Swirl batters with flat-bladed knife to make marble effect. Smooth top.
5. Bake 50 to 60 minutes or until cake tester inserted into cake comes out clean. Cool in pan on wire rack 10 minutes. Remove from pan and cool completely on rack.

Raisin Cake

1 cup butter, room
  temperature
1-1/2 cups sugar
5 eggs
1 teaspoon vanilla
  extract
2-1/4 cups sifted
  all-purpose flour
1/2 teaspoon salt
1 cup dark raisins
1 tablespoon
  all-purpose flour

1. Preheat oven to 350F (175C). Grease and flour 12-cup Bundt pan or 10-inch tube pan.
2. Prepare Butter Cake using ingredients listed above according to directions on page 87.
3. Place raisins in small bowl, sprinkle with 1 tablespoon flour and toss to coat. Fold raisins into cake batter.
4. Spoon batter into prepared pan and smooth top.
5. Bake 50 to 60 minutes or until cake tester inserted into cake comes out clean. Cool in pan on wire rack 10 minutes. Remove from pan and cool completely on rack.

Macaroon Cake

1 cup butter, room
  temperature
1-1/2 cups sugar
5 eggs
1 teaspoon almond
  extract
2-1/4 cups sifted
  all-purpose flour
1/2 teaspoon salt
Filling:
1 egg white
2 tablespoons sugar
3/4 cup finely ground
  almonds

1. Preheat oven to 350F (175C). Grease and flour 12-cup Bundt pan or 10-inch tube pan.
2. Prepare Butter Cake using ingredients listed above according to directions on page 87.
3. To make filling, place egg white in small bowl, add sugar and beat until foamy. Stir in ground almonds.
4. Spoon cake batter into prepared pan. Spoon filling on top of batter. Cut lightly through batter with flat-bladed knife. Smooth top.
5. Bake 50 to 60 minutes or until cake tester inserted into cake comes out clean. Cool in pan on wire rack 10 minutes. Remove from pan and cool completely on rack.

Hazelnut Cake

1 cup butter, room
  temperature
1-1/2 cups sugar
5 eggs
1 teaspoon vanilla
  extract
2-1/4 cups sifted
  all-purpose flour
1/2 teaspoon salt
1 cup toasted finely
  chopped hazelnuts

1. Preheat oven to 350F (175C). Grease and flour 12-cup Bundt pan or 10-inch tube pan.
2. Prepare Butter Cake using ingredients listed above according to directions on page 87.
3. Fold toasted hazelnuts into cake batter.
4. Spoon cake batter into prepared pan and smooth top.
5. Bake 50 to 60 minutes or until cake tester inserted into cake comes out clean. Cool in pan on wire rack 10 minutes. Remove from pan and cool completely on rack.

Cakes with Fruit Topping

Unlike a fruit flan, where fresh or cooked fruit is arranged in a prebaked pastry shell, these cakes have fruit placed on top of the cake batter. Baking powder and whole eggs, beaten into the batter, serve as the leavening agents.

Cherry Cake

(Illustrated in springform pan)
1 cup butter, room temperature
1-1/2 cups sugar
4 eggs
2-1/2 cups all-purpose flour
1 teaspoon baking powder
1-1/2 lbs. dark sweet cherries or red tart cherries, pitted
To decorate:
2 tablespoons sugar
1 teaspoon cinnamon

1. Preheat oven to 350F (175C). Grease and flour a 10-inch springform pan.
2. Beat butter and sugar in large bowl until light and fluffy. Add eggs, one at a time, beating well after each addition.
3. Sift flour and baking powder over butter mixture; fold in.
4. Pour batter into pan. Arrange cherries over batter.
5. To decorate, combine sugar and cinnamon and sprinkle over cherries.
6. Bake 50 to 60 minutes. Cool in pan 10 minutes. Remove side of pan; cool completely on rack.

Peach Cake

(Opposite, top left)
1-3/4 lbs. peaches
1 cup butter
1-1/2 cups sugar
4 eggs
2-1/2 cups all-purpose flour
1 teaspoon baking powder
To decorate:
2 to 3 tablespoons chopped almonds
3 tablespoons raisins

1. Simmer peaches in water 1 minute. Remove and peel. Cut peaches in half; remove pits and slice.
2. Preheat oven to 350F (175C). Grease and flour 10-inch springform pan.
3. Prepare cake batter according to directions for Cherry Cake.
4. Pour batter into pan. Arrange peach slices over; sprinkle with almonds and raisins.
5. Bake 50 to 60 minutes. Cool in pan 10 minutes. Remove side of pan; cool.

Pear Cake

(Opposite, top right)
1 cup butter
1-1/2 cups sugar
4 eggs
2-1/2 cups all-purpose flour
1 teaspoon baking powder
1-3/4 lbs. firm small pears, peeled, cored and halved
2 tablespoons crystal sugar
1 to 2 tablespoons finely chopped pistachios

1. Preheat oven to 350F (175C). Grease and flour 10-inch springform pan.
2. Prepare cake batter according to directions for Cherry Cake.
3. Pour batter into pan. Arrange pears, cut side down, over batter. Sprinkle crystal sugar and pistachios over.
4. Bake 50 to 60 minutes. Cool in pan 10 minutes. Remove side of pan; cool completely on rack.

Plum Cake

(Opposite, lower left)
1 cup butter, room temperature
1-1/2 cups sugar
4 eggs
2-1/2 cups all-purpose flour
1 teaspoon baking powder
1-3/4 lbs. Mirabella plums or other small plums, halved and pitted
Powdered sugar

1. Preheat oven to 350F (175C). Grease and flour 10-inch springform pan.
2. Prepare cake batter according to directions for Cherry Cake.
3. Pour batter into pan. Arrange plums, cut side down, over batter.
4. Bake 50 to 60 minutes. Cool in pan on wire rack 10 minutes. Remove side of pan; cool completely on rack. Dust top of cake with powdered sugar just before serving.

Apricot Cake

(Opposite, lower right)
1 (6- to 8-oz.) package dried apricots
1 cup butter, room temperature
1-1/2 cups sugar
4 eggs
2-1/2 cups all-purpose flour
1 teaspoon baking powder
3 tablespoons sliced, blanched almonds
3 to 4 tablespoons apricot jam

1. In small bowl, cover apricots with hot water and let stand.
2. Preheat oven to 350F (175C). Grease and flour 10-inch springform pan.
3. Prepare cake batter according to directions for Cherry Cake.
4. Pour batter into pan. Drain apricots, dry with paper towels, and arrange over batter. Sprinkle with sliced almonds.
5. Bake 50 to 60 minutes. Cool in pan 10 minutes.
6. Press apricot jam through sieve into small saucepan. Place over low heat; cook until jam is melted.
7. Remove saucepan from heat and brush jam over top of warm cake. Remove side of pan carefully; cool.

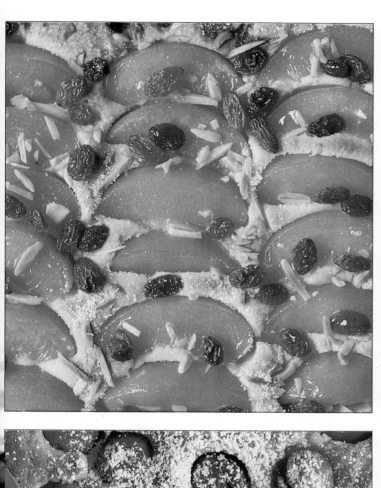

Fruit Cakes for Special Occasions

Fruit cakes, traditional at Christmas, and delicious at
any time, are best if they are made in advance
so the flavor of the cake has time to mellow. Wrap fruit
cake in foil and store in a cool place until
ready to serve. Don't forget to toss fruit and nuts in
flour before adding them to the cake batter.
This will prevent them from sinking to the bottom
of the cake.

Light Fruit Cake

1 cup currants or dark
  raisins
1 cup golden raisins
1/3 cup chopped
  candied citron
1/3 cup chopped
  candied lemon peel
1/2 cup halved red
  candied cherries
1-3/4 cups all-purpose
  flour
1 cup butter, room
  temperature
1-1/4 cups sugar
4 eggs
1 tablespoon grated
  orange or lemon
  peel
1 teaspoon baking
  powder
1/2 teaspoon ground
  cinnamon
1/4 teaspoon grated
  nutmeg
1/4 cup orange juice

1. Preheat oven to
300F (150C). Grease a
deep 8-inch-round
cake pan or 8-inch
springform pan. Line
bottom and side of pan
with parchment paper,
extending paper at
least 1 inch above rim
of pan. Grease paper.
2. Place currants,
golden raisins, citron,
lemon peel and
candied cherries in
bowl. Sprinkle 1/4 cup
flour over fruit and
toss to coat.
3. Beat butter in large
bowl until creamy.
Add sugar and beat
until light and fluffy.
4. Beat in eggs, 1 at a
time, beating well after
each addition. Stir in
orange peel.

5. Sift remaining 1-1/2
cups flour, baking
powder, cinnamon and
nutmeg onto sheet of
waxed paper. Add to
butter mixture
alternately with orange
juice, beating just until
blended. Fold in
reserved fruit mixture.
6. Spoon into pan and
smooth top.
7. Bake 2 to 2-1/2
hours or until cake
tester inserted in
center of cake comes
out clean and cake is
firm to the touch.
8. Cool completely in
pan on wire rack.
When cool, remove
and peel off paper.
Wrap in foil and store
in a cool place until
ready to serve.

Rich Holiday Fruit Cake

2 cups dark raisins
1 cup golden raisins
1 cup currants
1 cup whole candied
  cherries, coarsely
  chopped
1/2 cup chopped mixed
  candied fruit
2/3 cup ground
  almonds
2-1/4 cups sifted
  all-purpose flour
1 cup butter, room
  temperature
1-1/4 cups firmly
  packed brown sugar
3 tablespoons honey
4 eggs
1 teaspoon vanilla
  extract
Grated peel of 1
  orange
Grated peel of 1
  lemon
1 teaspoon baking
  powder

1/2 teaspoon grated
  nutmeg
1/2 teaspoon ground
  aniseed
1/2 teaspoon ground
  cardamom
1/2 teaspoon ground
  coriander
1/2 cup brandy or dark
  rum
Sweet sherry
Candied fruit

1. Preheat oven to
300F (150C). Grease
deep 9-inch-round
cake pan or 9-inch
springform pan. Line
bottom and sides of
pan with parchment
paper, extending paper
at least 1 inch above
rim of pan. Grease
paper.
2. Place raisins,
currants, cherries,
candied fruit, and
almonds in medium
bowl. Sprinkle 1/4 cup
flour over fruit and
toss to coat.
3. Beat butter in large
bowl until creamy.
Add brown sugar and
beat until light and
fluffy. Beat in honey.
4. Beat in eggs, 1 at a
time, beating well after
each addition. Beat in
vanilla.
5. Stir in orange and
lemon peels.
6. Sift remaining 2
cups flour, baking
powder, nutmeg,
aniseed, cardamom
and coriander onto
sheet of waxed paper.
Add to butter mixture
alternately with
brandy, beating just
until blended. Fold in
reserved fruit mixture.

7. Spoon into pan and
smooth top. Bake 2-1/2
hours or until cake
tester inserted in
center of cake comes
out clean and cake is
firm to the touch.
8. Cool completely in
pan on wire rack.
When cool, remove
from pan and peel off
paper.
9. Cut double
thickness of
cheesecloth large
enough to wrap
around cake twice.
Moisten cheesecloth
with sherry; wrap
cake. Overwrap with
foil. Store in a cool
place several weeks,
remoistening
cheesecloth with
sherry once a week.
When ready to serve,
decorate top of cake
with candied fruit.

Dundee Cake

(Illustrated page 61)
3/4 cup currants
3/4 cup dark raisins
3/4 cup golden raisins
1/3 cup ground
  blanched almonds
1/4 cup chopped
  candied lemon or
  orange peel
1/4 cup chopped citron
2 cups plus 2
  tablespoons
  all-purpose flour
1 cup butter, room
  temperature
1 cup sugar
4 eggs
Grated peel of 1
  lemon
1 teaspoon baking
  powder
1 teaspoon pumpkin
  pie spice (optional)

1. Preheat oven to
325F (165C). Grease
deep 8-inch-round
cake pan or 8-inch
springform pan. Line
bottom and side of pan
with parchment paper,
extending paper at
least 1 inch above rim
of pan. Grease paper.
2. Place currants,
raisins, ground
almonds, candied
lemon peel and citron
in bowl. Sprinkle 2
tablespoons flour over
fruit and toss to coat.
3. Beat butter in large
bowl until creamy.
Add sugar and beat
until light and fluffy.
4. Beat in eggs, one at
a time, beating well
after each addition.
Stir in lemon peel.
5. Sift remaining 2
cups flour, baking
powder and pumpkin
pie spice over butter
mixture and beat just
until blended. Fold in
reserved fruit mixture.
6. Spoon into pan and
smooth top.
7. Bake 2 to 2-1/2
hours or until cake
tester inserted in
center of cake comes
out clean and top of
cake is firm to the
touch.
8. Cool in pan on wire
rack 30 minutes.
Remove from pan,
peel off paper and cool
completely on wire
rack. Wrap in foil and
store in a cool place
until ready to serve.

A Very Famous & Controversial Cake

Whether Sachertorte originated at the Sacher Hotel or the world-famous Demel Bakery in Vienna is a controversy that has been left to the Austrian courts to resolve. This version includes a filling of apricot jam and therefore most closely resembles the Sachertorte made at the Sacher Hotel. Both versions are delicious and are traditionally served with strong hot coffee and "schlag" or vanilla-flavored whipped cream.

Sachertorte

1/2 cup butter, room temperature
1 cup sugar
6 eggs, separated
4 oz. semisweet chocolate, melted and cooled
1/3 cup finely ground almonds
1 cup sifted cake flour
Filling and Icing:
1/2 cup apricot jam
6 oz. semisweet chocolate

1. Preheat oven to 350F (175C). Grease and flour a 9-inch springform pan.
2. Beat butter in large bowl until creamy. Add 3/4 cup sugar and beat until light and fluffy.
3. Add egg yolks and beat until blended. Add melted chocolate and beat until well combined.
4. Fold in ground almonds and flour.
5. Beat egg whites in separate bowl until soft peaks form. Add remaining 1/4 cup sugar and beat until stiff peaks form.

6. Stir 4 heaping tablespoons beaten egg whites into chocolate batter to lighten. Fold in remaining beaten egg whites.
7. Pour mixture into prepared pan and smooth top.
8. Bake 50 to 60 minutes or until cake tester inserted in center of cake comes out clean.
9. Cool in pan on wire rack 10 minutes. Run tip of sharp knife around inside edge of pan. Remove side of pan carefully, invert cake onto rack, remove bottom of pan and cool completely on rack.
10. To make filling, press jam through sieve into small saucepan. Place saucepan over low heat and cook, stirring, until jam is melted. Set aside to cool.

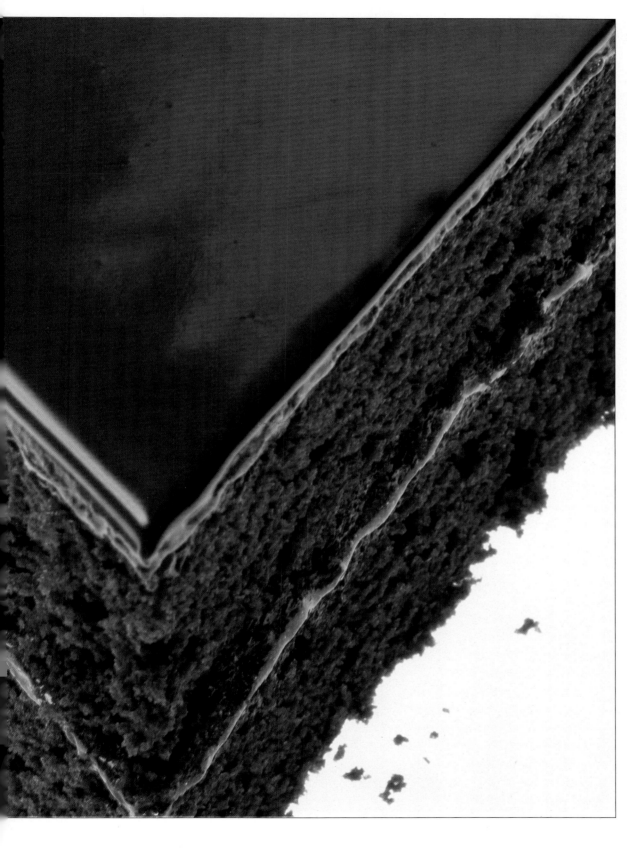

11. Cut cake in half horizontally to make 2 layers.

12. Place bottom layer on serving plate and spread with half the jam. Top with second layer. Spread remaining jam over top of cake. Let stand until jam is set.

13. To make icing, coarsely chop chocolate. Place half the chocolate in top of double boiler set over pan of simmering water. Stir over low heat until chocolate is melted.

14. Remove top of double boiler from heat. Add remaining chocolate and stir until all chocolate is completely melted and smooth.

15. Pour chocolate over cake and spread with long, thin metal spatula, covering top and side of cake completely.

16. Let stand until chocolate is almost set. Warm blade of long knife under hot water and wipe dry. Use warm knife to score top of cake into individual portions. Let stand until chocolate is completely set.

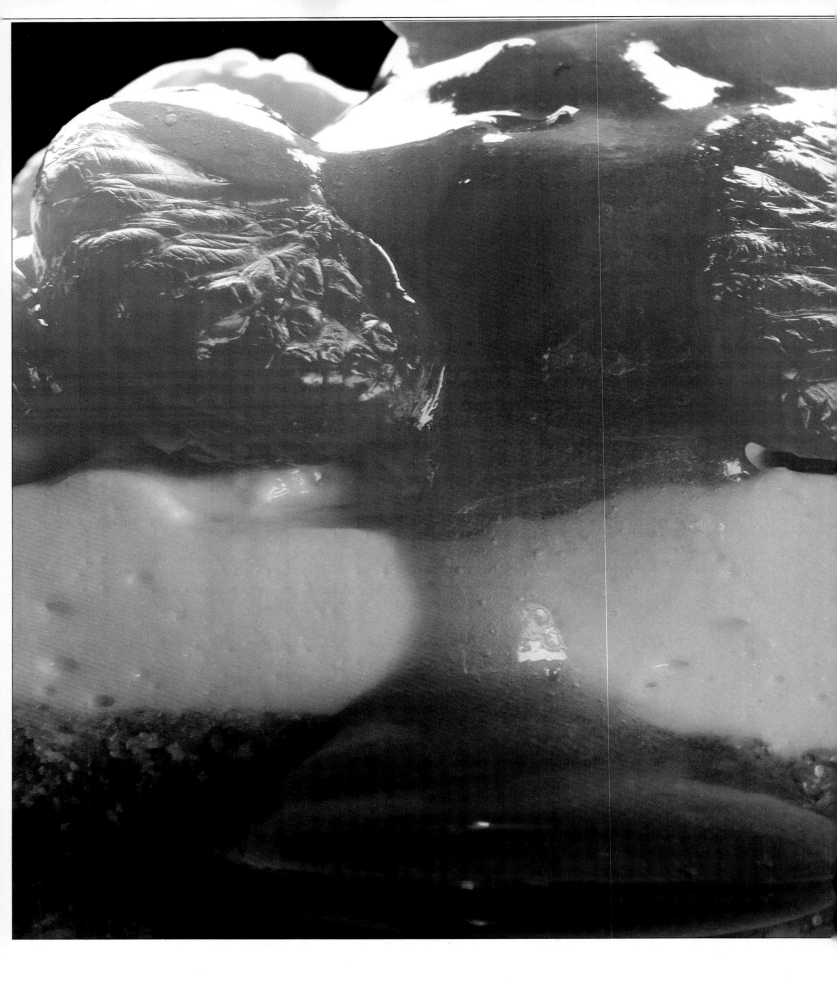

4. Jam Rings

1 recipe Shortcrust
   Cookies, page 101
1/2 cup strawberry or
   blackberry jelly
Powdered sugar

1. Prepare cookies
through Step 14.
2. Preheat oven to
425F (220C).
3. Cut pastry with
2-inch-scalloped cookie
cutter. Cut circle from
center of half the
cookies with smaller
scalloped cutter. Place
cookies and rings on
baking sheets.
4. Bake 8 to 10
minutes; cool.
5. Spread jelly over
cookie rounds. Dust
rings with sugar and
place over
jelly-covered rounds.
Yield: 2-1/2 dozen
cookies.

5. Decorated Stars

1 recipe Shortcrust
   Cookies, page 101
1 egg yolk beaten with
   2 tablespoons water
3 to 4 tablespoons
   sliced almonds
1-1/2 cups powdered
   sugar
2 to 3 tablespoons
   milk
1/2 teaspoon cinnamon

1. Prepare cookies
through Step 14.
2. Preheat oven to
425F (220C).
3. Cut into star
shapes. Brush 1/3 with
yolk mixture. Sprinkle
with almonds.
4. Bake 8 to 10
minutes; cool.
5. Combine sugar and
milk; stir cinnamon
into 1/2 of icing. Ice 1/2
of remaining cookies
with plain icing, 1/2
with cinnamon icing.
Yield: 5 dozen cookies.

6. Almond Diamonds

1 recipe Shortcrust
   Cookies, page 101
1 egg yolk beaten with
   2 tablespoons water
Whole blanched
   almonds, split

1. Prepare cookies
through Step 14.
2. Preheat oven to
425F (220C).
3. Cut pastry into 1″ x
2″ diamond shapes
with pastry wheel or
diamond-shaped
cookie cutter. Place on
baking sheets and
brush with beaten egg
yolk mixture. Top with
split almond halves.
4. Bake 8 to 10
minutes. Cool on wire
racks. Yield: 5 dozen
cookies.

7. Chocolate or Sugared Crescents

1 recipe Shortcrust
   Cookies, page 101
1 tablespoon cocoa
   powder
Powdered sugar

1. Prepare cookies
through Step 14.
2. Preheat oven to
425F (220C).
3. Cut pastry with
floured 2-inch
half-moon-shaped
cookie cutter.
4. Place on baking
sheets. Bake 8 to 10
minutes. Cool on wire
racks.
5. Blend cocoa with
1/3 cup powdered
sugar and sprinkle
over cookies.
Alternatively, dust
cookies with plain
powdered sugar. Yield:
5 dozen cookies.

8. Christmas Trees & Stars

1 recipe Shortcrust
   Cookies, page 101
3 to 4 tablespoons
   water or milk
Powdered sugar
Red and green food
   coloring

1. Prepare cookies
through Step 14.
2. Preheat oven to
425F (220C).
3. Cut pastry with star
and tree cookie cutters.
4. Bake 8 to 10
minutes; cool.
5. Blend water and 2
cups sugar. Set 1/3
icing aside. Spread 2/3
icing over cookies.
6. Blend 2 to 3
tablespoons sugar into
1/3 icing. Tint half
green and half red;
pipe around cookies.
Yield: 5 dozen cookies.

Variations on Shortcrust Pastry

The flavor of basic shortcrust pastry can be varied by the addition of seasoning such as nutmeg, cloves, cinnamon, cardamom, allspice, coriander, vanilla, citrus peel or cocoa. Additional egg yolk or butter will enrich the dough, and ground nuts or extra sugar will make the finished product more crisp.

Speculaas

3-3/4 cups all-purpose flour
1 cup firmly packed brown sugar
1/2 teaspoon ground cloves
1 teaspoon ground cinnamon
1 teaspoon ground cardamom
2 eggs
1 cup butter
2/3 cup ground hazelnuts or almonds

Oatmeal Raisin Cookies

1 cup butter
1-1/2 cups sugar
2 eggs
1-1/2 cups all-purpose flour
1 teaspoon baking soda
1/2 teaspoon salt
2 tablespoons milk
3 cups quick-cooking oatmeal
1 cup raisins

1. Preheat oven to 375F (190C). Grease baking sheets.
2. Beat butter and sugar in large bowl until light and fluffy. Beat in eggs, 1 at a time, beating well after each addition.
3. Stir flour, baking soda and salt together. Add to butter mixture and beat until blended. Beat in milk. Add oatmeal and stir with wooden spoon until blended. Stir in raisins.
4. Drop mixture by rounded teaspoonfuls onto baking sheets.
5. Bake 10 to 12 minutes or until golden brown. Cool on baking sheets 2 minutes. Remove and cool on wire racks. Makes about 7 dozen cookies.

1. Prepare cookie dough above according to directions on page 101 through Step 11, adding spices, and hazelnuts to flour mixture.
2. Preheat oven to 350F (175C).
3. Flour a 6-inch speculaas mold. Press small piece of dough into floured mold. Use taut piece of unwaxed dental floss to remove excess dough from top of mold.
4. Slam mold upside down on flat surface so cookie falls out of mold. Lift cookie with wide spatula and place on prepared baking sheet. Flour mold again before making next cookie.
5. Bake in preheated oven 15 to 18 minutes or until golden brown. Cool on baking sheet 2 minutes. Remove and cool completely on wire racks. Makes about 3 dozen cookies.

Almond Crescents

1 cup butter, room temperature
1 cup sugar
2 egg yolks
1 teaspoon almond extract
2-1/4 cups sifted all-purpose flour
1-3/4 cups ground blanched almonds
Powdered sugar

1. Beat butter and sugar until very creamy. Blend in egg yolks. Beat in almond extract.
2. Stir flour and almonds together. Fold into butter mixture gradually.
3. Divide dough into 4 pieces; shape each into log 1 inch thick. Wrap logs separately and refrigerate 30 minutes.
4. Preheat oven to 375F (190C).
5. Cut logs into 1/2-inch thick slices. Shape slices into crescents and place 1 inch apart on ungreased baking sheets.
6. Bake 9 to 11 minutes; cool on baking sheets 1 minute. Remove and cool on racks. Sprinkle with powdered sugar before serving. Yield: 7 dozen cookies.

Butter Rounds

3/4 cup butter, room temperature
1 cup sugar
3 egg yolks
1 teaspoon vanilla extract
2-1/2 cups sifted all-purpose flour
1/4 teaspoon salt
Sugar for rolling

1. Beat butter and 1 cup sugar until creamy. Beat in egg yolks and vanilla extract.
2. Stir flour and salt together. Add to butter mixture; blend. Cover and refrigerate dough at least 1 hour.
3. Halve dough. Shape into 2 logs 1-1/2 inches thick. Roll in sugar; wrap separately and refrigerate 30 minutes.
4. Preheat oven to 350F (175C). Grease baking sheets.
5. Slice logs 1/4 inch thick. Place 3/4 inch apart on baking sheets.
6. Bake 10 to 12 minutes; cool on baking sheets 3 minutes. Remove and cool completely on racks. Yield: 4-1/2 dozen cookies.

Checkerboard Cookies

1 recipe Shortcrust Cookies, page 101
2 oz. semisweet chocolate, melted
1 egg white, lightly beaten

1. Prepare cookies through Step 9.
2. Halve dough making 1 half slightly larger than the other. Add chocolate to small piece; knead. Wrap pieces separately and refrigerate 1 hour.
3. Set aside 1/4 of plain dough. Roll out chocolate dough and 3/4 plain dough to 1/4-inch thickness. Cut into equal-size rectangles. Brush plain dough with egg white and place chocolate dough on top. Cut into 2-1/4-inch strips.
4. Brush strips with egg white and stack, alternating chocolate and plain strips in checkerboard pattern (see photo). Roll out reserved plain dough to 1/8-inch thickness; wrap around stacked strips, enclosing strips completely; seal edge. Wrap in plastic wrap and refrigerate 1 hour.
5. Preheat oven to 400F (205C). Grease baking sheets.
6. Slice dough 1/4 inch thick. Bake 10 to 12 minutes; cool on baking sheets 2 minutes. Remove; cool on racks. Yield: 4 dozen cookies.

Cherry Bars

1/2 cup butter
2/3 cup sugar
1 egg
1 teaspoon almond extract
1 tablespoon milk
2 cups all-purpose flour
1/2 teaspoon baking powder
Topping:
1/2 cup sugar
2 tablespoons butter
6 tablespoons half and half, warmed
1/4 cup chopped red candied cherries
3/4 cup blanched slivered almonds

1. Grease and flour 13" x 9" baking pan.
2. Cream butter and sugar. Blend in egg, almond extract, and milk.
3. Stir in flour and baking powder. Press into pan; prick dough. Refrigerate 30 minutes.
4. Preheat oven to 375F (190C).
5. Melt sugar in skillet. Remove from heat; add butter, cream and cherries.
6. Spread topping over dough. Sprinkle with almonds.
7. Bake 17 minutes. Cut into bars or diamonds while warm. Yield: 4-1/2 dozen cookies.

Springerle Cookies

2 eggs
1-1/4 cups powdered sugar
2-1/4 cups cake flour
1/2 teaspoon baking powder
1/2 teaspoon salt
1 to 2 tablespoons aniseed, crushed
1 teaspoon grated lemon peel

1. Beat eggs and sugar until thick and lemon colored, 8 to 10 minutes.
2. Add sifted flour, baking powder and salt gradually. Stir in aniseed and lemon peel. Cover and refrigerate several hours.
3. Grease baking sheets.
4. Roll out dough to 1/4-inch thickness. Press springerle molds into dough. Place cookies on baking sheets. Cover; dry at room temperature 12 hours.
5. Preheat oven to 325F (165C).
6. Bake 15 to 18 minutes or until almost golden. Cool on baking sheets 1 minute. Remove and cool on racks. Yield: 2-1/2 dozen cookies.

Spritz Cookies

1 cup butter, room
   temperature
1 cup sugar
1 whole egg
3 egg yolks
1 teaspoon vanilla
   extract
2-3/4 cups cake flour
1/2 cup cornstarch
Candied fruit or
   chopped nuts

1. Preheat oven to
350F (175C).
2. Beat butter and
sugar in bowl until
creamy. Add whole
egg and egg yolks.
Beat until blended.
Beat in vanilla.
3. Sift flour and
cornstarch onto sheet
of waxed paper.
Gradually add to
butter mixture, beating
until blended.
4. Spoon dough into
large pastry bag fitted
with open-star tip or
pack dough into cookie
press fitted with star
plate.
5. Pipe dough in "S"
shapes, rings or
rosettes onto
ungreased baking
sheets about 1 inch
apart. Decorate with
pieces of candied fruit
or chopped nuts.
6. Bake in preheated
oven 10 to 12 minutes
or until golden.
Remove from baking
sheets and cool
completely on wire
racks. Makes about 5
dozen cookies.

Shortcrust Cookies without Kneading

This shortcrust cookie needs no kneading.
It contains enough milk that it
is piped out instead of being rolled. Using
a pastry bag fitted with a fluted tip
gives the cookies an attractive
zigzag effect. The dough can be piped
into rings, S-shapes, whirls or
straight lines.

Streusel (Crumb Topping)

2 cups all-purpose
   flour
1/2 cup sugar
1 teaspoon ground
   cinnamon
3/4 cup butter

1. Combine flour,
sugar and cinnamon.
Cut in butter until
mixture resembles
coarse crumbs.
Sprinkle over cookies,
cakes or pies before
baking.

Delicious Filled Tarts

Tarts for dessert are always special; they are lovely to
look at and delicious to eat. Make the pastry ahead
of time and keep the unfilled tarts in the
freezer, ready to use at any time. Fill them with flavored
whipped cream or smooth custard, then
add sliced fruit and, if desired, finish with a fruit
glaze of melted jam or jelly. Your guests
are sure to be impressed.

Pastry for Tarts & Tartlets

1-1/2 cups all-purpose
  flour
2 tablespoons sugar
1/2 teaspoon sugar
1/2 teaspoon salt
1/2 cup butter, chilled
1 egg yolk
2 to 3 tablespoons ice
  water

1. Stir flour, sugar and
salt in bowl. Cut in
butter with pastry
blender or 2 knives
until mixture
resembles coarse
crumbs.
2. Blend egg yolk with
2 tablespoons ice
water. Sprinkle over
flour mixture and toss
with fork until mixture
begins to bind
together, adding
remaining ice water
only if necessary.
3. Gather pastry
together and knead 3
to 5 strokes. Shape
into flattened ball,
wrap in plastic wrap or
waxed paper and
refrigerate 30 minutes.
4. To bake blind,
preheat oven to 400F
(205C).
5. Roll out pastry on
lightly floured surface
with floured rolling
pin to 1/8- to 1/4-inch
thickness.
6. To make large tart,
roll pastry 2-1/2 to 3
inches larger in
diameter than size of
pan to be used. Line

pastry in 9- or 10-inch
tart pan with
removable bottom.
Ease pastry into pan
and trim edge even
with rim of pan. Prick
lightly with fork. Line
pastry with foil,
parchment paper or
waxed paper and
weigh down with pie
weights or dried
beans. Bake in
preheated oven 10
minutes. Remove foil
and pie weights. Bake
5 to 6 minutes or until
golden. Cool
completely in pan on
wire rack before filling
or freezing.
7. To make small tarts,
place tart pans close
together (see page 24)
and line pans with
pastry. Prick lightly
with fork. Line pastry
with foil, parchment
paper or waxed paper
and weigh down with
pie weights or dried
beans. Bake in
preheated oven 6
minutes. Remove foil
and pie weights. Bake
5 to 6 minutes or until
golden. Cool
completely on wire
racks before filling or
freezing. Makes one 9-
or 10-inch tart/flan
pastry case or 10
(2-1/2- to 3-inch) tart
shells.

Note: If pastry is to be
filled before baking,
don't prick bottom of
pastry or bake blind.

Illustrated opposite:

An assortment of tarts
(clockwise from left to
right)
● Kiwi Tarts filled
with Vanilla Cream
(see page 233)
● Mandarin Tarts filled
with Ganache Cream
(see page 232)
● Strawberry Boats
filled with Vanilla
cream (see page 233)
● Orange Tarts filled
with Vanilla Cream
(see page 233)
● Mango and Papaya
Boats filled with
whipped cream

French Apple Flan

Pastry:
1-1/2 cups all-purpose
    flour
2 tablespoons sugar
1/2 teaspoon salt
1 egg
6 tablespoons butter

Filling:
2-1/2 lbs. tart cooking
    apples
Powdered sugar for
    sprinkling

1. Prepare pastry according to directions on page 101 through Step 10.
2. Roll out pastry on lightly floured surface and line 9- or 10-inch flan/tart pan with removable bottom.
3. Preheat oven to 425F (220C).
4. Peel and slice apples. Arrange apples in concentric circles in pastry-lined pan.
5. Sprinkle 2 to 3 tablespoons powdered sugar over apples. Bake in preheated oven 25 to 30 minutes or until apples are browned and edges are crisp.
6. Cool in pan on wire rack 10 to 15 minutes. Remove from pan and dust with powdered sugar before serving. Serve warm.

Fruit Flans the French Way

Fruit flans—thin, crisp, buttery shortcrust pastry topped with sliced fruit and baked in the oven—are always an ideal choice to finish a meal. Don't worry if the pastry darkens and the edges of the fruit turn brown and crisp during baking—this is just as it should be. Dust the flan with powdered sugar just before serving and serve warm, plain or topped with flavored whipped cream or ice cream.

Tart Tatin

For an unusual and striking dessert make an upside-down apple flan, created by the Tatin sisters of northern France many years ago.

Roll out Shortcrust Pastry 1/8 inch to 1/4 inch thick and set aside. Melt 3/4 cup sugar and 1/4 cup butter in heatproof 9- or 10-inch cake pan or deep pie pan until syrupy. Arrange peeled and quartered apples in single layer, rounded side down, in syrup. Cook apples over moderate heat 8 to 10 minutes or until slightly softened.

Preheat oven to 450F (230C). Cover apples with pastry, pressing pastry edges against sides of pan to seal. Bake in preheated oven 20 to 25 minutes or until pastry is golden brown.

Cool in pan on wire rack 5 minutes. Invert tart onto serving plate and serve warm.

You can also make upside-down fruit flans with pears, peaches or other fruit.

Variations

You can use any fruit suitable for baking. Substitute pears, peaches, plums or nectarines for apples.

Additions

Before baking the fruit flan, sprinkle fruit with 2 to 3 tablespoons slivered or sliced blanched almonds.

Fruit flans can also be glazed. Heat red currant jelly or apricot, peach or strawberry jam until melted. Brush over baked fruit flan. Let stand until set.

Sometimes fruit flans are filled with vanilla or flavored custard (see page 233). Spread custard over bottom of pastry-lined pan after baking. Top with sliced fruit.

The Glorious Cheesecake

Cheesecakes, almost as old as civilization have undergone many changes from the first known recipe of ancient Greece to the revolution that occurred when cream cheese was developed in the United States in 1872. A cheesecake can be crustless, it can have a shortcrust base, or it can have a crumb, nut, sponge, yeast or other crust on the bottom. No matter what crust you use, cheesecake will make a special treat for your next dinner party. But don't serve cheesecake to anyone who is counting calories!

New York Cheesecake

Shortcrust Pastry:
1-1/2 cups all-purpose flour
4 tablespoons sugar
1 egg
1/2 cup butter

Filling:
4 (8-oz.) packages cream cheese, room temperature
3/4 cup sugar
3 eggs
1 teaspoon vanilla extract or 1 teaspoon grated lemon peel
1/4 cup all-purpose flour
1 cup dairy sour cream
Strawberries, raspberries or blueberries for garnish (optional)

1. Preheat oven to 400F (205C). Prepare pastry according to directions on page 101 through Step 10.
2. Divide pastry in half. Press half of pastry onto bottom of a 9-inch springform pan and prick with a fork. Bake 10 minutes. Cool completely in pan on wire rack.
3. To make filling, beat cream cheese in large bowl until smooth. Add sugar and beat until light and fluffy.
4. Beat in eggs, 1 at a time, beating well after each addition. Beat in vanilla and flour until blended. Add sour cream and stir well.
5. Press remaining pastry around inside edge of pan to within 1 inch of rim.
6. Pour cheese mixture into pastry-lined pan. Bake 40 to 50 minutes or until edges are golden brown and center is set. Turn oven off and leave cheesecake in oven 1 hour. Remove from oven and let cool completely in pan on wire rack. Refrigerate in pan until ready to serve.
7. To serve, remove sides of pan, carefully lift cake from bottom of pan and slide cake onto serving plate. Decorate with fresh fruit, if desired.

Variation

To make strawberry-topped cheesecake, arrange strawberries over cooled cheesecake. Glaze with melted raspberry jelly or red currant jelly.

Coconut Refrigerator Cheesecake

Crumb Crust:
1/2 cup shredded or flaked coconut
1 cup vanilla wafer crumbs
1/3 cup butter, melted

Filling:
2 envelopes unflavored gelatin
3/4 cup sugar
1/4 teaspoon salt
2 eggs, separated
1 cup milk
3 cups small-curd cottage cheese
1 teaspoon vanilla or rum extract
2 to 3 tablespoons coconut-flavored liqueur (Cocoribe)
1 cup whipping cream
Toasted coconut for decoration

1. Preheat oven to 350F (175C). Grease 9-inch springform pan.
2. To make crust, stir coconut, wafer crumbs and melted butter in bowl until well combined. Press crumb mixture onto bottom and partly up sides of prepared pan. Bake in preheated oven 8 to 10 minutes. Cool completely in pan on wire rack.
3. To make filling, stir gelatin, sugar and salt in medium saucepan. Beat egg yolks and milk until blended. Add to gelatin mixture and stir until blended. Place saucepan over low heat and cook, stirring, until gelatin is dissolved and mixture is slightly thickened. Remove pan from heat and let cool.
4. Drain cottage cheese to remove excess liquid and discard liquid. Beat cottage cheese in large bowl or food processor until smooth. Add cooled gelatin mixture and beat until blended. Add vanilla and coconut liqueur and beat until blended. Refrigerate until mixture mounds when dropped from spoon.
5. Beat egg whites until stiff peaks form. Fold beaten egg whites into cheese mixture. Beat cream until firm. Fold whipped cream into cheese mixture. Pour mixture into prepared crust. Refrigerate several hours or until set.
6. To serve, run tip of sharp knife around inside edge of pan and release side of pan. Place cheesecake on serving plate and sprinkle top with toasted coconut.

Honey Cheese Pie

1 pastry recipe (see New York Cheesecake)

Filling:
2 cups ricotta cheese
4 eggs
1/2 cup honey
1 teaspoon grated lemon peel
2 teaspoons ground cinnamon

1. Prepare pastry according to directions on page 101 through Step 10.
2. Preheat oven to 400F (205C).
3. Roll out pastry to 1/8-inch thickness and use to line 10-inch pie plate. Trim and flute pastry edge and prick pastry with fork. Line pastry with foil and fill with pie weights. Bake in preheated oven 10 minutes. Remove foil and pie weights and bake 5 to 6 minutes. Cool completely in pan on wire rack.
4. Lower oven temperature to 375F (190C).
5. To make filling, drain ricotta cheese to remove excess liquid; discard liquid. Place cheese in bowl and beat until smooth.
6. Add eggs and beat until well blended. Beat in honey. Add lemon peel and 1 teaspoon cinnamon and beat well. Pour mixture into cooled pastry shell.
7. Bake in preheated oven 30 to 35 minutes or until center is set. Cool completely in pan on wire rack. Sprinkle top of pie with remaining 1 teaspoon cinnamon just before serving.

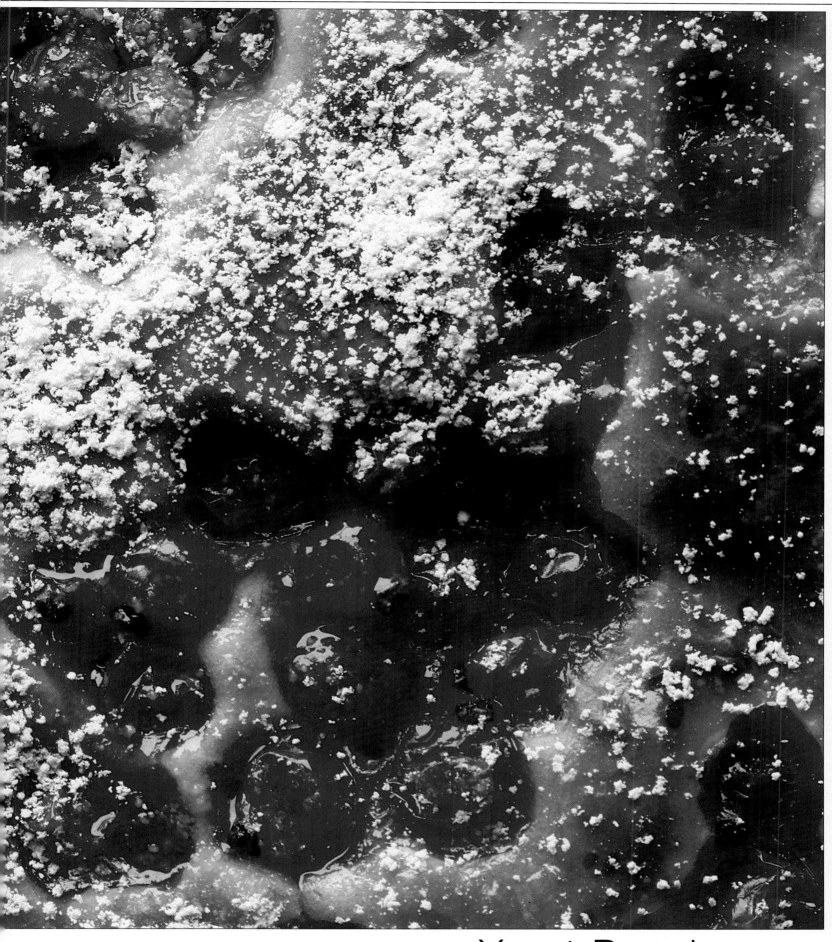

Yeast Dough—
Tempting Treats with
a Special Aroma

The Magic of Yeast

Yeast

Yeast is a very small living organism that requires a certain amount of warmth, liquid and sugar (molasses or honey) to make it function. When used properly it acts, as if by magic, to make dough rise.

Yeast is available in several forms. Active dry yeast is sold in 1/4-ounce packages that contain approximately 1 tablespoon of yeast, or in small jars. The packages are dated and, if kept in a cool dry place, will stay fresh until the expiration date. This is the yeast used in the recipes that follow. "Instant" or "rapid" yeast is also available and is sold in 1/4-ounce packages. It is also possible to buy fresh cake or compressed yeast that must be stored in the refrigerator and used promptly, or may be wrapped in foil and stored in the freezer for up to six months.

There are many people who find working with yeast so satisfying they have turned it into a special hobby. And there are also those who find the process of kneading dough a wonderful way to release tension. Whatever reason you have for making yeast dough, the results can be wonderfully satisfying once you learn the rules. Many aspects of cooking benefit from flexibility and imagination. But the action of yeast is a chemical action, and certain rules must be followed in order to make it work properly. Follow the instructions in the recipes carefully and use the hints and tips as added guidance.

How Yeast Works

When yeast is combined at the right temperature with the correct amount of moisture and sugar, it multiplies and produces bubbles of carbon dioxide that cause the dough to expand. The liquid must be between 105-115F(40-45C). If the liquid used is too cold, the yeast will not be activated. If the liquid is too hot, it will kill the yeast and the carbon dioxide bubbles will not be produced. Once the dough has been mixed and kneaded, it must be covered and placed in a warm, draft-free place in order to rise properly.

Hints and Tips

If you doubt whether or not your yeast is still alive, you will find out during the first step given in most recipes. When yeast and sugar are stirred into a small amount of warm water and allowed to stand 5 to 10 minutes, the mixture will bubble and foam if the yeast is still alive. This procedure is called "proofing." If the yeast does not react, discard it and start again with yeast that is alive.

Don't knead dough on a cold marble slab. A lightly floured wooden surface, tabletop height, is best.

To knead dough, flour hands, place the dough on the work surface and shape it into a ball. Pick up the edge of the dough farthest from you and bring it forward over the dough toward you. Push the dough down with the heels of your hands in a rolling motion. Give the dough a quarter turn and repeat the motion. Knead until the dough is smooth and elastic.

To tell whether or not dough had doubled in bulk, press two fingers an inch into the center of the dough. If the indentations remain, the dough has doubled. If the indentations fill in, recover and let dough rise another 10 to 15 minutes. Test again.

Basic Yeast Dough

Equipment:
Pastry board
Rolling pin
Yeast thermometer
(optional)
15" x 10" jelly-roll pan

Ingredients:
1/4 cup butter
1 cup milk
2 (1/4-oz.) packages
 active dry yeast (2
 tablespoons)
1/4 cup sugar
2 eggs, lightly beaten
About 4 cups
 all-purpose flour
l teaspoon salt
Topping for Sweet
 Dough:
4 tablespoons butter
3 tablespoons sugar

Oven Temperature:
375F (190C)

Baking Time:
20 minutes

Servings:
Makes one 15" x 10"
yeast cake

Storage:
Baked yeast dough can
be wrapped in foil or
plastic storage bags
and frozen for 3 to 5
months. Thaw bread,
wrapped, at room
temperature. Reheat in
300F (150C) oven 5 to
10 minutes.

Preparation

1. Measure ingredients and set aside to come to room temperature.

2. Melt butter in small saucepan and let cool to room temperature.

3. Place milk in small saucepan over low heat; warm (105-115F/40-45C).

4. Sprinkle yeast and 2 tablespoons sugar over milk. Stir well.

5. Let stand 5 to 10 minutes or until mixture is foamy.

6. Pour yeast mixture into large bowl.

7. Add melted butter and eggs and stir until thoroughly blended.

8. Add 3 cups flour, remaining 2 tablespoons sugar and salt.

9. Stir to make stiff dough that comes away from sides of bowl.

10. On floured surface, knead in enough flour to make smooth dough.

11. Knead dough until smooth and elastic, 8 to 10 minutes.

12. Place dough in greased bowl and turn to coat on all sides.

13. Cover with towel and place in warm, draft-free place to rise until doubled.

14. Knead dough lightly on a board and let rest 5 minutes.

15. Roll dough out on lightly floured surface to rectangle, 15" x 10".

16. Fit dough into greased 15" x 10" jelly-roll pan.

17. Dot with 3 tablespoons butter. Let rise, uncovered, 15 minutes.

18. Sprinkle top with 4 tablespoons sugar.

19. Bake in preheated 375F (190C) oven 20 minutes or until golden.

20. Remove from oven, let cool 10 minutes. Cut into squares and serve warm.

Cakes Made with Yeast

Yeast dough can be used to make many different kinds of cakes, shaped in a variety of ways. Three of the cakes on these pages are baked flat and cut after baking. The fourth recipe is for rolled and shaped dough that makes individual small cakes or buns. They are all appropriate to serve at breakfast or brunch, with coffee or tea at any time of day, or as dessert for lunch or supper.

Almond Butter Cake

(Illustrated top)
1 recipe Basic Yeast
    Dough, page 117
1/2 cup butter, room
    temperature
5 to 6 tablespoons
    sugar
1/2 cup sliced almonds

1. Prepare Basic Yeast Dough recipe through Step 16.
2. Preheat oven to 375F (190C).
3. Spread butter evenly over dough. Let rise 15 minutes.
4. Sprinkle sugar and almonds over dough.
5. Bake 20 to 25 minutes or until golden brown.
6. Let cool in pan on wire rack 10 minutes. Cut into squares and remove from pan. Serve warm.

Streusel Cake

(Illustrated bottom)
1 recipe Basic Yeast
    Dough, page 117
2 cups all-purpose
    flour
1/2 cup sugar
1 teaspoon ground
    cinnamon
3/4 cup butter
1 egg yolk beaten with
    1 tablespoon milk

1. Prepare Basic Yeast Dough recipe through Step 16.
2. Preheat oven to 375F (190C).
3. Mix flour, sugar and cinnamon in bowl. Cut in butter until mixture resembles coarse crumbs.
4. Brush top of dough with beaten egg yolk. Sprinkle crumbs evenly over dough. Let rise 15 minutes.
5. Bake 20 to 25 minutes.
6. Let cool in pan on wire rack 10 minutes. Cut into squares and remove from pan.

Almond Meltaway

1 recipe Basic Yeast
  Dough, page 117
10 tablespoons butter
1/2 cup sugar
1 cup light cream
1-3/4 cups chopped
  blanched almonds

1. Prepare Basic Yeast
Dough recipe through
Step 16.
2. Let dough rise 15
minutes.
3. Preheat oven to
375F (190C).
4. Melt butter in
medium saucepan over
low heat. Add sugar
and cook, stirring,
until sugar is
dissolved. Add cream
and bring to a boil.
5. Remove from heat
and stir in chopped
almonds. Set aside to
cool slightly.
6. Spread almond
mixture evenly over
dough.
7. Bake in preheated
oven 25 to 30 minutes
or until top is
browned.
8. Let cool in pan on
wire rack 10 minutes.
Cut into squares.

Variation

Almond Meltaway is
also delicious filled.
Remove cake from pan
uncut. Split in half
horizontally. Spread
Vanilla Cream (see
page 233) over bottom
half and replace top
half. Cut into serving
pieces.

Snail Buns

(Illustrated page 45)
1 recipe Basic Yeast
  Dough, page 117
2 tablespoons butter,
  melted
3/4 cup currants
1/2 cup firmly packed
  brown sugar
1 teaspoon grated
  orange peel
1 teaspoon ground
  cinnamon
1 egg yolk beaten with
  1 tablespoon milk

1. Prepare Basic Yeast
Dough recipe through
Step 14.
2. Grease two
8-inch-round cake
pans.
3. Roll out dough on
lightly floured surface
to 18″ x 12″ rectangle.
Brush dough with
melted butter.
4. Combine currants,
sugar, orange peel and
cinnamon in small
bowl. Sprinkle mixture
evenly over dough.
5. Roll up dough,
jelly-roll style, starting
at narrow end. Cut roll
into 16 slices.
6. Arrange 8 slices flat
in each prepared pan,
spacing them evenly
apart to allow enough
room for expansion.
7. Cover and let rise
30 to 40 minutes.
8. Preheat oven to
375F (190C).
9. Brush tops with
beaten egg yolk
mixture. Bake in
preheated oven 25 to
30 minutes or until
lightly browned.
10. Remove from pans
immediately and cool
on wire racks. Cut or
pull buns apart. Makes
16 buns.

Fresh Fruit Flans

Fruit flans, made with a sweet yeast dough, topped with fresh fruit, and sprinkled with a sugar topping or brushed with a glaze, are a special summer treat. Take advantage of fresh fruit when it is in season and make these delicious flans.

Tips

To prevent dough from getting soggy, sprinkle fine, dry unseasoned bread crumbs or finely ground nuts over dough before adding fruit.

After dough has been placed in pan, allow at least 20 minutes for dough to rise before adding fruit. Otherwise, the weight of the fruit will prevent the dough from rising adequately.

Plum Flan

1 recipe Basic Yeast Dough, page 117
4 tablespoons fine dry bread crumbs
2 to 2-1/2 lbs. small purple plums, halved and pitted
6 tablespoons crystal sugar
1/2 teaspoon ground cinnamon

1. Prepare Basic Yeast Dough recipe through Step 16.
2. Sprinkle bread crumbs over dough. Let rise 20 minutes.
3. Preheat oven to 350F (175C).
4. Arrange plums, skin side down, in a single layer over dough.
5. Combine sugar and cinnamon and sprinkle over plums.
6. Bake 35 to 40 minutes or until browned. Cool in pan on wire rack 10 to 15 minutes.

Toppings for Fruit Flans

There are several ways to give a finished touch to a freshly baked fruit flan. (Illustrated above)
1. Sprinkle fruit with coarse or crystallized sugar before and after baking.
2. Brush fruit with melted red currant jelly after baking.
3. Sprinkle rum-soaked golden or dark raisins over fruit before baking.
4. Sprinkle fruit with streusel topping (see page 106) before baking.

5. Sprinkle fruit with superfine or powdered sugar after baking.
6. Sprinkle fruit with shredded or flaked coconut before baking.
7. Cover fruit with fruit glaze: Combine 1 cup sugar, 3 tablespoons cornstarch and 1 cup water in saucepan. Cook over low heat until mixture is clear. Remove pan from heat and stir in 4 tablespoons flavored gelatin until dissolved. Let cool. Spoon over baked fruit flan.
8. Sprinkle with sliced almonds, chopped peanuts, pistachio

nuts, pine nuts or other chopped nuts before baking.
9. Brush with apricot glaze: Press 1 cup apricot jam through sieve into a small saucepan. Add 3 tablespoons water and 2 tablespoons sugar. Bring to a boil and boil rapidly 4 minutes. Pour or spoon over baked fruit flan.
10. Pipe meringue (see page 218) in a decorative pattern over baked fruit flan. Place in preheated 400F (205C) oven 5 to 6 minutes or until meringue is lightly browned.

11. Top servings with ice cream, sweetened whipped cream or fruit-flavored yogurt.

Apple Flan

3/4 cup raisins
1/4 cup dark rum
1 recipe Basic Yeast Dough, page 117
4 tablespoons fine dry bread crumbs
2-1/2 to 3 lbs. tart apples, peeled, cored and sliced
2 tablespoons lemon juice
1/3 cup sugar
1 teaspoon ground cinnamon
1/3 cup sliced almonds

1. Place raisins in bowl and add rum. Set aside.
2. Prepare Basic Yeast Dough recipe through Step 16.
3. Sprinkle bread crumbs evenly over dough. Let rise 20 minutes.
4. Place apple slices in large bowl and sprinkle with lemon juice, sugar and cinnamon. Toss to coat.
5. Arrange apple slices over dough. Drain raisins and scatter raisins over apples. Sprinkle almonds over apples. Let rise 30 minutes.
6. Preheat oven to 350F (175C).
7. Bake in preheated oven 30 to 35 minutes or until apples are tender. Cool in pan on wire rack 10 minutes.

Swiss Fruit Flans—Always a Favorite

Cherry Flan

(Illustrated above)
1/2 recipe Basic Yeast
   Dough, page 117
1 (16-oz.) can pitted
   red tart cherries or
   dark sweet cherries,
   drained

Custard Mixture:
4 eggs
1 cup light cream
3 to 4 tablespoons
   sugar
1/2 teaspoon ground
   cinnamon
Powdered sugar for
   sprinkling

1. Prepare 1/2 recipe Basic Yeast Dough according to directions on page 117 through Step 14.(Use half the ingredients or make a full recipe and freeze half the dough for use another time.)
2. Preheat oven to 350F (175C). Grease 10- or 11-inch black steel ovenproof pan or deep pie dish.
3. Roll out dough on lightly floured surface to 1/2-inch thickness. Line prepared pan with dough and scatter cherries over dough.
4. Beat eggs, cream, sugar and cinnamon in bowl until blended. Pour egg mixture over cherries.
5. Bake in preheated oven 30 to 40 minutes or until center is set. Sprinkle with powdered sugar and serve immediately.

Fruit flans, made with sweet yeast dough and filled with
custard and fruit, are a specialty of Switzerland.

Cranberry Flan

(Second photo, page 122)
Wash and pick over 2 cups fresh cranberries. Drain well and pat dry with paper towels. Spread cranberries over yeast dough (see Cherry Flan, opposite page). Increase sugar in custard mixture to 6 tablespoons or to taste. Proceed as directed for Cherry Flan.

Pear Flan

(Illustrated above)
Peel, halve and core 3 to 4 small firm pears. Place pears, cut side down, over yeast dough (see Cherry Flan, opposite page). Omit cinnamon in custard mixture and substitute 1/2 teaspoon almond extract. Proceed as directed for Cherry Flan.

Blueberry Flan

(Illustrated above)
Wash and pick over 1-1/2 cups fresh blueberries. Drain well and pat dry with paper towels. Spread blueberries over yeast dough (see Cherry Flan, opposite page). Add 1/2 teaspoon grated lemon peel to custard mixture. Proceed as directed for Cherry Flan.

Gugelhupf—The Cake with the Funny Name

Gugelhupf is a famous German/Austrian yeast cake, baked in a special deep tube pan with fluted sides. One of the truly confusing things about the cake is the many ways its name can be spelled—Gugelhupf, Guglhupf, Gougelhof, Gougelhopf, Kougelhupf and even Kugelhupf. But, no matter how you spell it, this cake is an all-time favorite.

The History of the Gugelhupf

Larousse Gastronomique suggests the Gugelhupf may have become popular in France because it was a favorite of Marie Antoinette. But the more likely origin of its popularity grew out of the friendship between Antonin Carême, the "king of cooks" in France at the turn of the nineteenth century, and M. Eugène, personal chef to the Austrian Ambassador to France. M. Eugène reportedly gave the recipe to Carême, who made it popular.

According to some food historians, the first tall, cone-shaped cakes were made in Roman times. There was no "chimney" in the center and the shape was symbolic of the rotating sun.

The unusual name given to the cake by the Germans probably is derived from its shape. The German word "kegel" means truncated cone.

"Hupfen" in German means to jump and, in all likelihood, refers to the fact that the yeast causes the dough to rise so high.

Gugelhupf

1 cup raisins
1/4 cup dark rum
1 cup warm milk (105-115F/40-45C)
1 (1/4-oz.) package active dry yeast
1/2 cup granulated sugar
3-1/2 cups all-purpose flour
3/4 cup butter, room temperature
3 eggs
1 teaspoon salt
3/4 cup slivered or chopped almonds
Powdered sugar for sprinkling

1. Place raisins in small bowl. Stir in rum and set aside.
2. Place warm milk in medium bowl. Sprinkle yeast and 1 tablespoon granulated sugar over. Stir to dissolve. Let stand 5 to 10 minutes or until foamy.
3. Add 1 cup flour and stir until well blended. Cover bowl with clean towel and set aside in a warm, draft-free place to rise until doubled in bulk.
4. Generously grease gugelhupf pan or 10-inch turk's head mold.
5. Beat butter and remaining granulated sugar in large bowl until light and fluffy. Beat in eggs, 1 at a time, beating well after each addition. Beat in salt.
6. Beat in yeast-flour mixture. Add remaining 2-1/2 cups flour and beat until smooth. Stir in rum-soaked raisins and almonds until blended.
7. Pour or spoon batter into prepared pan. Cover with clean towel and set aside to rise until doubled in bulk, about 1-1/4 hours.
8. Preheat oven to 375F (190C).
9. Bake 40 to 45 minutes or until cake tester inserted into cake comes out clean. Remove from pan and cool completely on wire rack. Sprinkle with powdered sugar just before serving.

Variations

A Gugelhupf can be eaten for breakfast with butter or jam or served as a dessert. The filling can be varied by replacing the raisins and almonds in the basic recipe:
1. Add 1/2 cup chopped candied orange peel and 1/2 cup chopped candied lemon peel.
2. Blend 1-1/2 cups finely chopped almonds or hazelnuts with 1 egg white and 2 to 3 tablespoons sugar. Stir into dough.
3. Use raisins and almonds in basic recipe. Cover baked Gugelhupf with melted chocolate and sprinkle with chopped nuts.
4. Add 1 teaspoon ground ginger, 1 teaspoon ground cinnamon and 1/2 teaspoon ground nutmeg to dough along with raisins and almonds.

Stollen—Traditional German Christmas Cake

Stollen is a German fruit cake traditionally served at
Christmas. As with other fruit cakes, it
should be made a few weeks ahead of time to allow the
flavors to blend. Wrap the cake in foil to
keep it nice and moist.

Christmas Stollen

1 cup raisins
1/4 cup dark rum
1 cup warm milk
2 (1/4-oz.) packages
 active dry yeast
3/4 cup granulated
 sugar
1/2 cup butter, melted
2 eggs, lightly beaten
1 teaspoon salt
About 4-1/4 cups
 all-purpose flour
1 teaspoon cinnamon
1 teaspoon cardamom
1/4 teaspoon grated
 nutmeg
3/4 cup chopped
 blanched almonds
1/2 cup chopped
 candied orange peel
1/2 cup chopped
 candied lemon peel

4 tablespoons butter,
 melted for brushing
Powdered sugar

1. Place raisins in small bowl. Stir in rum and set aside.
2. Place warm milk in large bowl. Sprinkle yeast and 1 tablespoon granulated sugar over. Stir to dissolve. Let stand 5 to 10 minutes or until foamy.
3. Add 1/2 cup melted butter and eggs to yeast mixture and stir until blended.
4. Add remaining sugar, salt, 1 cup flour, cinnamon, cardamom and nutmeg. Stir until blended.

5. Stir in soaked raisins, almonds, orange peel, lemon peel and 2-1/2 cups flour to make stiff dough.
6. Place dough on lightly floured surface and knead in flour to make smooth dough.
7. Place dough in greased bowl and turn to coat. Cover and set aside in a warm, draft-free place to rise until doubled in bulk.
8. Punch down dough and halve. Knead each piece 2 minutes.
9. Grease baking sheet.

10. Roll out each piece of dough to 11" x 7" oval. Brush with 1 tablespoon melted butter. Fold in half lengthwise to make traditional stollen shape. Place on baking sheet.
11. Cover with towel and set aside to rise until doubled in bulk, about 45 minutes.
12. Preheat oven to 375F (190C).
13. Bake 25 to 30 minutes or until loaves sound hollow when tapped on bottom. Remove from baking sheet; cool.

14. Brush with remaining melted butter while warm and sprinkle with powdered sugar. Let cool completely. Wrap in foil until ready to serve. Makes 2 Stollen.

The Shape of Brioche

A typical brioche is round, fluted on the side and has a small ball on top. Brioche pans come in many sizes. However, brioche dough can also be baked in a loaf pan, shaped into a ring, shaped like a pie or a tall cylinder.

Tips on Making Brioche Dough

Use unsalted butter only.

Allow dough to rise slowly overnight in the refrigerator for best results.

Brioche dough can be frozen but, because of the high butter content, should not be kept frozen longer than one month. Defrost slowly in the refrigerator before using. When defrosted, knead and bake as directed in recipe.

Freeze baked brioche while still slightly warm. Thaw slowly and reheat briefly in the oven.

Brioche—in the Best French Tradition

Brioche is made from a yeast dough rich in butter and eggs. It is neither savory nor sweet and can be used in many ways. Serve it for breakfast with butter and jam or as an accompaniment at lunch with soup or salad. You can also scoop out the centers and add a sweet or savory filling. You can even add cheese or fruit to the dough before baking.

Brioche

About 4-1/2 cups
   all-purpose flour
2 (1/4-oz.) packages
   active dry yeast
1/2 cup warm milk
   (105-115F/40-45C)
6 eggs
1/4 cup sugar
l teaspoon salt
1 cup unsalted butter,
   room temperature
1 egg yolk beaten with
   1 tablespoon milk
   for brushing

1. Sift flour onto clean work surface and make well in center. Add warm milk and yeast and stir with fingers.
2. Add eggs, sugar and salt to well and mix, drawing in flour from outside edge. Knead dough vigorously about 15 minutes, lifting dough from work surface with dough scraper.
3. Knead butter with heal of hand to soften. Add butter to dough. Knead and squeeze butter into dough until butter is incorporated.

Lift dough from work surface and "slam" back onto surface several times.
4. Place dough in greased bowl and turn to coat. Cover and refrigerate 2 hours. Stir down dough and knead 2 minutes. Recover dough and refrigerate overnight.
5. Grease 24 small brioche molds. Divide dough into 24 pieces. Roll pieces into pear-shaped balls. Pinch off small end of balls and shape in 24 small balls with slightly tapered end. Place large balls in prepared pans. Poke hole in center of each and place small ball in hole, tapered end down. Cover filled molds with clean towel and set aside in a warm, draft-free place to rise until doubled in bulk.
6. Preheat oven to 425F (220C).
7. Lightly brush tops of brioches with egg yolk mixture. Bake 15 to 18 minutes or until golden brown. Remove from pans and cool on wire racks. Makes 24 small Brioches.

Spicy Sausage in Brioche

(Illustrated opposite page)
Grease 9″ x 5″ loaf pan. Wrap spicy sausage in brioche dough and shape dough into loaf. Place in prepared pan. Make slash down center of loaf and let rise until doubled in bulk. Bake in preheated 375F (190C) oven 40 to 50 minutes or until loaf sounds hollow when tapped on bottom. Slice and serve as unusual appetizer.

Savarin—A Special Yeast Cake, Perfect for Filling

Savarin

Dough:
1/2 cup warm milk
  (105-115F/40-45C)
1 (1/4-oz.) package
  active dry yeast
4 tablespoons
  granulated sugar
About 2-1/2 cups
  all-purpose flour
3 eggs, beaten
1/2 teaspoon salt
1/4 cup butter, melted
  and cooled
Syrup:
1 cup granulated sugar
1/2 cup water
1/2 cup dark rum
Glaze:
2/3 cup apricot jam
2 tablespoons water or
  rum
Filling:
Fresh strawberries,
  rinsed and hulled
Powdered sugar

1. Generously grease a 6-1/2-cup (9-inch) ring mold.
2. To make dough, place warm milk in large bowl and sprinkle yeast and 1 tablespoon granulated sugar over. Stir to dissolve. Let stand 5 to 10 minutes or until foamy.
3. Add 1-1/2 cups flour, beaten eggs, salt and remaining 3 tablespoons granulated sugar. Beat vigorously with wooden spoon until thoroughly blended.
4. Beat in remaining 1 cup flour. Add melted butter and stir until well blended.
5. Spoon dough into prepared mold. Cover and let rise in a warm, draft-free place until dough has risen to within 1 inch of rim of pan, about 1 hour.
6. Preheat oven to 375F (190C).
7. Bake 25 to 30 minutes or until wooden pick inserted in center comes out clean. Remove from pan and cool on wire rack.
8. To make syrup, place granulated sugar and water in medium saucepan. Bring to a boil over moderate heat, stirring. Boil rapidly 8 minutes, without stirring, or until mixture is syrupy. Remove from heat and let cool 5 minutes. Stir in rum.
9. Prick bottom and top of cake all over with prongs of fork. Place cake, rounded side up, in deep serving dish. Spoon or pour syrup over cake. Let stand 3 to 4 hours,

Savarins are usually soaked in rum, but also can be soaked in kirsch or a flavored syrup. They can be filled with fresh fruit for a delicious treat or made even more delicious with a filling of whipped cream or pastry cream under the fruit.

spooning syrup over cake periodically until cake has absorbed syrup.

10. To make glaze, press apricot jam through sieve into small saucepan. Place saucepan over low heat and cook, stirring, until melted. Remove from heat and let cool 2 minutes. Stir in water. Brush glaze liberally over cake.

11. To serve, fill center of Savarin with strawberries and sprinkle with powdered sugar. Makes 1 Savarin.

Baba au Raisins

(Illustrated on page 48.) Prepare dough as directed for Savarin, adding 1 cup rum-soaked raisins along with melted butter. Spoon dough into 10 well-greased baba molds. Bake 15 to 20 minutes. Proceed as directed for Savarin. Serve with rhubarb sauce, poached rhubarb and fresh mint. Makes 10 Babas.

Filling Variations

Fill center of Savarin (page 130) with red currants. Spoon lightly sweetened whipped cream around bottom of Savarin or in the center.

A savarin can be filled with raspberries, strawberries, blackberries, blueberries, sliced peaches, cherries or almost any fruit. Sprinkle with rum and chopped nuts or toasted flaked coconut.

Braided & Rolled
Yeast Cakes

Braided and rolled yeast cakes with delicious fillings make wonderful coffee cakes. Serve them for breakfast or brunch, or any time you choose with a steaming hot cup of coffee or freshly brewed tea.

Fruited Braid

(Illustrated opposite
   page)
1 recipe Basic Yeast
   Dough, page 117
1/2 cup chopped
   candied lemon peel
1/2 cup chopped
   candied orange peel
   or citron
1 egg yolk beaten with
   1 tablespoon milk

1. Prepare Basic Yeast
Dough according to
directions on page 117
through Step 14,
adding candied lemon
and orange peel along
with flour (Step 8).
2. Grease baking
sheet.
3. Divide dough in
half, set 1 piece aside
and divide other piece
into 3 equal-size
pieces. Shape into
three 10-inch long
strands.
4. Place strands on
lightly floured surface
and pinch top ends
firmly together. Braid
strands, pinch ends
together and tuck
under. Repeat with
remaining piece of
dough.
5. Place fruited braids
on prepared baking
sheet. Cover with
clean towel and set
aside in a warm,
draft-free place to rise
until doubled in bulk,
about 1 hour.
6. Preheat oven to
350F (175C).
7. Brush tops of braids
with beaten egg yolk
mixture. Bake in
preheated oven 35 to
40 minutes or until
golden brown. Remove
from baking sheet and
cool on wire rack.
Makes 2 loaves.

Poppy Seed Twist

(Illustrated opposite
   page)
1 recipe Basic Yeast
   Dough, page 117
Filling:
1 cup poppy seed,
   ground
1-3/4 cups milk
1/3 cup granulated
   sugar
1/4 cup raisins,
   chopped
1/4 cup cornstarch
1 egg yolk, beaten
Powdered sugar

1. Prepare Basic Yeast
Dough recipe through
Step 14.
2. For filling, place
poppy seed and 1-1/4
cups milk in saucepan.
Bring to a boil over
moderate heat. Lower
heat and simmer 10
minutes. Stir in sugar
and raisins.
3. Blend cornstarch
with remaining milk
until smooth. Add to
poppy seed mixture
with egg yolk. Blend.
Cook, stirring, until
thickened (don't allow
mixture to come to a
boil). Let cool.
4. Grease baking
sheet.
5. Roll out dough on
lightly floured surface
to 16″ x 14″ rectangle.
Halve dough
lengthwise. Spread
filling over pieces of
dough to within 1/2
inch of edges. Roll up
pieces lengthwise to
make two long rolls.
Pinch seams to seal.
6. Place rolls side by
side and pinch top
ends together. Twist
rolls over each other in
spiral. Place on baking
sheet. Cover and let
rise until doubled.
7. Preheat oven to
350F (175C).
8. Bake 30 to 35
minutes or until
golden brown. Remove
from baking sheet and
cool on wire rack.
Sprinkle with

powdered sugar before
serving. Makes 1 loaf.

Nut Braid

(Illustrated left)
1 recipe Basic Yeast
   Dough, page 117
Filling:
2 cups finely chopped
   pecans, walnuts or
   hazelnuts
1/2 cup dry bread
   crumbs
1/2 cup granulated
   sugar
6 tablespoons dark
   rum
Icing:
1-1/2 cups powdered
   sugar
1 to 2 tablespoons
   warm water or milk

1. Prepare Basic Yeast
Dough recipe through
Step 14.
2. To make filling,
combine nuts, bread
crumbs, granulated
sugar and rum in bowl
until blended.
3. Grease baking
sheets.
4. Halve dough. Set 1
piece aside. Roll out
other piece on lightly
floured surface to 15″
x 12″ rectangle.
5. Sprinkle half of nut
mixture over dough.
Roll up, jelly-roll style,
starting from long end.
Pinch seam to seal and
place on baking sheet.
Snip top of roll with
scissors to make zigzag
pattern. Repeat with
remaining dough and
nut filling. Cover and
let rise until doubled
in bulk.
6. Preheat oven to
350F (175C).
7. Bake 30 to 35
minutes or until
golden brown. Remove
from baking sheets
and cool on wire racks.
8. Stir powdered sugar
and water in bowl
until smooth. Drizzle
over top of filled rolls.
Let stand until icing is
set. Make 2 loaves.

Homemade Pizza—The Best Kind of All

Pizza, that wonderful Italian creation, is clearly one of America's most popular foods. In spite of the proliferation of pizza parlors all over the United States, pizza can be made easily at home. Combine your favorite foods and make imaginative toppings to please the varied tastes of all your family and guests.

Pizza

Dough:
1-1/2 cups warm water (105-115F/40-45C)
1 (1/4-oz.) package active dry yeast
1 teaspoon sugar
l teaspoon salt
About 4-1/4 cups all-purpose flour
2 to 3 tablespoons olive oil
Pizza Sauce (opposite)
1 lb. mozzarella cheese, shredded
Toppings (opposite)

1. To make dough, place warm water in large bowl, sprinkle yeast and sugar over. Stir to dissolve. Let stand 5 to 10 minutes or until foamy.
2. Add salt and 2 cups flour and stir until blended. Stir in 1-1/2 cups flour to make stiff dough that comes away from sides of bowl.
3. Place dough on lightly floured surface and knead in enough remaining flour to make smooth dough.
4. Place dough in greased bowl and turn to coat. Cover and let rise in a warm, draft-free place until doubled in bulk.
5. Preheat oven to 450F (230C).
6. Lightly oil two 14-inch pizza pans or two 15″ x 12″ baking sheets. Punch dough down and halve.
7. Roll out each piece of dough to a 15-inch circle and place on pans. Pinch up edges of dough to make rim and brush with olive oil.
8. Spread half of sauce over each pizza. Sprinkle with cheese and add additional toppings as desired.
9. Bake 20 to 22 minutes or until crust is golden.
10. Cut into wedges and serve hot. Makes 2 pizzas.

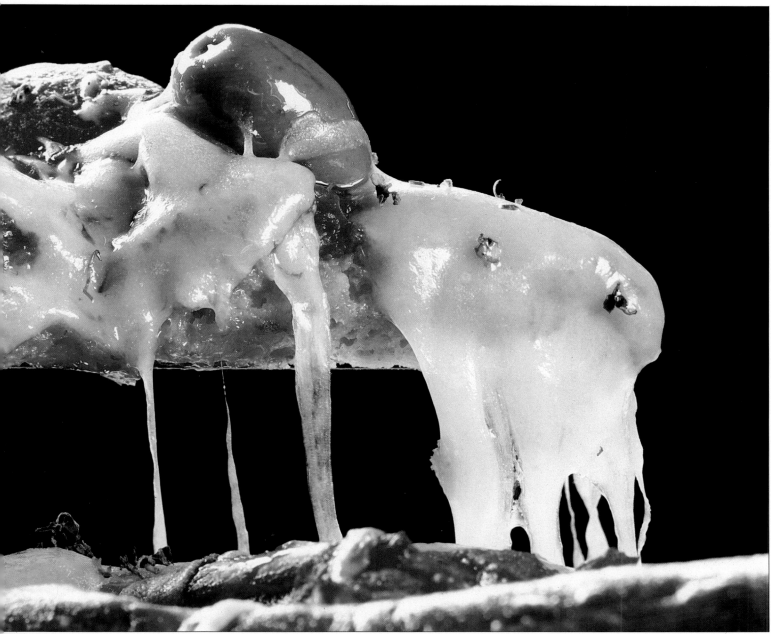

Pizza Sauce

2 tablespoons
vegetable or olive
oil
1 medium onion,
chopped
1 clove garlic, minced
1 (16-oz.) can crushed
tomatoes
4 tablespoons tomato
paste
1 teaspoon dried
Italian seasoning
1/2 teaspoon dried
oregano
Salt and freshly
ground pepper to
taste

Crushed red pepper to
taste

1. Heat oil in medium
saucepan. Add onion
and sauté until almost
transparent. Add garlic
and sauté 2 minutes.
2. Add crushed
tomatoes, tomato
paste, Italian
seasoning, oregano,
salt and pepper; stir
well. Bring to a boil
over moderate heat.
Lower heat and
simmer 15 minutes,
stirring occasionally.
Add crushed pepper

and remove saucepan
from heat. Spoon over
pizzas.

Pizza Toppings

Add 1 or more of the
following toppings
before baking:
1. Sautéed
mushrooms: Slice 1/2
lb. mushrooms. Sauté
in 2 tablespoons
vegetable oil 3 to 4
minutes.
2. Pepperoni or
salami: Thinly slice 1/4
lb. pepperoni or
salami.

3. Green or red
peppers: Seed, core
and cut into thin
strips.
4. Anchovy fillets:
Drain and cut into
thirds.
5. Three cheese
topping: Use 1/3
shredded mozzarella,
1/3 grated Parmesan or
Romano and 1/3
shredded Cheddar
cheese.
6. Pitted or stuffed
olives: Use whole or
sliced.
7. Italian sausage: Use
fully cooked sausage,

sweet or hot. Cut into
thin slices or crumble.
8. Meatballs: Fully
cook and slice.
9. Prosciutto or boiled
ham: Thinly slice and
cut slices into thin
strips.
10. Tuna: Drain and
flake.
11. Artichoke hearts or
bottoms: Drain and cut
into small pieces.
12. Seafood: Use small
cooked shrimp,
drained chopped
clams, drained mussels
or cooked squid.

Deep-Dish Pizza

Pizza does not always have to be made in the traditional
flat shape. It can also be made in a springform
pan or deep-dish pie plate. Fill it to the brim with sauce,
vegetables, meat and cheese and serve it as a
light meal with a crisp green salad.

Deep-Dish Vegetable Pizza

(Illustrated above)
1/2 recipe Pizza
   Dough, page 134
Filling and topping:
2 tablespoons
   vegetable oil
1 large onion, sliced

1 small green or red
   pepper, seeded,
   cored and cut into
   thin strips
1/4 lb. mushrooms,
   thinly sliced
1 small zucchini,
   trimmed and sliced
Salt and freshly
   ground pepper to
   taste

1/2 cup tomato sauce
1/4 cup grated
   Parmesan or
   Romano cheese
8 slices bacon,
   partially cooked
2 cups shredded
   mozzarella cheese

1. Prepare pizza dough according to directions on page 134. Divide dough in half. Wrap and freeze half of dough for use another time.
2. Grease a 10-inch springform pan, deep-dish pizza pan or deep-dish pie plate.
3. Roll out dough on lightly floured surface to 13-inch circle and line pan, pressing dough up sides of pan. Let dough rise 20 to 25 minutes.
4. Preheat oven to 400F (205C).
5. Lightly prick bottom of dough with fork. Bake in preheated oven 15 to 20 minutes or until golden. Remove from oven and cool in pan on wire rack.
6. To make filling, heat oil in medium skillet. Add onion, green pepper, mushrooms and zucchini. Sauté 3 to 4 minutes or until vegetables are very crisp. Season with salt and pepper and remove from heat.
7. Spread tomato sauce over bottom of crust and sprinkle with Parmesan cheese. Spoon vegetables over sauce. Place half the bacon slices over vegetables. Scatter mozzarella cheese over vegetables and top with remaining bacon.
8. Bake in preheated oven 15 to 20 minutes or until top is golden brown. Cut into wedges and serve hot.

137

Quick Sauceless "Pizza"

(Illustrated right)
1 (1-lb.) package
   frozen pizza dough
   or frozen white or
   whole-wheat bread
   dough, thawed
Onion Topping:
2 tablespoons olive oil
1/3 cup grated
   Parmesan or
   Romano cheese
5 to 6 medium onions,
   thinly sliced or cut
   into rings
1 to 2 teaspoons
   caraway seed
Salt and freshly
   ground pepper to
   taste
1 cup shredded Swiss
   or Gruyère cheese
1 cup shredded
   mozzarella or
   Monterey Jack
   cheese

1. Oil 15″ x 12″ baking
sheet. Roll out dough
on lightly floured
surface and fit onto
oiled pan. Let rise 20
to 30 minutes.
2. Preheat oven to
425F (220C).
3. Sprinkle dough
with oil and sprinkle
Parmesan cheese over
oil. Scatter onions
evenly over cheese and
sprinkle with caraway
seed. Season with salt
and pepper and scatter
Swiss and mozzarella
cheese over top.
4. Bake in preheated
oven 20 to 25 minutes.
Cut into serving pieces
and serve hot.

Quick Pizza

Keep frozen pizza or bread dough on hand so you can
make pizza quickly and easily when unexpected guests
appear. Top the dough with whatever you have
on hand and serve it piping hot from the oven.

. . . Ideal Food for an Informal Party

Be sure to have lots of napkins on hand and a wide variety of good things to drink. Soft drinks, beer and a good Italian red wine are ideal accompaniments for pizza.

Variations

Sauceless "pizzas" can be topped with a wide variety of vegetables, depending on what is in season.

Leek and Bacon "Pizza"

(Illustrated at left) Thoroughly rinse 2-1/4 lbs. (1 large bunch) leeks under cold running water. Thinly slice. Cut 4 to 6 slices bacon into chunks and partially cook. Sprinkle Parmesan cheese over dough. Scatter leeks and bacon over cheese and bake as directed for Quick Sauceless "Pizza".

Spinach and Pepper "Pizza"

Thaw 1 (10-oz.) package frozen chopped spinach. Drain well and squeeze out excess liquid. Seed and core 1 medium red pepper. Cut into thin strips. Sprinkle Parmesan cheese over dough. Scatter spinach and red pepper strips over cheese. Season with salt and pepper. Bake as directed for Quick Sauceless "Pizza".

Artichoke and Mushroom "Pizza"

Drain 1 (14-1/2 oz.) can artichoke hearts. Sauté a 1/2 lb. sliced mushrooms in 2 tablespoons butter. Sprinkle Parmesan cheese over dough. Cut artichoke hearts into quarters and scatter over dough along with mushrooms. Season with salt and pepper and 1/2 teaspoon dried tarragon. Proceed as directed for Quick Sauceless "Pizza".

Yeast Doughnuts—Sinfully Delicious

Crisp, sugary doughnuts, filled with jam or custard are always a welcome snack. Just be sure to make enough to satisfy everyone.

Hints and Tips

For best results, use an electric deep-fryer that controls the temperature of the cooking fat. If an electric deep-fryer is not available, be sure to use a deep-fat thermometer to check the temperature of the fat.

Don't crowd the pan. Fry only a few doughnuts at a time.

Use good quality fresh oil or shortening for frying. Don't reuse oil or shortening that has been used previously to cook strongly flavored food.

Use a slotted spoon to remove cooked doughnuts from fat.

Be sure to drain doughnuts on paper towels.

Jelly Doughnuts

1/4 cup warm water
  (105-115F/40-45C)
1 (1/4-oz.) package
  active dry yeast
3 tablespoons
  granulated sugar
1/3 cup butter, room
  temperature
1 teaspoon salt
1/2 cup milk, scalded
About 2-1/2 cups
  all-purpose flour
2 eggs, lightly beaten
Vegetable oil for
  deep-frying
Jelly or jam for filling
Powdered or
  granulated sugar

1. Place warm water in large bowl and sprinkle yeast and 1 teaspoon sugar over. Stir to dissolve. Let stand 5 to 10 minutes or until foamy.
2. Add butter, remaining 2 tablespoons granulated sugar and salt to milk and stir until butter is melted. Let cool to lukewarm.
3. Add milk mixture to yeast and stir until blended. Add 2 cups flour and beaten eggs and stir to make stiff dough that comes away from sides of bowl.
4. Place dough on lightly floured surface and knead in enough remaining flour to make smooth and elastic dough, 8 to 10 minutes.
5. Place dough in greased bowl and turn to coat. Cover and let rise in a warm, draft-free place until doubled in bulk.
6. Grease baking sheets and sprinkle with flour.
7. Punch dough down and roll out on lightly floured surface to 1/2-inch thickness. Cut dough with floured 2-1/2- to 3-inch biscuit or cookie cutter. Place dough circles on prepared baking sheets. Cover and let rise until doubled.

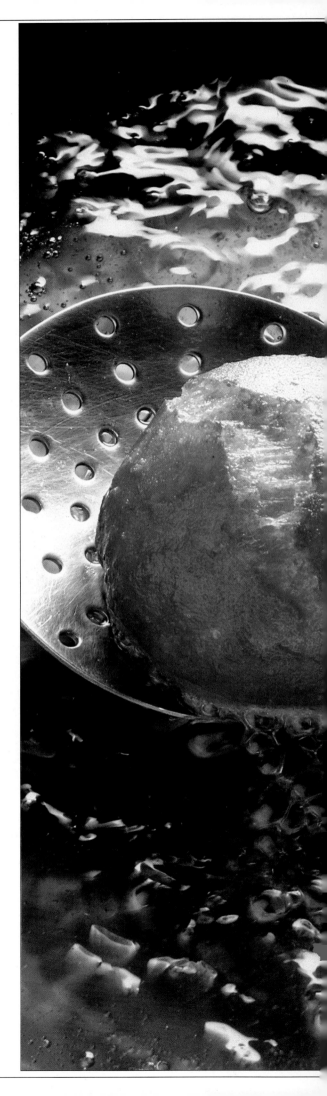

8. Heat oil in deep-fat fryer to 350F (175C) on deep-fat thermometer. Lift doughnuts with pancake turner and gently lower into hot fat. Deep-fry 2 to 3 doughnuts at a time, 1 minute on each side, turning once, or until doughnuts are golden brown.

9. Remove with slotted spoon and drain on paper towels.

10. Pierce doughnuts with sharp knife from 1 side almost through to the other side. Spoon jelly into pastry bag fitted with large plain tip and press small amount of jelly into doughnuts through opening. Sprinkle sugar over doughnuts. Makes 12 to 14 Jelly Doughnuts.

Variations

Raisin Doughnuts: Omit jelly and knead 3/4 cup raisins into dough. Deep-fry as directed for Jelly Doughnuts.

Custard Doughnuts: Omit jelly and fill doughnuts with Vanilla Cream, page 233.

Iced Doughnuts: Combine 1-1/2 cups powdered sugar with 1 to 2 tablespoons milk. Spread over tops of cooled doughnuts. Sprinkle with chopped nuts or colored candy sprinkles. Let stand until icing is set.

Cinnamon Doughnuts: Combine equal amounts of cinnamon and superfine sugar. Sprinkle over hot doughnuts.

Our Daily Bread

Shaping the Dough

In addition to making bread in a loaf pan, the dough can
be shaped in almost any way imaginable. Twists,
rolls and braids are among the most popular shapes.

Basic Instructions

Prepare Basic White
Bread according to
directions on page 144
through Step 5.

Punch dough down
and shape (see
opposite page). Place
on greased baking
sheet, cover and let
rise 30 to 45 minutes.
Brush with egg wash
for shiny crust or with
water for crisp crust.
Bake in preheated 375F
(190C) oven 20 to 35
minutes (depending on
size and shape).
Remove from baking
sheet and cool on wire
rack.

Spiral Loaf

Pinch off walnut-size ball of dough. Divide remaining dough into 8 equal-size pieces. Shape into 1/2- to 3/4-inch thick ropes and arrange in spiral pattern. Place ball of dough in center.

Pretzels

Divide dough into 14 equal-size pieces. Shape into 18- to 20-inch long pencils. Twist each "pencil" into pretzel shape. Sprinkle with coarse salt before baking.

Crescents

Divide dough into 12 to 16 equal-size pieces. Shape into 7-inch long ropes. Shape ropes into crescents. To make double crescents, join crescents back-to-back in center with small piece of dough.

Round Loaf

Shape into a slightly flattened round. Pinch and tuck ends under. After rising, cut "X" on top of loaf.

Club Rolls

Divide dough into 10 equal-size pieces. Shape into 4" x 2" rectangles. Cut slash down center of each roll before rising.

Baguettes

Divide dough in half. Shape into 2 loaves and taper ends. After rising, cut several diagonal slashes on top of loaves.

Cloverleaf Rolls

Cut dough into 36 equal-size pieces. Shape into small balls. Place 3 balls close together in clusters on greased baking sheet or in greased muffin cups. After rising, snip top of balls with scissors.

Breadsticks

Cut dough into 20 equal-size pieces. Shape into 8- to 10-inch long pencils.

Oval Rolls

Cut dough into 10 to 12 equal-size pieces. Roll out to 4-inch circles or 6-inch ovals.

Twist

Cut dough in half. Shape into two 16-inch ropes. Twist ropes together and tuck ends under.

Snails

Cut dough into 12 to 16 equal-size pieces. Shape into 15-inch long ropes. Wind ropes loosely to form spirals.

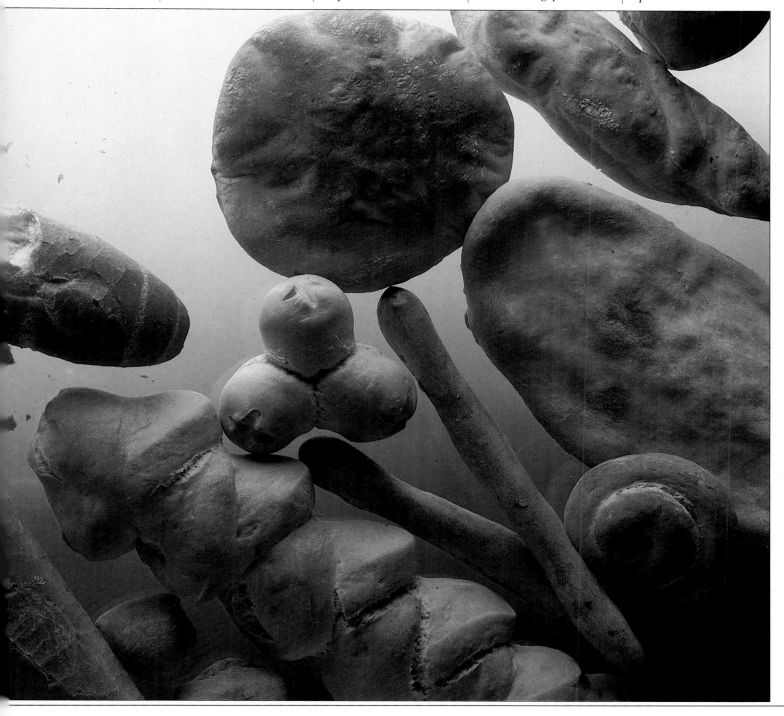

Simple Rolls with Flavorful & Decorative Toppings

Rolls

1 cup warm water
(105-115F/40-45C)
1 (1/4-oz.) package
active dry yeast
2 teaspoons sugar
About 3 cups bread
flour or all-purpose
flour
1 teaspoon salt
Cornmeal for
sprinkling
l egg beaten with l
tablespoon water
For Decoration:
Grated cheese
Sesame seed
Caraway seed
Finely chopped
pistachio nuts
Sea salt or coarse salt
Unprocessed wheat
bran
Black sesame seed

1. Place warm water in large bowl and sprinkle yeast and 1 teaspoon sugar over. Stir to dissolve. Let stand 5 to 10 minutes or until foamy.
2. Add 2 cups flour, salt and remaining sugar and stir until well blended. Stir in 1/2 cup flour or enough remaining flour to make soft dough.
3. Turn dough out onto a lightly floured surface and knead in enough remaining flour to make smooth dough. Knead until smooth and elastic, 8 to 10 minutes. Place dough in greased bowl and turn to coat entire surface of dough. Cover with a clean towel and set aside in a warm, draft-free place to rise until doubled in bulk, about 1 hour.
4. Grease baking sheet and sprinkle with cornmeal. Set aside.
5. Punch dough down and cut into 7 equal-size pieces. Shape into slightly flattened balls and pinch and tuck ends under. Place balls, seam side down, on prepared baking sheet in circle with 1 ball in center. Allow enough room between balls for expansion. Cover and let rise until almost doubled.
6. Preheat oven 400F (205C). Brush tops of rolls with egg wash and sprinkle with topping as desired (see photo). Bake in preheated oven 10 to 15 minutes or until golden brown. Remove from baking sheet and cool on wire rack or serve warm. Break ring apart to serve.

Flavoring is often added to dough. When flavoring is also
sprinkled on top, it provides a clue to the
possible hidden flavor inside, and adds a decorative and
flavorful touch to the finished product.

Additional Toppings

By varying the ingredients used as topping, you can make a different-flavor roll every time you make this recipe. Add a little seed or chopped nuts to the dough along with the flour to flavor the inside of the roll. Sprinkle on top of rolls before baking.

Walnuts: Use coarsely chopped or broken into small pieces.

Hazelnuts: Roast in the shell in a hot oven a few minutes. Remove shells and rub off skins. Crush nuts coarsely in mortar and pestle or with rolling pin.

Cashew Nuts: Use coarsely chopped or broken into small pieces.

Almonds: Use sliced, slivered or coarsely chopped blanched almonds.

Cereal and Grains: Add to rolls to increase nutritional value.

Variations on Basic White Bread

Once you have learned how to make a golden brown wholesome loaf of white bread, there are many things you can add to the dough to enhance the bread. Flavor and appearance can both be changed dramatically.

Raisin Bread

(Illustrated opposite page, top left)
1/4 cup warm water (105-115F/40-45C)
1 (1/4-oz.) package active dry yeast
2 tablespoons sugar
1 teaspoon salt
3 tablespoons butter
1 cup milk, scalded
About 3-1/4 cups all-purpose flour
3/4 cup raisins
1 egg beaten with 1 tablespoon milk or water for egg wash

Prepare recipe for Basic White Bread according to directions on page 144. Add raisins after the first addition of flour. Proceed as directed in recipe.

Tomato Bread

(Illustrated opposite page, top right) Prepare recipe for Basic White Bread according to directions on page 144. Add 2 to 3 tablespoons tomato paste with milk mixture. Proceed as directed in recipe.

Herb Bread

(Illustrated opposite page, second row left) Prepare recipe for Basic White Bread according to directions on page 144. Add 3 to 4 tablespoons freshly chopped herbs with the first addition of flour. Proceed as directed in recipe. Almost any combination of herbs will do; try parsley, dill, basil and thyme.

Prune Bread

(Illustrated opposite page, second row right) Prepare recipe for Basic White Bread according to directions on page 144. Add 1 cup snipped pitted prunes after first addition of flour. Proceed as directed in recipe.

Cocoa Bread

(Illustrated opposite page, third row left) Prepare recipe for Basic White Bread according to directions on page 144. Add 1/3 cup cocoa powder with the first addition of flour. If desired, add 1 to 2 tablespoons additional sugar. Proceed as directed in recipe.

Carrot Bread

(Illustrated opposite page, third row right) Prepare recipe for Basic White Bread according to directions on page 144. Add 1 cup shredded or grated carrots with the first addition of flour. Proceed as directed in recipe.

Onion Bread

(Illustrated opposite page, bottom row left) Sauté 1 cup chopped onion in 2 tablespoons butter until onions are lightly browned. Prepare recipe for Basic White Bread according to directions on page 144. Add sautéed onion with the first addition of flour. (It may be necessary to add a little more flour during kneading.) Proceed as directed in recipe.

Pepper Bread

(Illustrated opposite page, bottom right) Dice 1/2 red, 1/2 green and 1/2 yellow pepper. Sauté in 2 tablespoons butter about 3 minutes. Prepare recipe for Basic White Bread according to directions on page 144. Add sautéed peppers with the first addition of flour. (It may be necessary to add a little more flour during kneading.) Proceed as directed in recipe.

Tips

You can vary the flavor of the dough in many different ways:

Add a little extra salt, if desired, when making a savory dough.

Be sure to knead the dough well so the added ingredients will be evenly distributed throughout the dough.

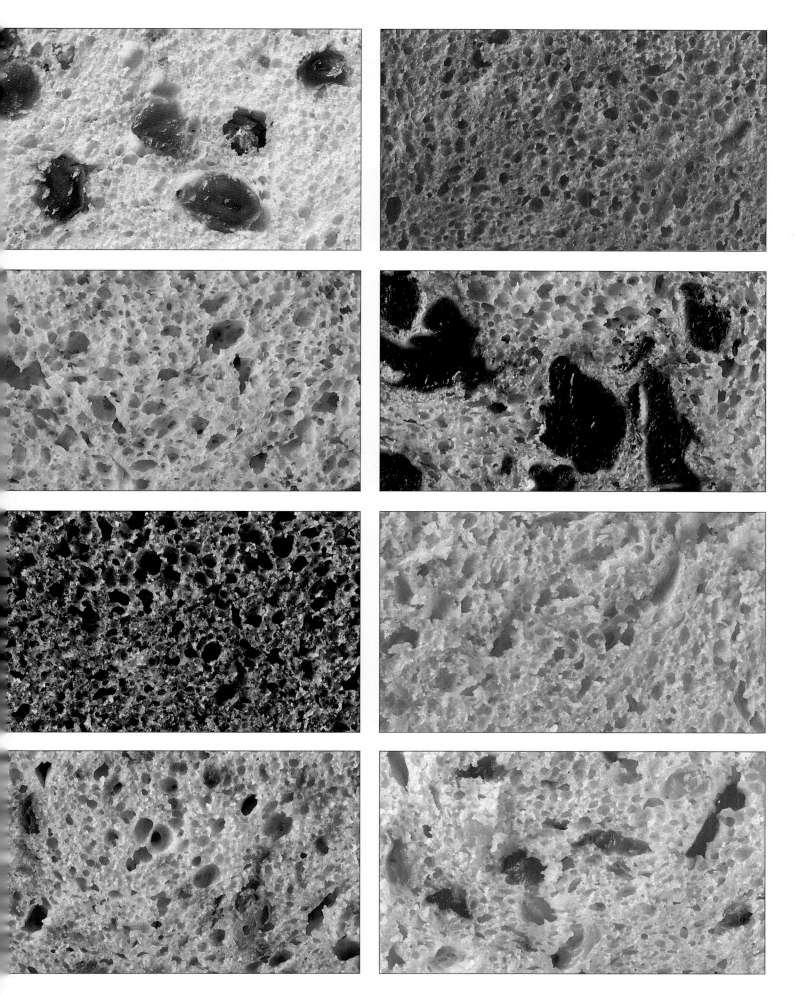

High Fiber Breads—Good to Eat & Good for You

Oat Bread

1 cup regular rolled
    oats
2 cups boiling water
1/2 cup firmly packed
    brown sugar
2 tablespoons butter
2 teaspoons salt
1/2 cup warm water
    (105-115F/40-45C)
1 (1/4-oz.) package
    active dry yeast
2 cups whole-wheat
    flour
3 to 3-1/2 cups
    all-purpose flour

1. Place oats in large
bowl. Add boiling
water, brown sugar,
butter and salt and stir
well. Let stand 40
minutes or until cool.
2. Place warm water in
small bowl. Sprinkle
yeast over and stir to
dissolve. Let stand 5 to
10 minutes or until
foamy. Stir yeast into
cooled oat mixture.
3. Stir in whole-wheat
flour. Add all-purpose
flour, 1 cup at a time,
stirring to make soft
dough.
4. Place dough on a
lightly floured surface
and knead in enough
all-purpose flour to
make smooth dough.
Knead until smooth
and elastic.

5. Place dough in
greased bowl and turn
to coat. Cover and let
rise in a warm,
draft-free place until
doubled in bulk, about
1-1/2 hours.
6. Grease two 8'' x 4''
loaf pans. Punch
dough down and
divide in half. Shape
each piece of dough
into a loaf and place in
prepared pans. Cover
and let rise until
dough reaches rims of
pans.
7. Preheat oven to
375F (190C). Brush
tops of loaves with
water and bake in
preheated oven 30 to

35 minutes or until
bread sounds hollow
when tapped on
bottom. Remove from
pans and cool on wire
rack. Makes 2 loaves.

Wheat Bran Bread

1/4 cup warm water
    (105-115F/40-45C)
1 (1/4-oz.) package
    active dry yeast
2 tablespoons butter
2 tablespoons brown
    sugar
1 teaspoon salt
1 cup milk, scalded
1/2 cup unprocessed
    wheat bran
About 3 cups
    whole-wheat flour

The more we learn about good nutrition, the more we realize the importance of eating foods that are high in fiber. The trick is to find foods that also taste good. These delicious breads fall into a special category—the more high fiber bread you eat, the better it is for you.

1. Place warm water in large bowl, sprinkle yeast over and stir to dissolve. Let stand 5 to 10 minutes or until foamy.
2. Add butter, brown sugar and salt to hot milk and stir until butter is melted. Let cool to room temperature. Stir milk mixture into yeast until blended. Stir in bran and enough whole-wheat flour to make soft dough.
3. Place dough on a lightly floured surface and knead in enough whole-wheat flour to make smooth dough.

Knead until smooth and elastic.
4. Place in greased bowl and turn to coat. Cover and let rise in a warm, draft-free place until doubled in bulk, about 1-1/2 hours.
5. Grease 8" x 4" loaf pan. Punch dough down. Shape dough into a loaf and place in prepared pan. Cover and let rise until dough reaches rim of pan.
6. Preheat oven to 375F (190C). Brush top of loaf with water and bake in preheated oven 30 to 35 minutes or until bread sounds

hollow when tapped on bottom. Remove from pan and cool on wire rack. Makes 1 loaf.

Graham Bread

Prepare recipe for Wheat Bran Bread according to directions (near left). Omit unprocessed bran and decrease whole-wheat flour to 2 to 2-1/2 cups. Substitute 1 cup graham flour. Proceed as directed in recipe.

Buckwheat (Kasha) Bread

Prepare recipe for Oat Bread according to directions (far left). Omit rolled oats and decrease all-purpose flour to 3 cups. Substitute 1 cup medium buckwheat groats (Kasha). Proceed as directed in recipe.

Bread & Rolls from Home & Around the World

Just about every country and ethnic group has its own special kind of bread, some that are eaten all year and some that are made for holidays and special occasions.

Challah is a traditional Jewish Sabbath bread made with eggs and sometimes colored with saffron. It is delicious fresh or toasted, baked plain or topped with sesame or caraway seeds.

Panettone is an Italian Christmas cake similar to the German Christmas cake, Stollen. Panettone can be made in a soufflé dish or coffee can as suggested in the recipe on the right, or you can buy a special panettone pan.

Dinner rolls, familiar all over the United States, differ from rolls served in Europe because most Americans prefer to serve rolls warm. It is unusual to be served warm bread in Europe, whereas in the United States many people form their first impression of a restaurant based on whether or not the bread or rolls arrive at the table nicely

warmed and carefully wrapped in a napkin to keep them that way.

Pita bread, the Greek and adopted American name for pocket bread from the Middle East, is very versatile. It can be filled with all kinds of wonderous mixtures or broken into small pieces and served with a dip. It is sometimes added to salad in the Middle East or used as an eating utensil to scoop up other food.

Challah

1/4 cup warm water (105-115F/40-45C)
1 (1/4-oz.) package active dry yeast
2 tablespoons sugar
3 tablespoons butter
1-1/2 teaspoons salt
1/8 teaspoon ground saffron (optional)
1/2 cup milk, scalded
About 3 cups bread flour or all-purpose flour
2 eggs, lightly beaten
1 egg beaten with 1 tablespoon water for egg wash
Sesame seed for sprinkling

1. Place water in large bowl, sprinkle yeast and 1 teaspoon sugar over and stir to dissolve. Let stand 5 to 10 minutes or until foamy.
2. Add butter, salt, remaining sugar and saffron to hot milk and stir until butter is melted. Cool to room temperature.
3. Add milk mixture to yeast mixture and stir to mix. Stir in 1 cup flour until blended. Add eggs and 1 cup flour and stir vigorously. Stir in enough remaining flour to make soft dough.
4. Place dough on a lightly floured surface and knead in enough remaining flour to make smooth dough. Knead until smooth and elastic, 8 to 10 minutes.
5. Place dough in greased bowl and turn to coat. Cover and set aside in a warm, draft-free place to rise until doubled in bulk, about 1 hour.

6. Grease baking sheet. Punch dough down and divide into 2 pieces, making 1 piece slightly larger than the other. Cut each piece into 3 equal-size pieces. Shape 3 large pieces into ropes 18 inches long. Shape 3 small pieces into ropes 14 inches long. Braid 3 large ropes, pinching and tucking ends under. Place on prepared baking sheet. Braid 3 short ropes, pinching and tucking ends under. Place on top of large braid. Cover and let rise until doubled.
7. Preheat oven to 375F (190C). Brush loaf all over with egg wash and sprinkle sesame seed on top. Bake in preheated oven 40 to 50 minutes or until braid sounds hollow when tapped on bottom. Remove from baking sheet and cool on wire rack. Makes 1 loaf.

Panettone

(Illustrated above)
2/3 cup warm milk
  (105-115F/40-45C)
2 (1/4-oz.) packages
  active dry yeast
1/2 cup sugar
6 egg yolks
1/2 cup butter, melted
  and cooled
1 teaspoon salt
2 teaspoons grated
  lemon peel
1 to 2 teaspoons
  aniseed, crushed
About 3-1/2 cups
  all-purpose flour
3/4 cup raisins
1/2 cup chopped mixed
  candied fruit
1/3 cup toasted
  chopped almonds
1 egg beaten with 1
  tablespoon water for
  egg wash

1. Place milk in large
bowl, sprinkle yeast
and 1 teaspoon sugar
over and stir to
dissolve. Let stand 5 to
10 minutes or until
foamy.
2. Add egg yolks,
melted butter,
remaining sugar, salt,
lemon peel and
crushed aniseed and
beat vigorously with a
wooden spoon until
well blended.
3. Add 2 cups flour,
raisins, fruit and
almonds and stir until
blended. Stir in

enough remaining
flour to make soft
dough.
4. Place dough on a
lightly floured surface
and knead in enough
remaining flour to
make smooth dough.
Knead until smooth
and elastic, 8 to 10
minutes.
5. Place dough in
greased bowl; turn to
coat. Cover and let rise
in a warm, draft-free
place until doubled,
about 1-1/2 hours.
6. Grease two 6-inch
(1-quart) soufflé dishes
or two 1-pound coffee
cans. If using soufflé
dishes, line sides of
dishes with greased
parchment paper,
extending paper 2
inches above rim of
dish.
7. Punch dough down
and divide in half.
Shape each piece into
a flattened ball and
place in dishes or cans.
Cover and let rise until
doubled.
8. Preheat oven to
375F(190C). Brush tops
of loaves with egg
wash. Bake 30 to 40
minutes or until cake
tester inserted in
center comes out
clean. Remove from
dishes or cans and cool
on wire rack. Makes 2
Panettone.

Party Dinner Rolls

(Illustrated above)
1/4 cup warm water
  (105-115F/40-45C)
1 (1/4-oz.) package
  active dry yeast
2 tablespoons sugar
1/2 cup butter
1 teaspoon salt
2/3 cup milk, scalded
1 egg, beaten
About 3 cups
  all-purpose flour
1 egg beaten with 1
  tablespoon water for
  egg wash

1. Place water in large
bowl, sprinkle yeast
and 1 teaspoon sugar
over and stir to
dissolve. Let stand 5 to
10 minutes or until
foamy.
2. Add remaining
sugar, butter and salt
to hot milk and stir
until butter is melted.
Cool to room
temperature.
3. Stir milk mixture
and beaten egg into
yeast mixture until
blended. Add 2-1/2
cups flour and stir
with a wooden spoon
to make soft dough.

4. Place dough on a
lightly floured surface
and knead in enough
remaining flour to
make smooth dough.
Knead until smooth
and elastic, 8 to 10
minutes.
5. Place dough in
greased bowl and turn
to coat. Cover and let
rise in a warm,
draft-free place until
doubled in bulk, about
1 hour.
6. Grease a 12-cup
muffin pan. Punch
dough down and
divide into 12
equal-size pieces.
Shape into slightly
flattened balls and
place in prepared
muffin cups. Cover
and let rise until
doubled.
7. Preheat oven to
400F (205C). Brush
tops of rolls with egg
wash. Bake 18 to 22
minutes or until tops
are golden brown.
Remove from pan and
cool on wire rack.
Serve warm. Makes 12
rolls.

Pita Bread

(Illustrated on pages
  50-51)
1-1/2 cups warm water
  (105-115F/40-45C)
1 (1/4-oz.) package
  active dry yeast
1 teaspoon sugar
2 teaspoons salt
About 5 cups
  all-purpose flour
Cornmeal for
  sprinkling

1. Place warm water in
large bowl, sprinkle
yeast and sugar over
and stir. Let stand 5 to
10 minutes or until
foamy.
2. Add salt and 3 cups
flour and stir until well
blended. Stir in
remaining flour to
make soft dough.
3. Place dough on a
lightly floured surface
and knead in enough
remaining flour to
make smooth dough.
Knead until smooth
and elastic.
4. Place dough in
greased bowl and turn
to coat. Cover and let
rise in a warm,
draft-free place until
doubled, about 1 hour.
5. Grease 2 large
baking sheets and
sprinkle with
cornmeal. Punch
dough down and
divide into 12
equal-size pieces. Roll
out each piece of
dough on a lightly
floured surface to a
6-inch circle. Place on
baking sheets about 1
inch apart. Cover and
let rise 15 minutes.
6. Preheat oven to
475F (245C). Bake 8 to
10 minutes or until
tops are puffed and
golden brown, rotating
baking sheets after 4
minutes. Remove from
baking sheets; cool.
Makes 12 circles.

155

Sourdough Starters

Sourdough, which was used in many countries even before yeast was discovered, makes most of us think of San Francisco. During the Gold Rush, miners carried sourdough starter with them and used it to make pancake batter each morning, saving a portion of the starter to be used the next day. Sourdough adds a special flavor to bread and, when properly cared for, starters can be kept going for several years.

Tips on How to Make a Starter

Make the starter several days before you plan to use it. Use a large glass, plastic or pottery bowl. Don't use a metal bowl or stir the starter with a metal utensil.

Store the starter in the refrigerator.

When you remove the amount of starter needed for a recipe, replenish the starter with equal amounts of flour and water. If you use 1 cup of starter, replace it with 1 cup of flour and 1 cup of water.

Sourdough Starter

(Illustrated top 6 photos)
1 (1/4-oz.) package active dry yeast
2 cups warm water (105-115F/40-45C)
2 cups all-purpose flour or whole-wheat flour

1. Sprinkle yeast into clean, dry non-metallic bowl.
2. Add warm water slowly.
3. Stir with wire whisk to dissolve yeast.
4. Add flour gradually, stirring constantly.
5. Stir flour-water mixture thoroughly to break up any lumps.
6. Cover bowl with clean towel and let stand at room temperature 2 days. Stir mixture down occasionally. Yield: 3 cups Starter.

Sourdough Rye Bread

(Illustrated bottom 6 photos)
2-1/2 cups medium rye flour
2 cups all-purpose flour
1 tablespoon sugar
2 teaspoons salt
1 (1/4-oz.) package active dry yeast
1-1/2 cups warm water (105-115F/40-45C)
1 cup Starter (made with all-purpose flour)
Cornmeal

1. Combine rye flour, all-purpose flour, sugar, salt and dry yeast in large bowl.
2. Add warm water and Starter and stir well to make stiff dough. Let stand 15 minutes.
3. Place dough on a lightly floured surface and knead 10 to 15 minutes.
4. Place dough in greased bowl and turn to coat. Cover and let rise in a warm, draft-free place until doubled in bulk, about 1-1/2 hours.
5. Punch dough down. Grease baking sheet and sprinkle with cornmeal.
6. Shape dough into large round loaf, place on prepared baking sheet and cut "X" on top of loaf. Cover and let rise until doubled. Bake in preheated 375F (190C) oven 45 to 50 minutes or until bread sounds hollow when tapped on bottom. Remove from baking sheet and cool on wire rack. Makes 1 large loaf.

The Sweet Smell of Sourdough Breads

White Bread

1 cup Starter (made with all-purpose flour)
1 (1/4-oz.) package active dry yeast
1 tablespoon sugar
1-1/2 cups warm water (105-115F/40-45C)
2 teaspoons salt
About 4-1/2 cups bread flour or all-purpose flour
Cornmeal

1. Place Starter, yeast, sugar and warm water in large bowl and stir well. Let stand 5 to 10 minutes or until foamy.
2. Add salt and 4 cups flour and stir to make stiff dough. Place dough on a lightly floured surface; knead in flour to make soft dough. Knead until smooth and elastic, 8 to 10 minutes.
3. Place dough in greased bowl; turn to coat. Cover and let rise in a warm, draft-free place until doubled, about 1-1/2 hours.
4. Grease baking sheet and sprinkle with cornmeal. Punch dough down and shape into large oval or round loaf. Place on baking sheet. Cover and let rise until doubled.
5. Preheat oven to 375F (190C). Cut diagonal slashes across top of loaf and brush with water. Bake 45 to 50 minutes or until bread sounds hollow when tapped on bottom. Cool on wire rack. Makes 1 large loaf.

Multi-Grain Bread

1 cup Starter (made with whole-wheat flour)
1 cup quick-cooking rolled oats
1 cup warm skim milk (105-115F/40-45C)
3 cups medium rye flour
1-1/2 cups warm water (105-115F/40-45C)
l (1/4-oz.) package active dry yeast
2 tablespoons sugar
1/4 cup butter, melted and cooled
2 teaspoons salt
3 to 3-1/2 cups whole-wheat flour

1. Place Starter, rolled oats and skim milk in large bowl and stir. Add rye flour and 1 cup warm water and stir well. Cover bowl; let stand 1 hour.
2. Sprinkle yeast and sugar over remaining 1/2 cup warm water; stir to dissolve. Let stand 5 to 10 minutes or until foamy. Add to oat mixture; stir well. Stir in melted butter and salt.

The aroma of sourdough bread as it bakes is quite different from the aroma of other breads. It fills the air with the promise of a special treat to be enjoyed when the bread comes out of the oven. Sourdough starter can be used to make white bread or dark bread and the breads that fall in between.

3. Stir in 3 cups whole-wheat flour to make soft dough. Place dough on a lightly floured surface; knead in flour to make stiff dough. Knead until smooth and elastic, 8 to 10 minutes.
4. Place dough in greased bowl and turn to coat. Cover; let rise in a warm, draft-free place until doubled, about 2 hours.
5. Grease two 8'' x 4'' loaf pans or 2 baking sheets. Punch dough down and halve. Shape into loaves and place in pans or shape into slightly flattened ovals and place on baking sheets. Cover and let rise until doubled.
6. Preheat oven to 400F (205C). Cut slash down center of oval loaves. Bake 25 to 30 minutes or until bread sounds hollow when tapped on bottom. Cool on wire rack. Makes 2 loaves.

Black Bread

2 cups Starter (made with whole-wheat flour)
1 cup warm water (105-115F/40-45C)
3 tablespoons dark molasses
1 tablespoon unsweetened cocoa powder
1 tablespoon powdered instant coffee
1 (1/4-oz.) package active dry yeast
1 tablespoon caraway seed, crushed
2 teaspoons salt
2 cups dark rye flour
2 to 2-1/2 cups whole-wheat flour

1. Place Starter, warm water, molasses, cocoa, coffee, and yeast in large bowl and stir well. Let stand 10 minutes or until foamy. Add caraway seed, salt and rye flour and stir well.
2. Stir in 2 cups whole-wheat flour to make soft dough. Place dough on a lightly floured surface; knead in flour to make stiff dough. Knead until smooth and elastic, about 10 minutes.
3. Place dough in greased bowl; turn to coat. Cover and let rise in a warm, draft-free place until doubled, about 2 hours.
4. Grease 9'' x 5'' loaf pan. Punch dough down and shape into loaf. Place in pan. Cover and let rise until dough reaches rim of pan.
5. Preheat oven to 350F (175C). Bake 45 to 50 minutes or until bread sounds hollow when tapped on bottom. Cool on wire rack. Makes 1 loaf.

Salami Sandwich

Arrange thin slices of salami, tomato and cucumber on slices of dark bread. Garnish with sweet peppers.

Roquefort-Pear Sandwich

Arrange thinly sliced canned pear halves on pumpernickel slices. Top with crumbled Roquefort cheese and walnut halves.

Prosciutto Sandwich

Arrange thin slices of prosciutto on slices of dark bread. Top with tiny gherkins.

Bologna-Egg Sandwich

Spread egg salad on sliced bologna; fold over. Arrange on bread slices. Garnish with wedges of hard-cooked egg and chopped parsley.

Roast Beef Sandwich

Arrange thin slices of rare roast beef on slices of bread. Top with horseradish and mustard-pickles.

Egg-Shrimp Sandwich

Spoon hot, cooked scrambled eggs onto toast. Top with tiny cooked shrimp; garnish with chives.

Liver Pâté Sandwich

Arrange slices of liver pâté on slices of dark bread. Top with sliced

mushrooms and radish sprouts.

Tartar Sandwich

Season freshly ground beef or top round with salt and pepper. Add capers, egg yolk and finely chopped onion and parsley, if desired. Spread over slices of dark bread; serve immediately. (Caution: If left at room temperature, Steak Tartar can be unsafe to eat.)

Savory Open Sandwiches . . .

Use slices of fresh bread or toast. Spread with softened butter or mayonnaise as desired. For added flavor, stir mustard into butter or mayonnaise. Sprinkle sandwiches with freshly ground pepper or a touch of paprika for a finishing touch.

Dieter's Sandwich

Spread creamy-style lowfat cottage cheese on slices of bread. Top with orange segments and fresh mint.

Apple Sandwich

Cook apple slices briefly in a small amount of water with a few raisins and a little sugar. Drain well and spoon on slices of bread.

Ricotta-Jelly Sandwich

Spread ricotta cheese on slices of bread. Top with red currant or raspberry jelly.

Deluxe Peanut Butter Sandwich

Spread peanut butter on slices of bread. Top with extra chopped roasted peanuts.

Plum Sandwich

Spread plum jam or plum puree over thickly buttered bread.

Cream Cheese-Honey Sandwich

Spread cream cheese on slices of bread. Top with an exotic-flavored honey.

. . . & Sweet Snacks

Raisin or fruit bread is always a good choice for sweet sandwiches. Spread with softened cheese or sweet butter and sprinkle with finely chopped nuts.

Chocolate-Cream Cheese Sandwich

Stir melted semisweet chocolate into softened cream cheese; spread on bread slices. Top with sliced bananas and flaked coconut.

Fruit Sandwich

Spread honey butter on bread slices. Top with sliced kiwifruit and strawberries.

161

Puff Pastry—The
Ultimate in Baking
Know-How

Crisp & Light Puff Pastry—The Pastry with Paper-Thin Layers & Layers & Layers . . .

Tips on Storage

The basic recipe for Puff Pastry will make about 2-3/4 pounds. Since considerable time and effort are necessary to make puff pastry, it is not really worthwhile to make a smaller amount. Wrap the dough in plastic wrap and store in the refrigerator up to two days. To freeze, divide and wrap in plastic wrap. Overwrap with foil. Store in the freezer up to three months. Thaw in the refrigerator 24 hours before using.

After the dough has been cut into shapes, collect the scraps, stack them and wrap them in plastic wrap. Refrigerate and let rest in the refrigerator 45 to 60 minutes before rolling and shaping.

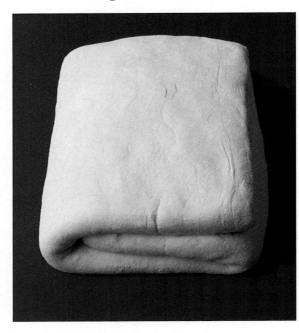

The French call puff pastry "mille feuille" which, literally translated, means a thousand layers. Although this is certainly an exaggeration, professionally made puff pastry can have as many as a hundred light and airy layers!

How The Pastry Gets Its Layers

Puff pastry dough is wrapped around a block of well-chilled butter and then rolled out into a rectangle. The rectangle is folded into thirds and rolled again. Rolled dough must be permitted to rest in the refrigerator before it can be rolled and folded again. The more often the rolling and folding process is repeated, the more layers there will be. The layers are created in the pastry by the thin layers of butter that are between the layers of dough. When the pastry is baked, the butter creates steam which causes the pastry to rise in layers.

The Versatility of Puff Pastry

Puff pastry can be used in many ways. Fill small shapes for appetizers or large shapes for main dishes or desserts; use as a cake base or layer with custard or whipped cream; or flavor with cheese and serve as an elegant snack.

Puff Pastry

Equipment:
Sifter
Marble work surface, if available
Dough scraper
Rolling pin

Ingredients:
4 cups sifted all-purpose flour
2-1/4 cups unsalted butter, well chilled
1 teaspoon salt
1 cup plus 2 tablespoons ice water

Chilling Time:
15 hours

Oven Temperature:
425F (220C)

Baking Time:
18 to 20 minutes

Yield:
Approximately 2-3/4 pounds

Tips on Preparation

All butter used must be thoroughly chilled before it is rolled in.

A cold work surface, such as marble, will keep the pastry and butter cool, which is vitally important.

Resting the dough allows the butter layers to get firm and the dough to relax.

For the best result, make the dough at least one day before baking to allow it to rest.

Don't make puff pastry on a hot, humid day.

Preparation

1. Measure ingredients carefully.

2. Sift flour onto clean cool work surface, preferably marble.

3. Cut 4 tablespoons butter into small pieces and scatter over flour.

4. Cut butter into flour until mixture resembles large, coarse crumbs.

5. Make well in center of flour. Add salt to well and pour in ice water.

6. Rub salt between fingers to dissolve.

7. Push flour over water with dough scraper.

8. Knead and push flour until dough comes together.

9. Shape dough into an 8-inch square.

10. Wrap dough in plastic wrap and chill 12 hours.

11. Wrap remaining butter in plastic wrap and pound with rolling pin.

12. Roll out butter to a 9″ x 5″ rectangle, 1/2 inch thick.

13. Roll out dough on floured surface to a 12-inch square, 1/2 inch thick.

14. Place butter over half of dough and fold dough over butter.

15. Press edges of dough firmly together to enclose butter.

16. Roll dough to a 16″ x 8″ rectangle.

17. Fold lengthwise in thirds, folding bottom third up over center.

18. Rotate 90 degrees and roll dough to a 16″ x 8″ rectangle.

19. Fold into thirds, wrap in plastic wrap and chill for 45 minutes.

20. Flour dough and work surface. Roll out dough to a 16″ x 8″ rectangle.

21. Repeat steps 19 and 20 twice more.

22. Roll out dough to 12″ x 8″ rectangle; wrap. Chill for 45 minutes.

23. Roll out 1/4 dough to an 11-inch square, 1/8 inch thick. Freeze remainder.

24. Cut in a 10-inch circle, using the side of a springform pan as a guide.

25. Brush baking sheet lightly with cold water.

26. Place pastry circle on baking sheet carefully.

27. Prick pastry with fork.

28. Place in preheated 425F (220C) oven.

29. Bake 15 minutes. Lower heat to 375F (190C). Bake 5 to 6 minutes.

30. Remove pastry from oven and cool on a wire rack.

Fruit with Puff Pastry

Once the puff pastry has been made, it can be turned
into a magnificent dessert almost (but not quite)
as quickly as you can make a pot of fresh coffee to serve
with it.

Strawberries on Puff Pastry

1/4 recipe Puff Pastry,
  page 165
1-1/2 pints fresh
  strawberries
1 (10-oz.) jar red
  currant jelly
1 tablespoon sugar

1. Preheat oven to
425F (220C).
2. Roll out pastry on
lightly floured surface
to an 11-inch square.
Cut pastry in a 10-inch
circle using the side of
a springform pan as a
guide. Place pastry
circle on a wet baking
sheet and bake
according to directions
on page 165.
3. Remove pastry from
baking sheet and cool
on a wire rack.
4. Wash and hull
strawberries and place
on a double thickness
of paper towels to dry.
5. Place pastry base on
a flat serving plate.
Arrange strawberries
in concentric circles
over cooled pastry.
6. Place red currant
jelly and sugar in small
saucepan. Place over
low heat and cook,
stirring, until mixture
comes to a boil. Boil
rapidly 1 minute.
Remove pan from heat
and let cool slightly.
7. Brush red currant
jelly over strawberries
liberally. Let stand
until glaze is set.

Variations
Use a different fruit or
a combination of fruits
such as fresh or
poached apricots,
peaches, kiwifruit or
mangoes. For an
added touch, spread a
thin layer of custard
over the baked pastry
base before adding
fruit. Sprinkle glazed
fruit with chopped or
sliced nuts. To glaze,
choose a jelly with a
flavor that will
compliment the flavor
of the fruit.

Tip
Serve fruit-topped
pastry as soon as
possible because the
juice from the fruit will
make the pastry base
soggy if allowed to
stand too long.

Puff Pastry Treats

Use puff pastry to make appetizers or small pastries.
Appetizers made from puff pastry freeze well
so you can keep all kinds of treats in the freezer,
ready to serve when unexpected company appears.

Cheese Straws

(Illustrated top row)
1/4 recipe Puff Pastry,
   page 165
1 cup grated Swiss,
   Gruyère, Cheddar or
   Parmesan cheese
1 teaspoon paprika

1. Preheat oven to
425F (220C).
2. Roll out pastry on
lightly floured surface
to 10″ x 8″ rectangle.
3. Sprinkle cheese and
paprika over bottom
half of pastry.
4. Fold top half of
pastry over cheese,
covering cheese
completely. Press
edges firmly together
with rolling pin.
5. Cut pastry into
strips, 1/2 inch wide,
and twist strips as
illustrated. Brush
baking sheet lightly
with cold water. Place
twisted pastry strips
on wet baking sheet
about 1 inch apart.
Press ends of pastry
strips down onto
baking sheet.
6. Bake in preheated
oven 15 to 18 minutes
or until golden brown.
Remove from baking
sheet and cool on wire
rack. Makes 20 Cheese
Straws.

Apricot Windmills

(Illustrated center row)
1/4 recipe Puff Pastry,
   page 165
1 (17-oz.) can apricot
   halves, drained
1/2 cup apricot jam
1 tablespoon sugar

1. Preheat oven to
425F (220C).
2. Roll out pastry to a
12-inch square; cut in
nine (4-inch) squares.
Cut pastry squares
diagonally from
corners in toward
center. Fold every
other point in to center
and press to secure.
3. Brush large baking
sheet with cold water.
Place windmills on
sheet 1 inch apart.
4. Select the 9 best
apricot halves.
5. Place 1 apricot half,
cut side down, in
center of each shape.
6. Bake 15 to 18
minutes. Remove from
baking sheet and cool.
7. Press apricot jam
through sieve into
small saucepan. Stir in
sugar. Cook over low
heat, stirring, until
mixture comes to a
boil. Boil rapidly 1
minute. Remove from
heat and cool slightly.
Spoon over apricots
and pastry. Let glaze
set. Makes 9
Windmills.

Small Palmiers

(Illustrated bottom
  row)
1/4 recipe Puff Pastry,
   page 165
About 1/2 cup sugar

1. Roll out pastry to a
12″ x 10″ rectangle
and brush with cold
water. Sprinkle 5 to 6
tablespoons sugar
evenly over pastry.
2. Starting from long
edge, roll pastry in to
center. Repeat from
opposite side (see
photo). Rolls should
touch in center. Wrap
pastry roll in plastic
wrap and refrigerate 30
minutes.
3. Preheat oven to
425F (220C). Brush
baking sheet lightly
with cold water.
4. Cut pastry into
1/4-inch-thick slices.
Place slices on wet
baking sheet about 1
inch apart. Sprinkle
slices with remaining
sugar.
5. Bake 10 to 12
minutes or until
golden brown. Remove
from baking sheet
immediately and cool
on wire rack. Makes
about 40.

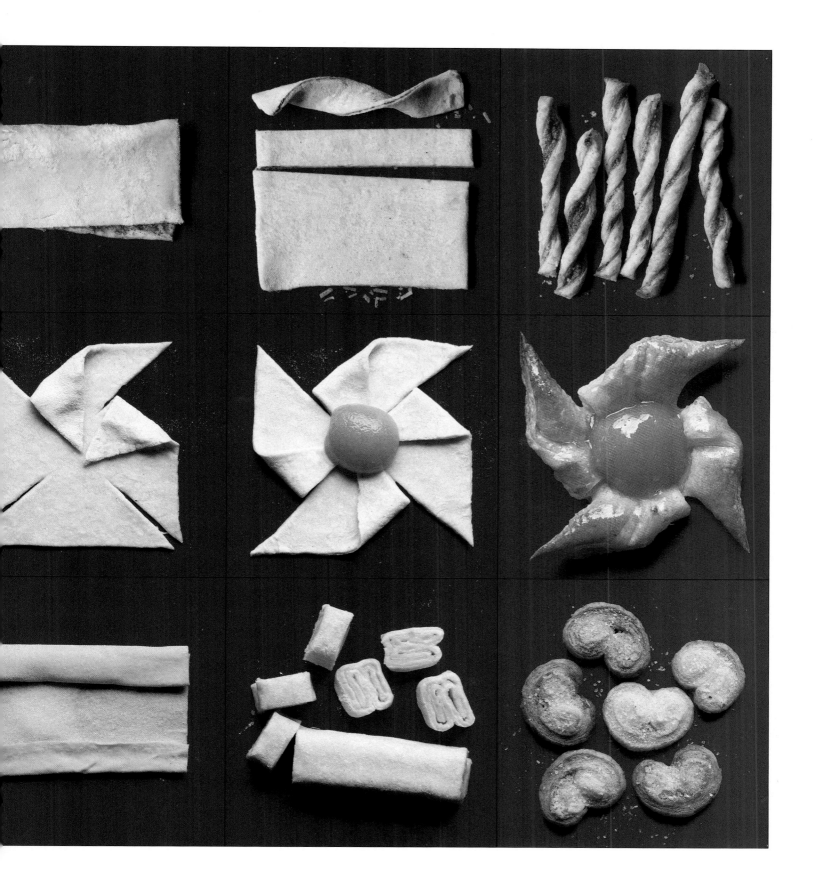

Crisp Pastry Cases . . .

Not Just for Dessert

When a special appetizer is needed, cut and shape puff pastry and fill it with almost anything. Try some of the filling suggestions that follow or make up your own. Whether you hide tiny shrimp or bits of sausage in a pastry case, or make an elaborate and highly seasoned filling, piping hot puff pastry appetizers are always a hit with before-dinner drinks.

You can use the same recipes for light meals by making larger shapes and increasing the amount of filling. Just be sure to serve them promptly while the pastry is still warm and flaky.

Pastry Shapes

Puff pastry can be cut into many shapes and filled with savory or sweet fillings. Pastry cut into rectangular or square shapes can be folded into triangles or crescent shapes or rolled to make croissants or long parcels.

Roll out pastry to 1/8-inch thickness and cut into desired shapes. For large pastry shapes, spoon 1 to 2 tablespoons of filling (see filling suggestions) onto center of pastry. For small pastry shapes fill with 1 to 2 teaspoons of filling. Brush pastry edges with egg wash (1 egg beaten with 1 tablespoon water).

Fold pastry over filling and press edges together firmly to enclose filling. Refrigerate 30 minutes. Brush tops of filled pastries with egg wash and sprinkle with poppy seed, sesame seed, caraway seed or finely chopped nuts.

Bake on ungreased baking sheets in preheated 425F (220C) oven 12 to 15 minutes for small shapes, 15 to 20 minutes for large shapes, or until puffed and golden brown. Serve warm.

Apricot-Curry Filling

(Illustrated opposite page, top left)
1 lb. fresh apricots
1 cup chopped walnuts
1/3 cup raisins, chopped
1 tablespoon curry powder
3 to 4 tablespoons flaked coconut

1. Blanch apricots in boiling water 1 to 2 minutes. Peel, halve, discard pits and chop coarsely.
2. Combine apricots, walnuts, raisins, curry and coconut and mix well. Spoon onto center of pastry shapes and bake as directed. Makes 3-1/2 cups.

Turkey Filling

(Illustrated opposite page, top center)
1/4 lb. cooked turkey breast, diced
1/4 lb. beef bologna, diced
1/4 lb. cooked ham, julienned
1 egg, lightly beaten
1 cup grated Parmesan cheese
Salt and freshly ground pepper
Freshly grated nutmeg (optional)

1. Combine turkey, bologna and ham in a bowl. Add beaten egg and mix well. Add cheese, salt, pepper and nutmeg and blend. Spoon onto center of pastry shapes and bake as directed. Makes 3-1/4 cups.

Ground Meat Filling

(Illustrated opposite page, top right)
1 lb. lean ground beef
1 onion, diced
1 to 2 tablespoons chopped parsley
1 egg
1 cup fresh soft bread crumbs
Salt and freshly ground pepper

1. Brown beef in skillet until meat is no longer pink. Drain off fat and let cool.
2. Place beef in a bowl. Add onion, parsley, egg, bread crumbs, salt and pepper and mix well. Spoon onto center of pastry shapes and bake as directed. Makes about 3 cups.

. . . with Savory Fillings

Spinach-Ricotta Filling

(Illustrated center left)
1 lb. fresh spinach, rinsed
1 cup ricotta cheese
2 eggs, lightly beaten
1 cup grated Parmesan cheese
Salt and pepper

1. Place spinach in large skillet and cook, covered, over moderate heat, just until wilted. Drain well, cool and chop.
2. Place spinach in a bowl, add remaining ingredients and mix well. Spoon onto center of pastry shapes and bake as directed. Makes about 3 cups.

Tomato & Red Pepper Filling

(Illustrated center)
2 tablespoons butter or margarine
2 red bell peppers, diced
4 large ripe tomatoes, blanched, peeled, diced
2 tablespoons chopped fresh basil
1 to 2 teaspoons paprika
2 egg yolks, beaten
Salt and pepper

1. In skillet, sauté peppers in butter 3 minutes. Add tomatoes and cook, stirring, until peppers are barely tender. Let cool.
2. Place tomato-pepper mixture in a bowl. Add remaining ingredients and mix well. Spoon onto center of pastry shapes and bake as directed. Makes about 3 cups.

Bacon & Scallion Filling

(Illustrated center right)
1/2 lb. bacon, diced
2 bunches scallions, thinly sliced
Pepper to taste

1. Cook bacon in a skillet until crisp; drain on paper towels.
2. Place bacon in a bowl, add scallions and pepper and mix well. Spoon onto center of pastry shapes and bake as directed. Makes about 1-3/4 cups.

Chinese Filling

(Illustrated bottom left)
3/4 lb. lean boneless pork, diced or ground
4 to 6 mushrooms, chopped or sliced
1/2 teaspoon cornstarch
2 teaspoons soy sauce
2 teaspoons dry sherry
1 teaspoon sesame oil
1/2 lb. peeled cooked shrimp, chopped
1/4 cup chopped scallions
Salt and freshly ground pepper

1. Brown pork in a skillet until meat is no longer pink. Add mushrooms and sauté 3 minutes.
2. Blend cornstarch, soy sauce, sherry and oil until smooth. Add to skillet and cook, stirring, until slightly thickened. Remove from heat and let cool.
3. Spoon mixture into a bowl. Add shrimp, scallions, salt and pepper and mix well. Spoon onto center of pastry shapes and bake as directed. Makes about 2-1/2 cups.

Mushroom Filling

(Illustrated bottom center)
3 tablespoons vegetable oil
2 onions, chopped
3/4 lb. mushrooms, chopped
1-1/2 cups fresh soft bread crumbs
Salt and pepper

1. Heat oil in medium skillet. Sauté onions and mushrooms until onions are transparent; cool.
2. Spoon onion-mushroom mixture into a bowl. Add bread crumbs, salt and pepper and mix well. Spoon onto center of pastry shapes and bake as directed. Makes about 2-1/2 cups.

Spicy Meat & Raisin Filling

(Illustrated bottom right)
1/2 lb. ground beef
2 onions, chopped
2 tablespoons raisins
1 to 2 dried chili peppers, finely chopped
1/2 teaspoon caraway seed (optional)
Salt and pepper

1. Brown beef in a skillet; drain off fat. Add onions and sauté until transparent. Stir in remaining ingredients and cook 1 minute; cool.
2. Spoon onto center of pastry shapes and bake as directed. Makes about 1-1/2 cups.

Deep-Dish Pies

Deep-dish pies are one crust pies with a crust on the
top instead of the bottom. This is a good way to
make a pie when the consistency of a filling would make a
bottom crust soggy.

The Right Dish

Standard pie plates are
usually 1 to 1-1/2
inches deep. To make
a deep-dish pie you
will need a pie dish
that is 2 to 2-1/2 inches
deep. If you don't own
one, use a casserole or
other deep ovenproof
dish instead.

Deep-dish pies are
easy to make. Only
one crust is needed
and almost any fruit
can be used.

Decoration

Once you have rolled
out the puff pastry and
cut the correct-size
circle, gather the
scraps and stack them
(don't roll the scraps
into a ball). Roll out
the stack of scraps to
about 1/4-inch
thickness and cut out
small pastry shapes
with a pastry wheel,
small aspic cutters or
cookie cutters. Cut
leaves, moons, stars,
fluted circles or other
pastry shapes. Brush
the bottom of the

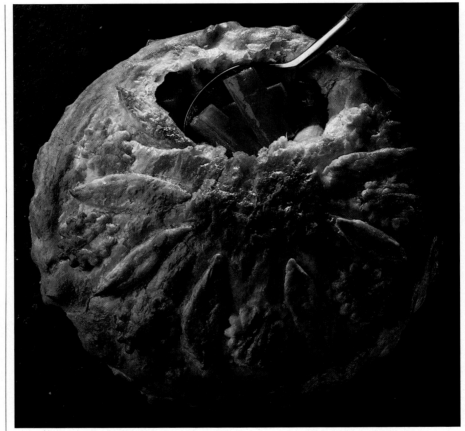

pastry shapes with egg
wash and place on the
pastry-topped pie in a
decorative pattern.
Brush top of shapes
with egg wash.

Deep-Dish
Rhubarb Pie

1-3/4 lbs. fresh
    rhubarb (about 6
    cups cut in 1-inch
    pieces)
1/4 teaspoon salt
1 teaspoon ground
    cinnamon
3/4 cup sugar
3 tablespoons
    cornstarch
1/4 recipe Puff Pastry,
    page 165
Egg wash (1 egg
    beaten with 1
    tablespoon water)

1. Preheat oven to
425F (220C).
2. Place rhubarb, salt,
cinnamon, sugar and
cornstarch in large
bowl and toss gently
until rhubarb is well
coated. Spoon into
deep 9- or 10-inch pie
dish or casserole.
3. Roll out pastry on a
lightly floured work
surface to a 1/4-inch
thickness. Cut out a
circle 1 to 2 inches
larger than the
diameter of the dish
you are using.
4. Brush rim of pie
dish with water and
place pastry circle over
rhubarb carefully.
Press pastry edge
firmly to rim of dish.
5. Brush pastry with
egg wash and cut 1 or
2 vents in pastry.
6. Stack pastry scraps
and roll out. Cut into
decorative shapes.
Brush bottom of pastry
shapes with egg wash
and arrange
decoratively on top of
pie. Brush with egg
wash.
7. Bake 15 minutes.
Lower oven
temperature to 375F
(190C) and bake 35 to
40 minutes or until
pastry is golden brown
and rhubarb is tender.
Cool on a wire rack.

Variation

Substitute firm red
plums, peaches or
apricots for the
rhubarb.

Hot Apple Tarts for Dessert

Few things are more American than apple pie, but it is the French who deserve credit for the simple, but delicious, apple tart. Serve them plain or with some of the toppings suggested below.

Serving Ideas

Prepare the tarts ahead of time and place them in the refrigerator. Bake them while you are eating your main course and you will be able to serve them piping hot directly from the oven. You can also freeze the tarts before baking and bake them frozen. Just add a few minutes to the baking time.

Serve tarts with fruit sorbet, ice cream, whipped cream, fruit puree or fresh fruit. To glaze the apple slices, brush with melted jelly when the tarts come out of the oven.

Apple Tarts

1 to 2 tablespoons lemon juice
4 to 5 small tart apples, peeled and thinly sliced
1/2 cup superfine sugar
1/3 recipe Puff Pastry, page 165

1. In a medium bowl sprinkle lemon juice on apples and toss lightly. Sprinkle 5 to 6 tablespoons sugar over apples and toss gently.
2. Preheat oven to 450F (230C). Brush large baking sheet lightly with cold water.
3. Roll out pastry on a lightly floured surface to a 18″ x 12″ rectangle, 1/8 inch thick. Cut in six (4-1/2-inch) circles. Place on baking sheet 1 inch apart and prick with a fork.
4. Arrange apple slices on top of pastry circles in circular pattern, overlapping slices slightly and leaving 1/2-inch border of pastry all the way around. Sprinkle remaining sugar over pastry edges.
5. Bake 15 to 18 minutes or until pastry is golden brown. Remove from baking sheets and cool on wire racks. Serve warm. Makes 6.

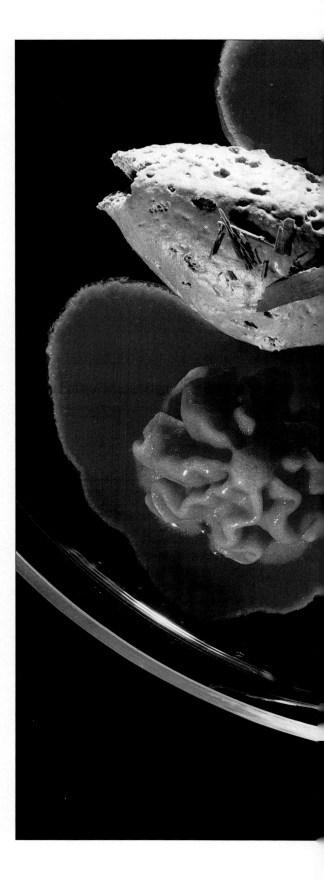

Pastry Cream Slice

(Illustrated page 54)
1/4 recipe Puff Pastry,
   page 165

Vanilla Cream:
3/4 cup granulated
   sugar
5 tablespoons
   all-purpose flour
1/4 teaspoon salt
2 cups milk
6 egg yolks
2 teaspoons vanilla
   extract
Powdered sugar

1. Preheat oven to
425F (220C). Brush
baking sheet lightly
with cold water.
2. Roll out pastry to a
12-inch square and cut
in three (12" x 4")
strips. Place strips on
sheet and prick with
fork. Bake as directed
on page 165; cool.
3. To make Vanilla
Cream, stir granulated
sugar, flour and salt in
a saucepan. Add milk
and stir. Stir over low
heat until mixture
boils. Remove from
heat.
4. Beat egg yolks in
medium bowl. Stir in
about 1/2 cup hot milk
mixture slowly; blend.
Return to saucepan.
5. Cook over low heat,
stirring, until mixture
thickens. (Do not boil.)
Remove from heat and
pour into bowl. Stir in
vanilla. Cover surface
with waxed paper and
let cool completely.
6. To assemble, place
1 pastry strip on a flat
plate; spread with half
of cooled custard. Top
with second strip;
spread with remaining
custard. Top with
remaining strip. Chill 1
to 2 hours.
7. Before serving, dust
with powdered sugar.
Makes 6 to 8 servings.

Dutch Cherry Gâteau

1/2 recipe Puff Pastry, page 165

Cherry Filling:
3/4 lb. fresh dark sweet cherries
1 tablespoon lemon juice
1/4 cup granulated sugar
1/4 teaspoon cinnamon
1/3 cup water
1 tablespoon cornstarch
2 cups whipping cream
3 to 4 tablespoons powdered sugar

Glacé Icing:
1 cup sifted powdered sugar

1. Preheat oven to 425F (220C). Brush two baking sheets lightly with cold water.
2. Cut pastry into 3 equal-size pieces. Roll out each to a 9-inch square. Cut squares in 8-inch circles using an 8-inch cake pan as a guide. Place pastry circles on baking sheets and prick with fork. Bake as directed on page 165. Remove from sheets and cool on wire racks.
3. To make filling, set 8 cherries aside for decoration. Place remaining cherries, lemon juice, granulated sugar, cinnamon and water in medium saucepan and stir well. Bring to a boil over low heat. Remove 2 tablespoons cherry liquid and set aside to use in Glacé Icing.

An Unforgettable Gâteau

4. Blend cornstarch with 2 tablespoons water until smooth. Add to cherries and cook, stirring, until thickened. Remove from heat and let cool.

5. Place 1 pastry circle on flat plate. Spread cooled cherry filling over pastry to within 1/2 inch of pastry edge. Set aside.

6. Beat cream in medium bowl until soft peaks form. Add 3 to 4 tablespoons powdered sugar and beat until firm. Set aside 1 cup whipped cream. Spoon remaining whipped cream into pastry bag fitted with large open-star tip and pipe half over filling to pastry edge. Top with second circle. Pipe remaining cream over.

7. To make icing, blend reserved cherry liquid with 1 cup powdered sugar until smooth. Spread icing over remaining circle and place on top of gâteau.

8. Spoon reserved 1 cup whipped cream into pastry bag fitted with medium open-star tip. Pipe swirls on top of gâteau and decorate with cherries. Chill until ready to serve. Makes 6 to 8 servings.

Tip

To avoid squashing pastry layers more than necessary when cutting cake, score top layer in serving portions before you place it on top of cake.

Crisp puff pastry, whipped cream and fresh sweet cherries—a combination of flavors and textures that compliment each other superbly and make a dessert you will not be able to resist.

Croissants, Danish
Pastry, Strudel
& More

Versatile Croissants: Sweet or Savory

Croissants are slightly sweet and buttery and their mild flavor combines well with both sweet and savory fillings. Filled croissants have become so popular they might almost be classified as the newest "fast food." They are not really difficult to make and, when eaten fresh from the oven, are a taste treat very hard to beat.

Cheese Croissants

(Illustrated opposite page—top left)
Use 1 ounce of cheese cut into sticks or about 3 to 4 tablespoons grated or shredded cheese for each Croissant. Cheeses with mildly strong flavor blend well with the buttery flavor of the dough. Cheddar, Emmentaler, Gruyère, Swiss or Romano cheese are all good. Place cheese on base of triangle and sprinkle with sweet paprika. Roll up from base of triangle. Brush Croissant and tip of triangle with egg wash.

Ham Croissants

(Illustrated opposite page—top right)
Use good quality, thinly sliced, smoked ham such as prosciutto, Westphalian or Virginia ham. Cut slices into small pieces or thin julienne strips. Use the equivalent of 1 slice of ham for each Croissant. Place on base of triangle. Add a little chopped fresh herbs or shredded cheese, if desired. Roll up from base of triangle. Brush Croissant and tip of triangle with egg wash.

Nut Croissants

(Illustrated opposite page—bottom left)
Use 1 to 2 tablespoons nut filling for each Croissant. To make nut filling, combine finely chopped almonds or hazelnuts with a little sugar and cinnamon. Bind nut mixture with a little rum or milk. Spread filling on base of triangle and roll up from base. Brush Croissant and tip of triangle with egg wash. For variations use walnuts, pecans, peanuts, pistachio or macadamia nuts and a few raisins soaked in rum for extra flavor.

Chocolate Croissants

(Illustrated opposite page—bottom center)
Choose whatever kind of chocolate you wish, chopped or broken into small pieces so it will melt evenly. Use 1/2 ounce to 1 ounce of chocolate for each Croissant. If desired, add some ground or finely chopped nuts to the chocolate. Place the chocolate on the base of the triangle and roll up from base. Brush Croissant and tip of triangle with egg wash.

Apple Croissants

(Illustrated opposite page—bottom right)
Apple filling can be made ahead of time. Peel, core and coarsely chop tart apples. Place in small saucepan, add a little water or apple juice and cook until apples are barely tender. Sweeten to taste, add a little calvados or rum, if desired, and add a few raisins or sliced almonds for extra flavor. Allow the apple filling to cool before using to fill Croissants as directed in recipes at left.

Danish Pastry

In the tradition of Ripley's "Believe It or Not,"
the Danes call this pastry Viennese Pastry
and the Viennese call it Danish Pastry, as does most
of the world. Each country politely credits
the other as the creator. No matter who should get
the credit, Danish Pastry makes for
delicious eating anytime.

Apple Combs

(Illustrated far left and top right)
1 recipe Rolled-In Yeast Dough, page 181
Filling:
4 large tart apples, peeled, cored and sliced
1/4 cup apple juice
1 tablespoon lemon juice
1/2 cup sugar
2 tablespoons cornstarch
1/2 teaspoon ground cinnamon
1 egg beaten with 1 tablespoon water for egg wash
1 recipe Apricot Glaze, page 244

1. Prepare Rolled-In Yeast Dough; refrigerate.
2. Stir apples, apple juice, lemon juice, sugar, cornstarch and cinnamon in heavy saucepan. Cook over low heat, stirring, until apples are tender. Cool to room temperature.
3. Grease 2 baking sheets. Roll out half of dough to a 15" x 10" rectangle. Cut dough into six 5-inch squares.
4. Spoon 2 tablespoons filling onto center of each square. Brush edges with egg wash and fold dough over filling. Press edges to seal. Cut slits along 1 long edge of pastry. Place on baking sheets. Repeat with remaining half of dough.
5. Preheat oven to 400F (205C). Brush pastries with egg wash. Bake 20 to 25 minutes or until golden brown. Cool on wire racks. Brush with Apricot Glaze while warm.
Makes 12 Apple Combs.

Cheese Danish

(Illustrated lower left)
1 recipe Rolled-In Yeast Dough, page 181
Filling:
1 cup ricotta cheese
2 egg yolks
1/4 cup sugar
2 tablespoons raisins or currants, chopped
1 egg beaten with 1 tablespoon water for egg wash
1 recipe Apricot Glaze, page 244

1. Prepare Rolled-In Yeast Dough; refrigerate.
2. Blend cheese, egg yolks and sugar in medium bowl until smooth. Stir in raisins.
3. Grease 2 baking sheets. Roll out half of dough to a 15" x 10" rectangle. Cut dough into six 5-inch squares.
4. Spoon 1 to 2 tablespoons cheese filling onto center of each square. Fold edges of dough in to make circle of dough with rim. Place on prepared baking sheets. Repeat with remaining half of dough.
5. Preheat oven to 400F (205C). Brush edges of pastries with egg wash. Bake 15 to 18 minutes or until golden brown. Remove from baking sheets and cool on wire racks. Brush or spoon Apricot Glaze over top of pastry while warm. Makes 12 Cheese Danish.

Marzipan Rings

(Illustrated Center)
1 recipe Rolled-In Yeast Dough, page 181
Filling:
1 (7-oz.) package marzipan
1 cup milk
1 egg beaten with 1 tablespoon water for egg wash
1/2 cup sliced almonds
1 recipe Apricot Glaze, page 244

1. Prepare Rolled-In Yeast Dough; refrigerate.
2. Place marzipan and milk in container of food processor or blender and process until smooth.
3. Grease 2 baking sheets. Roll out half of dough to a 15" x 6" rectangle. Cut dough into six 5" x 3" rectangles.
4. Spread 1-1/2 tablespoons filling over each rectangle. Fold rectangles in half lengthwise. Cut slit lengthwise down center of each rectangle to within 1 inch of each end. Pick up ends and push through slit. Place on baking sheets. Repeat with remaining half of dough.
5. Preheat oven to 400F (205C). Brush pastries with egg wash and sprinkle with almonds. Bake 15 to 18 minutes or until golden brown. Cool on wire racks. Brush with Apricot Glaze while warm. Makes 12 Marzipan Rings.

Cherry Danish

(Illustrated top left)
1 recipe Rolled-In Yeast Dough, page 181
Filling:
1 (16-oz.) can dark pitted cherries
1/2 teaspoon ground cinnamon
3 tablespoons cornstarch
2 tablespoons water
1 egg beaten with 1 tablespoon water for egg wash
1 recipe Apricot Glaze, page 244

1. Prepare Rolled-In Yeast Dough; refrigerate.
2. Place cherries with their liquid and cinnamon in saucepan. Bring to a boil over low heat. Blend cornstarch with water; add to cherries and cook, stirring, until mixture thickens and comes to a boil. Cool to room temperature.
3. Grease 2 baking sheets. Roll out half of dough to a 15" x 10" rectangle. Cut dough into six 5-inch squares.
4. Brush pastry edges with egg wash. Bring 4 corners of squares into center and press down lightly to seal. Spoon 1 tablespoon filling onto center of each. Place on baking sheets. Repeat with remaining half of dough.
5. Preheat oven to 400F (205C). Brush edges with egg wash. Bake 15 to 18 minutes. Cool on wire racks. Brush with Apricot Glaze while warm. Makes 12 Cherry Danish.

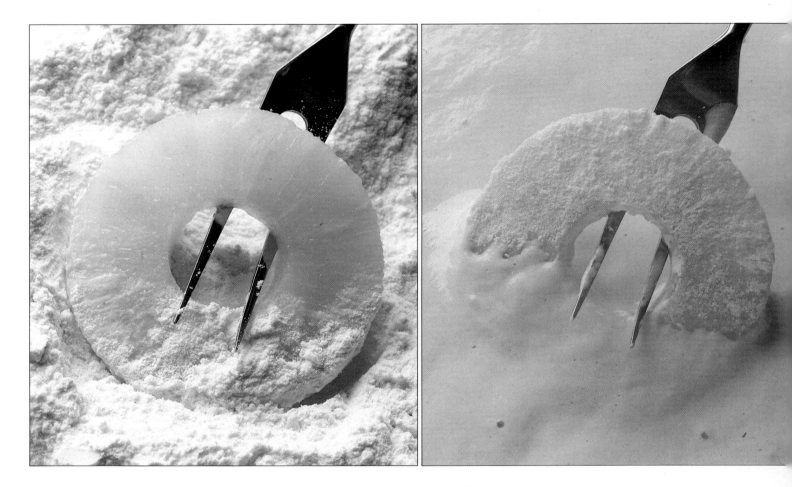

Fritters—Crisp, Juicy, Tender & Irresistible

Sweet or savory food can be dipped in batter and
deep-fried. Whether known as fritters or French beignets
they are a special and popular delicacy.
Choose almost any kind of fruit for a sweet fritter,
slice or chop the fruit, coat it in batter,
deep-fry and serve hot with honey, maple syrup or a light
coating of powdered sugar.

Tips for Deep-Frying

Fat used to deep-fry food must not have either a low burning or low smoking point. Therefore neither butter nor margarine can be used. Solid vegetable shortening is ideal. It is flavorless and odorless and, when properly handled, can be reused. Lard or bland cooking oil can also be used.

The critical factor in successful deep-frying is the temperature of the fat. If the fat is too hot, the fritter can burn on the outside before the inside is cooked. If the fat is not hot enough, the food being cooked will absorb the fat and be greasy and soggy. To eliminate guess work, use an electric deep-fat fryer or a deep-fat thermometer.

Don't fill the pan more than half full of fat. Fat will bubble up when food is added to it.

Don't fry too much food at one time. When food is added to the pan, it lowers the temperature of the fat. By the time the fat is reheated, the batter will have absorbed too much fat.

Use a long-handled slotted spoon or tongs to protect your hands from splattering fat.

Batter should be thick enough to coat the food and adhere to it.

Let batter stand in refrigerator at least 1 hour before adding beaten egg whites. Once egg whites are added; use promptly.

Fruit Fritters

2 eggs, separated
1 cup flat beer
1 tablespoon melted butter
1-1/4 cups sifted all-purpose flour
3 tablespoons granulated sugar
1/4 teaspoon salt
8 to 10 canned pineapple rings or 2 to 3 cups sliced fruit
Sifted powdered sugar
Shortening for frying
Crystal sugar

1. Beat egg yolks, beer and melted butter in medium bowl until thoroughly blended.
2. Sift flour, 1 tablespoon granulated sugar and salt over egg yolk mixture and stir until smooth. Cover and refrigerate 1 hour.
3. Beat egg whites in separate bowl until soft peaks form. Add remaining granulated sugar and beat until stiff peaks form. Fold egg whites into batter.
4. Heat 3- to 4-inches fat in deep-fryer to 360F (180C).
5. Pat pineapple rings dry and dip in powdered sugar. Shake off excess sugar and dip in batter.
6. Lower fruit into hot oil, 1 or 2 pieces at a time. Deep-fry 2 to 3 minutes or until golden brown, turning fruit over once. Remove and drain on paper towels. Repeat with remaining fruit and batter.
7. Sprinkle with sugar; serve warm.

Gingerbread Christmas Cookies

(Illustrated right column)
1 cup butter, room temperature
1 cup granulated sugar
1/3 cup molasses
1 egg
2-3/4 cups all-purpose flour
2 teaspoons cinnamon
2 teaspoons cardamom
1 teaspoon ginger
1 teaspoon baking powder
1 teaspoon salt
1/2 teaspoon nutmeg
1/4 teaspoon cloves
1/2 recipe Royal Icing, page 244
1 recipe Glacé Icing, page 244
Crystal sugar
Small colored candies

1. Cream butter and granulated sugar in large bowl. Beat in molasses and egg.
2. Sift flour, cinnamon, cardamom, ginger, baking powder, salt, nutmeg and cloves. Add to molasses mixture in small amounts, beating well after each addition to make soft dough. Knead dough in bowl 8 to 10 strokes or until smooth.
3. Divide dough in half and shape into 2 slightly flattened balls. Wrap each in plastic wrap and refrigerate 2 to 4 hours.
4. Preheat oven to 350F (175C).
5. Remove 1 piece of dough from refrigerator and roll out on lightly floured surface to 1/8-inch to 1/4-inch thickness. Cut dough with floured cookie cutters and place on ungreased baking sheets. Repeat with remaining piece of dough.
6. Bake 12 to 15 minutes; cool.
7. Prepare Royal Icing and Glacé Icing. Tint small amounts of each icing different colors.
8. Pipe icing decoratively on cookies (see illustrations). Decorate with crystal sugar and small colored candies. Allow icing to set.
Makes 12 to 22 cookies depending on size.

Lebkuchen

(Illustrated left top)
2 cups all-purpose flour
1/2 teaspoon baking soda
1/2 teaspoon cinnamon
1/2 teaspoon cardamom
1/4 teaspoon coriander
1/4 teaspoon nutmeg
1/2 cup chopped almonds
1/4 cup chopped candied orange peel
1/4 cup chopped candied lemon peel
2/3 cup honey
1/2 cup sugar
2 tablespoons butter
1 tablespoon lemon juice
1 recipe Glacé Icing, page 244

1. Preheat oven to 350F (175C). Grease 13" x 9" baking pan.
2. Sift flour, baking soda, cinnamon, cardamom, coriander and nutmeg into bowl. Add almonds, candied peel and stir to combine. Set aside.
3. Cook honey and sugar over low heat, stirring, until sugar is dissolved. Remove from heat, add butter and stir until butter is melted. Stir in lemon juice. Gradually stir in flour mixture to make sticky dough.
4. Spread in prepared pan. Bake 20 to 25 minutes or until lightly browned. Cool in pan.
5. Prepare Glacé Icing. Drizzle icing over Lebkuchen in pan while warm. Score into 2" x 1" bars. Let icing set. Cut bars along scored marks and remove from pan. Store in airtight containers. Makes 54 Lebkuchen.

Spice Swirls

(Illustrated left center)
3/4 cup butter
1 cup brown sugar
1 egg
2-1/4 cups all-purpose flour
1 tablespoon cocoa powder
1 teaspoon cinnamon
1/2 teaspoon nutmeg
1/2 teaspoon ginger
1/2 teaspoon baking soda
1/4 teaspoon allspice
1 egg white beaten with 1 tablespoon water
4 tablespoons granulated sugar
1/2 cup chopped raisins
1/2 cup finely chopped blanched almonds

1. Cream butter and brown sugar in large bowl. Beat in egg.
2. Sift flour, cocoa, cinnamon, nutmeg, ginger, baking soda and allspice. Stir into butter mixture. Knead until smooth, 8 to 10 strokes.
3. Divide dough in half and shape into 2 slightly flattened balls. Wrap in plastic wrap and refrigerate 1 hour.
4. Preheat oven to 375F (190C). Grease baking sheets.
5. Roll out 1 piece of dough on lightly floured surface to 12" x 8" rectangle. Brush with egg white mixture and sprinkle with 1/2 of granulated sugar, 1/2 of raisins and almonds.
6. Roll dough tightly, jelly-roll style, starting from long side. Cut into 1/2-inch-thick slices; place cut side down on baking sheets. Repeat steps 5 and 6 with remaining ingredients.
7. Bake 12 to 15 minutes. Cool on wire racks. Store airtight. Makes 4 dozen Swirls.

Honey Cake

(Illustrated left bottom)
1 cup honey
1/2 cup brown sugar
1/2 cup butter
2-1/2 cups all-purpose flour
1 tablespoon cocoa powder
2 teaspoons cinnamon
1 teaspoon baking soda
1 teaspoon cardamom
1/2 teaspoon cloves
1/2 teaspoon salt
2 eggs, lightly beaten
1 cup milk
1/2 cup ground almonds
Topping:
1/2 cup raisins
1/2 cup whole blanched almonds
1/3 cup chopped blanched almonds
1/3 cup red glacé cherries, chopped
1/4 cup chopped walnuts
1/4 cup each chopped candied lemon peel and orange peel
Crystal sugar

1. Heat honey, brown sugar and butter over low heat until butter is melted and sugar is dissolved; cool.
2. Preheat oven to 350F (175C). Grease 15" x 10" jelly-roll pan.
3. Sift flour, cocoa, cinnamon, baking soda, cardamom, cloves and salt.
4. Pour honey mixture into large bowl. Beat in eggs until blended. Add flour mixture alternately with milk, beating until blended. Add ground almonds; spread in pan.
5. Sprinkle raisins, almonds, cherries, walnuts, and candied peel over batter. Sprinkle with sugar.
6. Bake 35 to 40 minutes. Cool in pan on rack. Cut into bars; remove from pan. Makes 40 bars.

189

Strudels—Filo Leaves Wrapped Around Wonderful Fillings

Filo dough is probably one of the most difficult things a baker can hope to learn how to make. The technique for stretching it paper thin is a special skill that requires years of practice. Fortunately, frozen filo leaves are available in most supermarkets and are a very credible substitute for homemade dough.

Tips for Working with Filo Leaves

Thaw frozen filo leaves in the refrigerator 1 or 2 days. When filo leaves are thawed at room temperature the leaves tend to stick together.

Filo leaves will keep 3 to 4 weeks, in the refrigerator in an unopened package. Once opened, they will keep about 2 weeks if they are rewrapped in an airtight plastic bag.

Use a very sharp knife or scissors to cut filo leaves.
Use either unsalted or clarified butter to brush leaves. Be sure to brush butter over edges of leaves. Use a pastry brush at least 1-1/2 inches wide.

When you are ready to assemble the strudel, open the package of filo leaves and unfold the leaves very carefully. Place them flat on a dampened dish towel and cover with a large sheet of plastic wrap or another towel. Remove 1 leaf at a time and place it on a dampened towel. Brush with melted butter. Repeat process as often as directed in the recipe.

Cheese Strudel

(Illustrated opposite page)
1 (8-oz.) package
    cream cheese, room
    temperature
1 cup ricotta cheese or
    1 cup creamy cottage
    cheese, drained
1/2 cup sugar
1 teaspoon grated
    lemon peel
1 egg
2 egg yolks
1/2 cup golden raisins
1/2 lb. filo leaves (9 to
    10 leaves)
About 1/2 cup
    unsalted butter,
    melted and cooled
    for brushing
1/2 cup fine dry bread
    crumbs
Powdered sugar for
    sprinkling

1. To make filling,
place cream cheese,
ricotta cheese, sugar
and lemon peel in
container of food
processor or blender
and process until
smooth. Add egg and
egg yolks and process
until blended. Spoon
mixture into bowl and
stir in raisins. Cover
and set aside.
2. Unfold filo leaves
and place on
dampened towel.
Cover with plastic
wrap or clean towel.
Remove 1 filo leaf and
place on separate
damp towel. Brush
with melted butter and
sprinkle 1 tablespoon
crumbs over. Place
second filo leaf on top
of first, brush with
melted butter and
sprinkle with crumbs.
Repeat, with
remaining filo leaves,
butter and crumbs.
3. Preheat oven to
375F (190C). Grease
large baking sheet.
4. Spread cheese
filling on filo leaves in
3-inch wide strip, 2
inches in from 1 long
side and 1 inch in from
top and bottom. Fold
2-inch strip over filling
and fold in strips at
top and bottom. Lift
long side of towel and
gently roll Strudel,
jelly-roll style, patting
roll to keep its shape.
Brush seam with
melted butter.
5. Lift Strudel in towel
and gently roll onto
baking sheet, seam
side down. Brush all
over with melted
butter. Bake 40 to 45
minutes or until
golden brown.
6. Remove from oven
and cool on baking
sheet on wire rack 30
minutes. Slide off
baking sheet onto
serving plate and dust
with powdered sugar.
Serve warm or cold.
Makes 8 to 10
servings.

Dried Fruit
Strudel

(Illustrated above)
3/4 lb. dried mixed
    fruit (apricots, figs,
    pears, apples and/or
    peaches)
1/2 cup raisins
1/3 cup pistachio nuts
2 to 3 tablespoons
    brown sugar
1/2 lb. filo leaves (9 to
    10 leaves)
About 1/2 cup
    unsalted butter,
    melted and cooled
1/2 cup gingersnap
    crumbs
Powdered sugar

1. Place fruit and
raisins in bowl. Barely
cover with hot water;
let stand at room
temperature 1 hour.
2. Drain fruit and pat
dry with paper towels.
Coarsely chop fruit
and place in bowl.
Add nuts and sugar
and toss to coat.
3. Unfold filo leaves as
directed in Step 2 of
Cheese Strudel recipe
(see left). Brush with
melted butter and
sprinkle with crumbs.
4. Preheat oven to
375F (190C). Grease
large baking sheet.
5. Spoon fruit filling
on filo leaves as
directed in Step 4 of
Cheese Strudel recipe
(see left).
6. Lift Strudel in towel
and gently roll onto
baking sheet, seam
side down. Brush with
melted butter. Bake 40
to 45 minutes.
7. Remove from oven
and cool on baking
sheet on wire rack 30
minutes. Slide off
baking sheet onto
serving plate and dust
with powdered sugar.
Serve warm or cold.
Makes 8 to 10 servings

Pâte à Choux or
Choux Paste—
Light & Delicious

The Unique Batter That Is Cooked Before It Is Baked

Basics for Making Choux Paste

Water and butter should be cooked together until the butter has melted completely and the mixture comes to a boil. At this point the flour must be added immediately. If the water and butter are allowed to boil beyond the point where the butter is melted, evaporation will take place and the amount of liquid will be reduced. This will create an imbalance in the required ratio of liquid to flour.

In order to avoid lumps, flour must be added all at once and the batter stirred vigorously off heat or over very low heat until the liquid has been absorbed and the flour forms a ball that comes away from the sides of the pan. It should be cooked over low heat only long enough to be certain the flour ball is dry. There will be a thin film of dough in the saucepan when all the liquid has been absorbed.

Eggs should be added, 1 at a time, off heat. Each egg must be thoroughly beaten into the slightly cooled batter before the next egg is added. The number of eggs called for in the recipe can be altered depending on the size of the eggs used and the moisture content of the flour. The finished batter should be pliable but not runny and easy to pipe through a pastry bag.

Although the making of choux paste is sometimes thought of as a delicate procedure, "delicate" more aptly describes the finished product than the preparation. Choux paste is quick and easy to make. It is also very versatile because cream puffs can be filled with all kinds of mixtures, sweet or savory.

Why Choux Paste Is Cooked Before It Is Shaped and Baked

When flour is added to the hot mixture of melted butter and boiling water, the starch in the flour breaks down and swells, speeding the development of gluten and evenly distributing the fat. This turns the batter into a smooth, firm mixture rather than the more usual dry, crumbly mixture from which many kinds of cake and pastry are made. Without this procedure the batter would not puff up properly when baked. The eggs that are added to the flour mixture are the leavening agent that causes large air bubbles to form in the pastry.

Hints and Tips

Transfer the flour ball to a bowl and allow it to cool slightly before adding the eggs. Eggs should not be added to a very hot mixture, nor should they be added to a cold mixture.

Use unsalted butter.

If cream puffs are to be filled with a savory mixture, eliminate sugar from the batter. If desired, 1/4 cup grated cheese or 1/2 teaspoon freshly ground pepper or hot paprika may be substituted for the sugar.

If possible, shape the batter and bake it immediately. If this is not possible, cover the batter and store it in the refrigerator. Bring it to room temperature before shaping.

Shaping Choux Paste

The best method for shaping choux paste is filling a large pastry bag fitted with a large open-star tip and piping the desired shapes onto a prepared baking sheet. It is also possible to make cream puffs by using two large spoons and placing mounds of choux paste on the baking sheet. A light cake base can be made by spreading choux paste in a circle on a baking sheet or in the bottom of a prepared springform pan.

Baking Hints

The baking sheet or springform pan must be carefully greased and floured or lined with parchment paper.

Be sure to leave about 2 inches between choux paste shapes on the baking sheet. They will expand during baking.

Preheat the oven to the correct temperature and don't open the oven door during the first half of the baking period. Bake until the pastry is completely dry. If the pastry is removed from the oven too soon, it will collapse.

Split pastry while it is still warm and pull out any soft dough inside. Allow the pastry to cool before filling. Serve it as soon as possible after filling in order to prevent the bottom of the pastry from becoming soggy.

Basic Choux Paste

Equipment:
2-quart saucepan
Electric mixer
Pastry bag
Large piping tip

Ingredients:
1 cup water
1/2 teaspoon salt
1 tablespoon sugar
1/2 cup unsalted butter
1 cup all-purpose flour
4 eggs

Oven Temperature:
400F (205C)

Baking Time:
35 to 40 minutes

Cooling Time:
20 to 30 minutes

Servings:
12 large Cream Puffs or 32 small Profiteroles.

Storage:
Choux Paste should be baked promptly or covered and placed in the refrigerator. If it is allowed to stand, it can get crumbly and form a crust. Once Choux Paste has been baked, the pastry can be frozen. Wrap in plastic wrap and place in an airtight container or plastic bag. Freeze up to six months. Defrost at room temperature about 30 minutes. Crisp in hot oven at 425F (220C) on baking sheet 3 to 5 minutes. Don't fill baked pastry if you plan to freeze it. The filling will make the pastry soggy.

Preparation

1. Measure ingredients and set aside to come to room temperature.

2. Place water, salt and sugar in saucepan over moderate heat.

3. Add butter and bring to a boil, stirring, until butter is completely melted.

4. Add flour all at once, stirring constantly.

5. Lower heat and stir vigorously.

6. Cook until dough forms ball and comes away from sides of pan.

7. Transfer mixture to mixing bowl and let cool 2 minutes.

8. Add eggs, 1 at a time, beating well after each addition.

9. Beat until each egg is well incorporated before adding next egg.

10. Grease large baking sheet or line with parchment paper.

11. Sprinkle greased baking sheet with flour.

12. Spoon Choux Paste into pastry bag fitted with large piping tip and pipe.

Cream Puffs

1. Use a 1/2-inch open-star or plain tip.

2. Pipe mixture into 12 mounds about 2-1/2 inches apart.

3. Bake in preheated 400F (205C) oven 35 to 40 minutes.

4. Remove from baking sheet and cool completely on wire rack.

Profiteroles (Miniature Cream Puffs)

1. Pipe 32 walnut-size balls onto prepared baking sheet.

2. Bake in preheated 400F (205C) oven 20 to 25 minutes. Cool on wire rack.

3. Use piping tip to make hole in bottom of each Profiterole.

4. Pipe whipped cream or custard into Profiteroles.

Filled Cream Puffs—Never Too Many

Mandarin-Filled Cream Puffs

(Illustrated far left)
1 recipe Basic Choux
 Paste, page 197

Filling:
1 (11-oz.) can
 mandarin orange
 segments
2 cups whipping
 cream
2 to 3 tablespoons
 orange-flavored
 liqueur
Powdered sugar

1. Prepare Basic Choux Paste and 12 Cream Puffs.
2. Cut Cream Puffs in half horizontally, remove tops and any soft dough inside puffs. Reserve tops.
3. Drain oranges; discard liquid. Pat dry with paper towels; arrange in bottom of puffs.
4. Beat cream in medium bowl until soft peaks form. Add liqueur and 4 tablespoons powdered sugar. Beat until firm. Spoon into pastry bag fitted with large open-star tip.
5. Pipe whipped cream generously over oranges in bottom of puffs. Replace tops and refrigerate until ready to serve. Dust with powdered sugar just before serving.

Raspberry Cream Puffs

(Illustrated second from left)
1 recipe Basic Choux
 Paste, page 197

Filling:
1 pint fresh raspberries
2 to 3 tablespoons
 granulated sugar
2 cups whipping
 cream
Powdered sugar

1. Prepare Basic Choux Paste and 12 Cream Puffs.
2. Cut Cream Puffs in half horizontally, remove tops and any soft dough inside puffs. Reserve tops.
3. Place 2/3 raspberries in bowl. Sprinkle with granulated sugar and toss gently. Spoon into bottom of puffs. Puree remaining raspberries in blender or food processor; set aside.
4. Beat cream in medium bowl until soft peaks form. Add reserved raspberry puree and 4 tablespoons powdered sugar. Beat until firm. Spoon into pastry bag fitted with large open-star tip.
5. Pipe whipped cream generously over raspberries in bottom of puffs. Replace tops and refrigerate until ready to serve. Dust with powdered sugar just before serving.

On formal occasions cream puffs are eaten with a fork. However, if you are able to eat a deliciously filled cream puff when no one is watching, forget the fork and pick it up in your hand. You may need to hold a plate under your chin, and you certainly will need extra napkins, but you will experience a very special treat. And the next time you are served a cream puff at a dinner party, you may have difficulty resisting the temptation to pick it up in your hand.

Cream-Filled Puffs

1 recipe Basic Choux Paste, page 197

Filling:
2 cups whipping cream
1-1/2 teaspoons vanilla extract or 2 to 3 tablespoons liqueur of choice
Powdered sugar

Follow instructions for other Cream Puffs filled with flavored whipped cream.

Strawberry-Filled Cream Puffs

(Illustrated far right)
1 recipe Basic Choux Paste, page 197

Filling:
1-1/2 pints or 1 lb. fresh strawberries, rinsed and hulled
2 to 3 tablespoons granulated sugar
2 cups whipping cream
Powdered sugar

1. Prepare Basic Choux Paste and 12 Cream Puffs.
2. Cut Cream Puffs in half horizontally, remove tops and any soft dough inside puffs. Reserve tops.
3. Slice strawberries, sprinkle with granulated sugar; place in bottoms of puffs.
4. Beat cream in medium bowl until soft peaks form. Add 4 tablespoons powdered sugar. Beat until firm. Fill pastry bag fitted with large open-star tip. Pipe over strawberries in bottom of puffs. Replace tops and refrigerate until ready to serve. Dust with powdered sugar just before serving.

Glazes for Cream Puffs

Instead of dusting the tops of cream puffs with powdered sugar, spoon glaze over the tops.
Sugar Glaze: Blend 1 cup powdered sugar with 1 to 2 tablespoons warm water, milk, rum or lemon juice and stir until smooth. Spoon over filled puffs.
Chocolate Glaze: Melt 4 ounces semisweet chocolate in saucepan over low heat and stir until smooth. Spoon over filled puffs.
Apricot Glaze: Bring 1/3 cup apricot jam, 1 tablespoon sugar and 1 tablespoon water to a boil in small saucepan. Boil rapidly 1 to 2 minutes. Brush over filled puffs.
Caramel Glaze: Bring 3/4 cup sugar and 5 tablespoons water to a boil in heavy saucepan. Cook, stirring, until mixture turns golden brown. Spoon or drizzle over filled puffs.

199

Deep-Fried Choux Paste

This is a wonderful trio of ethnic recipes made from choux paste—deep-fried rather than baked in the oven. Beignets from France, churros from Spain and cruellers with a name that is a Dutch derivative, all are elegant snacks or perfect food for an old-fashioned tea.

Raisin Beignets

(Illustrated top)
1 recipe Basic Choux Paste, page 197
1/3 cup raisins
Vegetable oil
Powdered sugar

1. Prepare Basic Choux Paste according to directions on page 197, adding raisins after last egg has been beaten in.
2. Heat 2-inches oil in deep-fat fryer until temperature registers 375F (190C). Drop heaping teaspoonfuls of batter into hot oil. Deep-fry Beignets, a few at a time, until golden brown.
3. Remove with slotted spoon and drain on paper towels. Dust with powdered sugar.

Churros

(Illustrated bottom)
1 recipe Basic Choux Paste, page 197
Vegetable oil
1/2 teaspoon ground cinnamon
3 to 4 tablespoons granulated sugar

1. Prepare Basic Choux Paste according to directions on page 197.
2. Spoon Choux Paste into pastry bag fitted with medium open-star tip.

3. Heat 2-inches oil in deep-fat fryer until temperature registers 375F (190C). Pipe 5- to 6-inch lengths of dough into hot oil. Deep-fry Churros, a few at a time, until golden brown.
4. Remove with slotted spoon and drain on paper towels. Combine cinnamon and sugar. Dredge Churros in cinnamon sugar while still warm.

Cruellers

(Illustrated center)
1 recipe Basic Choux Paste, page 197
Vegetable oil
1 cup sifted powdered sugar
1 to 2 tablespoons warm water or milk

1. Prepare Basic Choux Paste according to directions on page 197.
2. Spoon Choux Paste into pastry bag fitted with large open-star tip. Pipe mixture into 2-1/2-inch circles on greased parchment paper.
3. Heat 2-inches oil in deep-fat fryer until temperature registers 375F (190C). Invert paper over hot oil until Cruellers drop off paper into oil. Deep-fry Cruellers, a few at a time, until golden brown. Remove with slotted spoon and drain on paper towels.

4. Blend sugar and water and stir until smooth. Spoon glaze over Cruellers and let stand until set.

Tips for Deep-Frying

Use fresh, unflavored vegetable oil or solid vegetable shortening that can be heated to a high temperature without burning or smoking. Don't use butter or olive oil.

Deep-fry only a few pastries at a time. Don't overcrowd the pan as it will cause the temperature of the oil to decrease and the pastry will not cook evenly.

Check the oil to be sure it is the correct temperature before frying the pastry. If you don't own a deep-fat thermometer, drop a 1-inch cube of white bread into the hot oil. If the oil is the correct temperature, the cube of bread will brown in 50 seconds.

Use a slotted spoon to remove the pastry from the hot oil. Drain the pastry on paper towels to remove excess fat.

A Toast to St. Honoré

St. Honoré was a French saint for whom this incomparable French pastry was named. It is truly one of the masterpieces of pâtisserie, but why it was named for St. Honoré is something of a mystery. He was Bishop of Amiens, France around 600 A.D. and is the patron saint of pastry cooks. But even an authoritative reference book such as *Larousse Gastronomique* cannot find any event in St. Honoré's life to explain a gastronomic connection. No matter the reason, pastry lovers all over the world are the beneficiaries of this special and delicious pastry.

Gâteau St. Honoré

1 recipe Basic Choux Paste, page 197
l sheet (1/2 of 17-1/4-oz. package) frozen puff pastry or homemade Puff Pastry, pages 164-165

Filling:
1/2 cup sugar
1/3 cup all-purpose flour
1/2 teaspoon salt
2 cups milk
5 egg yolks
2 teaspoons vanilla extract
3 egg whites

For caramel syrup:
3/4 cup sugar
5 tablespoons water

1. Prepare Basic Choux Paste according to directions on page 197.
2. Spoon into pastry bag fitted with large plain tip. Set aside.
3. Preheat oven to 400F (205C). Grease large baking sheet.
4. Roll out Puff Pastry on lightly floured surface to a 9- or 10-inch circle. Place on prepared baking sheet and prick lightly with fork.
5. Pipe reserved Choux Paste in spiral over pastry base, starting in center and piping out toward edge (see top left photo, opposite).
6. Pipe remaining Choux Paste into 14 walnut-size balls. Place around edge of prepared baking sheet, not on top of pastry base.
7. Bake in preheated oven 35 to 40 minutes or until both pastry base and balls are deep golden brown. Carefully remove base and balls from baking sheet and cool on wire rack.
8. To make filling, place sugar, flour and salt in medium saucepan. Stir well, add milk and stir until blended. Place pan over low heat and cook, stirring, until mixture thickens and comes to a boil. Remove from heat.
9. Place egg yolks in small bowl and beat well. Stir 4 to 5 tablespoons hot milk mixture into beaten egg yolks. Add mixture to saucepan.

Cook, stirring constantly, until mixture thickens and coats back of wooden spoon. Remove from heat and pour into bowl. Stir in vanilla. Place piece of waxed paper over surface of custard to prevent skin from forming. Set aside to cool.
10. Use piping tip to make hole in bottom of each small puff (see page 197). Spoon half the cooled custard into pastry bag fitted with plain tip and fill small puffs. Set remaining custard aside.
11. To make caramel syrup, bring sugar and water to a boil in small heavy saucepan. Cook, until syrup turns light brown in color. Dip

top of each filled puff into syrup carefully and place around outside edge of large pastry circle (see lower left photo, opposite). Be careful not to burn tips of fingers when dipping balls into syrup.
12. Beat egg whites until stiff peaks form. Fold beaten egg whites into remaining cooled custard. Spoon mixture into center of gâteau (see lower right photo, opposite). Refrigerate until ready to serve.

Note: This pastry is best when it is eaten as soon as possible after it has been assembled.

The Wonderful Versatility of Choux Paste

Swans, éclairs and special gâteaus are but a few of the wonderful pastries that can be made with choux paste. There is equal versatility to the fillings, icings and glazes that can be used with choux paste, but nothing is quite as dramatic as a finish of spun sugar, the typical finish for a croquembouche shown on the next page.

Swans

1. Prepare Cream Puffs according to directions on page 197. Pipe "question marks" for Swans' necks.

2. Cut Cream Puffs in half horizontally while still warm.

Éclairs

1. Prepare Basic Choux Paste (see page 197). Pipe into 4-inch long fingers or wavy lines on greased baking sheet.

2. Cut Éclairs in half horizontally while still warm. Let cool completely.

Choux Paste Gâteau

1. Prepare Basic Choux Paste according to directions on page 197. Spread in two 11-inch circles on greased baking sheets.

2. Bake each circle 15 to 20 minutes. Trim to 9 inches using 9-inch springform pan as a guide. Reserve trimmings.

Spun Sugar

1. Stir 3/4 cup sugar and 5 tablespoons water in small heavy saucepan over moderate heat.

2. Bring to a boil, stirring constantly, until mixture is syrupy.

3. Cut tops in half to make "wings" for Swans.

4. Fill bottom halves of puffs with sweetened whipped cream or custard cream.

5. Place neck in position and push wings into whipped cream at an angle on each side of Swan. Refrigerate until ready to serve. Dust with powdered sugar.

3. Brush tops of Éclairs with Apricot Glaze (see page 199). Let stand until set.

4. Pipe Mocha Buttercream (see page 229) into bottoms of Éclairs.

5. Replace tops and press down lightly. Refrigerate until ready to serve.

3. Spread 1/4 cup plum butter over 1 round. Spread 1 cup whipped cream over plum butter. Top with second round.

4. Spread 1/4 cup plum butter over top. Spread about 1-1/2 cups whipped cream over plum butter and around side of cake.

5. Break reserved trimmings into small pieces and scatter over top of cake. Dust with powdered sugar.

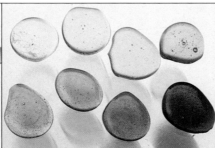

3. Lower heat and cook, stirring, until syrup turns light brown.

4. Syrup will change color from light to dark brown very quickly.

5. To use Spun Sugar, see recipe for Croquembouche, next page.

Croquembouche—
A Formidable Pastry Pyramid

The making of this impressive pyramid of sweet-filled profiteroles covered with spun sugar is a marvelous feat of baking. The beautiful web of delicate strands of sugar holds the profiteroles tightly in place—wonderful to look at, but somewhat difficult to serve and eat!

The Origin of the Name

Literally translated, croquembouche means "cracks in the mouth," an accurate description for this pastry. Croquembouche is a crisp and delicious pastry that crackles when you bite into it. It is made with a beautiful pyramid of profiteroles, filled with cream and held together with caramel spun into a fine web. Undoubtedly it will take some practice to learn how to handle spun sugar, but it is worth the effort. Practice very carefully in order to avoid burned fingers, but don't give up. There are very few desserts more delicious to eat, beautiful to behold and thoroughly impressive.

Making Spun Sugar

Wait for a cool dry day to make Spun Sugar. Be sure to make it within 3 or 4 hours of when you plan to serve it as it will not hold up longer than this. Use a heavy saucepan and don't be distracted while you are working. Dissolve the sugar completely in the water and then boil the syrup to evaporate all the water. As the syrup cooks, it will change color very quickly, going from clear to light brown—and then suddenly to dark brown or burned if it is cooked too long. Watch carefully and remove the pan from the heat as soon as the syrup turns light brown (290F/145C on a candy thermometer). Let it cool slightly, but don't let it harden. Spread your work surface with newspaper and place the plate with the pyramid of Profiteroles right next to the pan of syrup on the paper. Dip the prongs of a fork carefully into the syrup, lift the fork high out of the syrup and drape the sugar threads over the pyramid as quickly as possible. Repeat until the pyramid is covered with a web of sugar threads. Be very, very careful not to touch the hot syrup because it will burn your fingers.

Croquembouche

1 recipe Basic Choux
  Paste, page 197
1/2 recipe Shortcrust
  Pastry, page 101
2 cups whipping
  cream
2 teaspoons vanilla
  extract
1/4 cup powdered
  sugar
Spun Sugar:
1-1/4 cups granulated
  sugar
5 tablespoons water

1. Prepare Choux
Paste and make
Profiteroles.

2. Roll out Shortcrust Pastry to a 9-inch round and bake as directed on page 101 until golden, 8 to 10 minutes. Cool completely.
3. Beat cream in medium bowl until soft peaks form. Add vanilla and powdered sugar and beat until firm. Fill Profiteroles with whipped cream (page 197).
4. Place cooled pastry base on flat serving plate and set aside.
5. To make caramel syrup for Spun Sugar, place granulated sugar and water in heavy saucepan and bring to a boil over moderate heat. Cook until syrup is light brown in color. Remove pan from heat and let cool 2 minutes.
6. Lightly brush pastry edge with caramel syrup. Dip tops of filled Profiteroles carefully into syrup. Arrange Profiteroles close together around edge of pastry, piling Profiteroles in cone shape and using syrup to glue them together.
7. Reheat syrup if it is too hard, or make a new batch of syrup if too many particles from the Profiteroles have fallen into it.
8. Dip fork into syrup, lift fork out and drape sugar threads over pyramid of Profiteroles. Repeat to create web of Spun Sugar, covering pyramid and pastry edge completely.

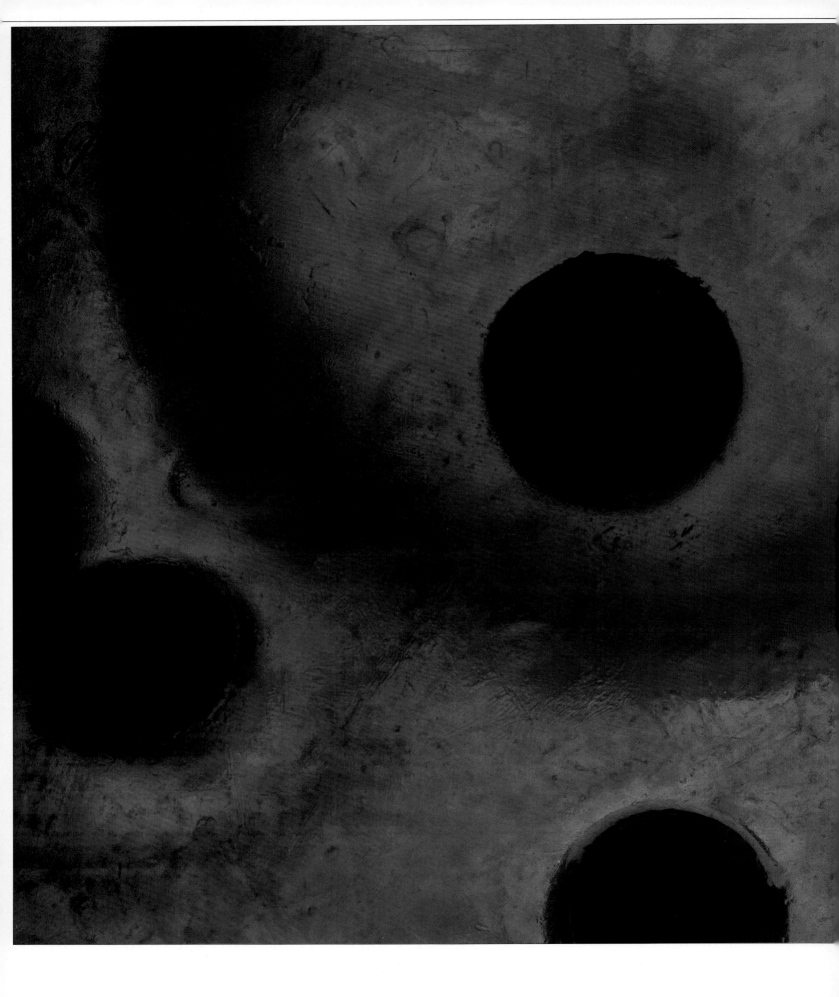

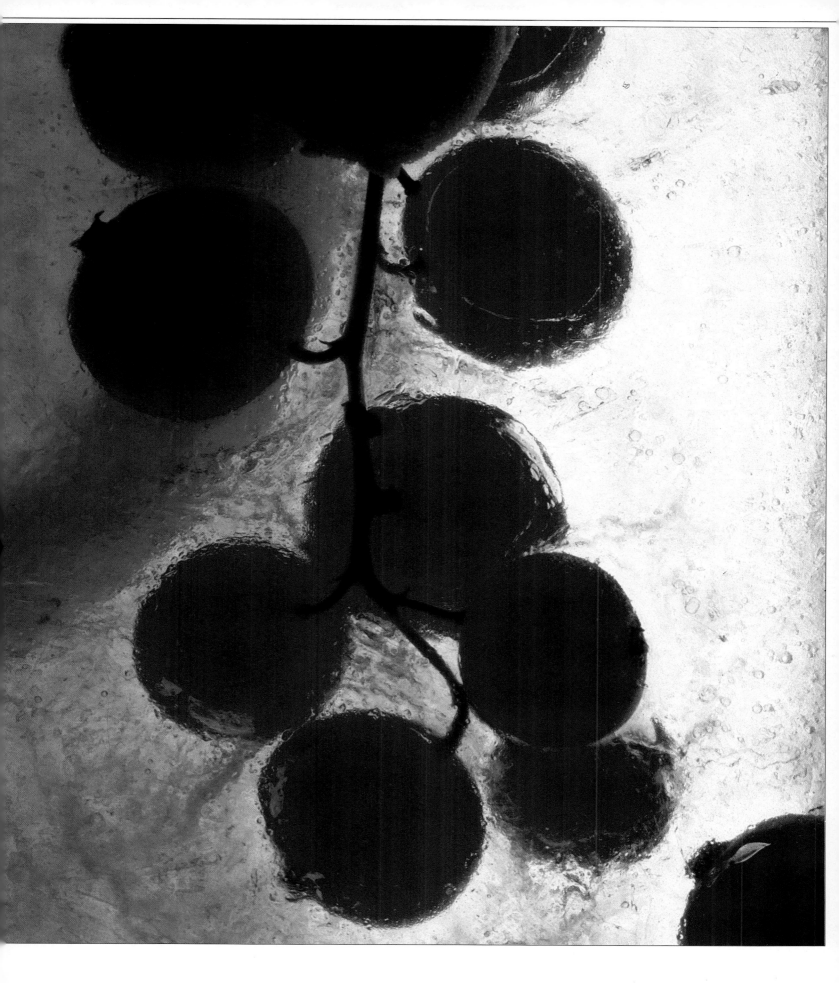

Dazzling Desserts

Sorbet

(Illustrated left)
Sorbet (or sherbet) is a light and refreshing ice made with fruit juice and fruit puree to which sparkling red or white wine, champagne or liqueur is often added. Although sorbet can be bought ready-made, the flavors available are likely to be limited. It is easy to make at home in the freezer or in an ice-cream maker. Sorbet can be served as a first course, between courses to clear the palate or as a meltingly delicious dessert with fancy little cookies or cakes to accompany it.

Ice Cream

(Illustrated right)
Although ice cream can be bought in an almost endless variety of flavors, quality varies greatly from one brand to another. When serving ice cream to company, use top quality ice cream that has a rich creamy flavor or, better still, make it yourself. New ice-cream makers are easy to use and provide an opportunity to use fresh ingredients. There are many models and sizes of ice-cream makers available in a wide range of prices.

Chillingly Delicious Freezer Treats

Children are not the only ones who find ice cream
the dessert of choice for almost any occasion.
Next time you have a patio party for adults,
arrange scoops of ice cream in a wide variety of
flavors on a large platter. Line a basket
with a colorful cloth and fill it with sugar cones.
Add a big dish of chocolate sprinkles,
provide lots of napkins and invite
your guests to help themselves.

When you think about ice cream and other
frozen dessert mixtures, let your imagination
take over. Frozen mixtures can be used to make all kinds
of desserts from the simple ice-cream cone
to an impressive Baked Alaska. Use frozen mixtures
between layers of cake; to fill crêpes, cream puffs or
meringue nests; on top of waffles,
brownies or plain cake; hidden under fresh fruit
and topped with a sprinkling of liqueur;
or simply spooned into a dish and served with cookies.

Frozen Mousse

(Illustrated center)
Frozen mousse is similar in many ways to an extra rich ice cream. However, it is not stirred during the freezing process in the same way ice cream is stirred. It can be used in many ways:

Freeze the mousse in a bombe mold, invert it on a plate and decorate elegantly to make an impressive dessert.

Freeze the mousse in a soufflé dish as illustrated. When using a soufflé dish, choose a dish that is too small to hold all of the mixture. Make a collar with a double thickness of greased waxed paper or foil that extends 2 inches above the rim of the dish. Wrap the collar around the dish and fill the collared dish with mousse. Freeze until the mousse is set. Remove the collar, decorate the top of the mousse with toasted shredded coconut, grated chocolate or finely ground nuts. Let it stand at room temperature about 10 minutes before serving.

Frozen mousse can also be used between cake layers to make a frozen cake as illustrated in the step-by-step photos on the opposite page and the pages that follow.

Frozen Mousse Cake

Equipment:
Double boiler or saucepan and heatproof bowl to fit over pan
Electric hand mixer
Grater
10-inch springform pan
Large pastry bag fitted with open-star tip

Ingredients:
1 recipe 10-inch-baked Genoise Sponge, page 71
5 egg yolks
2 cups sifted powdered sugar
Peel of 2 oranges
3 cups whipping cream
1/3 to 1/2 cup orange-flavored liqueur
1/2 cup orange juice

To decorate:
1-1/2 cups whipping cream
3 to 4 tablespoons granulated sugar

Freezing Time:
4 to 5 hours

Before Serving:
After icing cake, freeze at least 1 hour. Remove from freezer and place in refrigerator 50 minutes. Remove from refrigerator and let stand at room temperature 10 minutes before serving.

Servings:
8 to 10

Basic Mousse Mixture—Frozen Mousse Gâteau

1. Bake Genoise Sponge. Set out remaining ingredients.

2. Place egg yolks in top of double boiler or heatproof bowl.

3. Sprinkle sugar over yolks. Place over pan of simmering water.

4. Beat egg yolks and sugar with electric mixer until very thick.

5. Remove bowl from the heat and beat until mixture is cool.

6. Grate peel from both oranges and set aside.

7. Beat whipping cream in separate bowl until firm.

8. Fold cream, peel and 3 tablespoons liqueur into egg mixture; chill.

9. Cut cake in half horizontally to make 2 layers and place 1 in pan.

10. Sprinkle half of juice and remaining liqueur over layer.

11. Spread chilled mousse mixture over cake layer and smooth top.

12. Place remaining cake layer on top and press down gently.

13. Pour remaining juice over cake. Cover and freeze 4 to 5 hours.

14. Run tip of knife around inside edge of pan. Place cake on plate.

15. Beat cream until soft peaks form; beat in sugar. Spread on cake.

16. Decorate with remaining whipped cream. Freeze 1 hour.

More Frozen Mousse Cakes

Lemon-Orange Mousse Cake
Prepare and freeze cake (see page 211). Substitute 1/4 cup each lemon juice and orange juice for 1/2 cup orange juice. Use peel from 1 orange and lemon.

Pineapple Mousse Cake
Prepare and freeze cake (see page 211). Substitute arrack for liqueur and pineapple juice for orange juice; omit orange peel. Add 2/3 cup chopped candied pineapple.

Strawberry Mousse Cake
Prepare and freeze cake (see page 211). Omit orange peel and juice. Fold 1 cup lightly crushed strawberries into mousse mixture. Substitute kirsch for orange liqueur.

Cassata Mousse Cake
Prepare and freeze cake (see page 211), but use bottom layer only. Omit liqueur, peel and juice. Sprinkle cake with 3 tablespoons each brandy and crushed praline. Fold 1/3 cup each chopped walnuts and pistachios and 3/4 cup chopped maraschino cherries into mousse mixture.

Eight variations on a theme—some with one cake layer
and some with two. If only one layer is needed,
freeze the remaining layer for use another time.
No matter which cake you make, you will need enough
for second helpings.

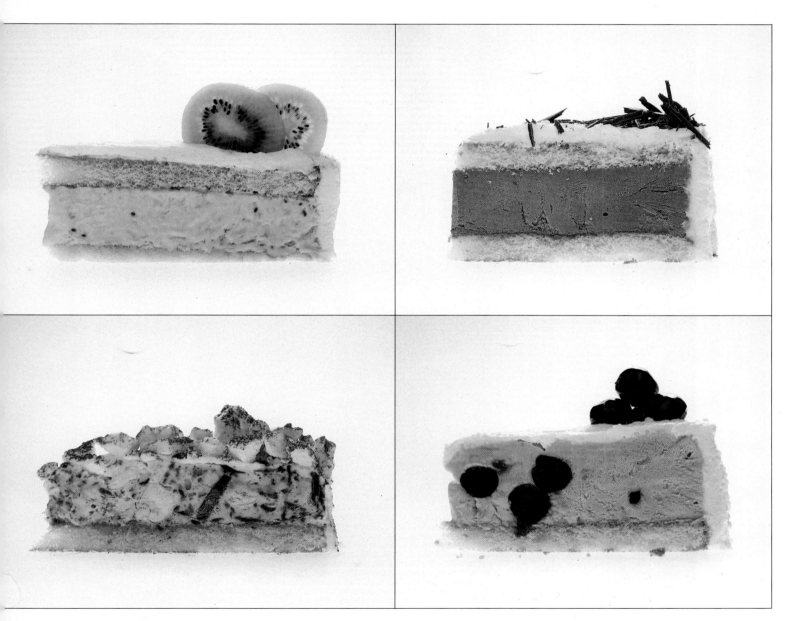

Kiwifruit Mousse Cake
Prepare and freeze cake (see page 211). Omit liqueur
and juice. Puree 4 kiwifruit in blender; fold into
mousse mixture with 3 tablespoons dark rum. Sprinkle cake
with 4 tablespoons rum.

Chocolate Mousse Cake
Prepare and freeze cake (see page 211). Omit liqueur,
peel and juice. Fold 6 ounces melted and cooled semisweet
chocolate into mousse mixture with 3 tablespoons
dark rum. Sprinkle cake layers with 4 tablespoons rum.

Chocolate-Meringue Mousse Cake
Prepare and freeze cake (see page 211), but use bottom
layer only. Omit liqueur, peel and juice. Fold
in 1 cup each chopped semisweet chocolate and crushed
meringue into mousse mixture. Sprinkle cake with
3 tablespoons brandy.

Blueberry Mousse Cake
Prepare and freeze cake (see page 211), but use bottom
layer only. Fold 1 cup fresh or frozen and thawed
blueberries into mousse mixture with liqueur and peel.

213

Jellied Fruit— An Unusual Idea

This attractive way to serve fruit is Far Eastern in origin. Fruit encased in shimmering gelatin retains its shape and flavor and will not dry out quickly.

Jellied Mandarin Oranges

1 (11-oz.) can
  mandarin oranges
1 envelope unflavored
  gelatin
2 tablespoons lemon
  juice
Orange juice
1/2 cup sugar

1. Drain oranges, reserving syrup. Place syrup in small saucepan and sprinkle gelatin over. Let stand 5 minutes to soften. Place over low heat and cook, stirring, until gelatin is dissolved. Remove from heat and let cool 2 minutes.
2. Pour mixture into a 2-cup glass measure. Add lemon juice and enough orange juice to measure 2 cups and stir to blend. Pour into medium bowl, add sugar and stir to dissolve.
3. Arrange orange segments, rounded side down, in ice cube trays, or small plastic or metal molds. Spoon gelatin mixture over, covering fruit completely.
4. Refrigerate 3 to 4 hours or until set. To serve, dip bottom of ice cube trays or molds in pan of hot water 30 seconds. Invert jellied fruit onto serving plate and arrange attractively. Refrigerate until ready to serve.

Hints and Tips
Many fruits can be jellied. However, neither fresh nor frozen pineapple nor pineapple juice can be used.

Tint liquid gelatin with food coloring to match color of fruit used.

Omit lemon juice and substitute 2 tablespoons compatibly flavored liqueur.

One envelope (1 tablespoon) unflavored gelatin is enough to set 2 cups of liquid. Be sure gelatin is dissolved before adding additional liquid.

Two Special Gelatin Desserts

Cool and refreshing cakes that require little or
no baking are ideal for summer entertaining,
or at any time of year.

Fruit-Glazed Refrigerator Cake

10-inch Genoise
 Sponge, page 71
4 tablespoons dark
 rum
1 (16-oz.) can sliced
 peaches
2 envelopes
 unflavored gelatin
1/2 cup granulated
 sugar
4 cups plain yogurt
1 cup whipping cream
2 tablespoons
 powdered sugar
3 ripe kiwifruit

Glaze:
1 cup granulated sugar
3 tablespoons
 cornstarch
1 cup water
4 tablespoons
 lemon-flavored
 gelatin

1. Cut cake in half
horizontally to make 2
layers. Place 1 layer in
bottom of a 10-inch
springform pan.
(Reserve 2nd layer for
use another time.)
Sprinkle rum over cake
and set aside.
2. Drain peaches,
reserving syrup. Set
peaches aside. Place
peach syrup in small
saucepan and sprinkle
gelatin over. Let stand
5 minutes to soften.
3. Place saucepan over
low heat and cook,
stirring, until gelatin is
completely dissolved.
Remove from heat and
pour into medium
bowl. Add granulated
sugar and stir until
dissolved. Let cool.

4. Add yogurt and stir
until thoroughly
blended. Chill until
slightly thickened.
5. Pour yogurt mixture
over cake and smooth
top. Refrigerate 2 to 3
hours or until
completely set.
6. Beat cream in
medium bowl until
soft peaks form. Add
powdered sugar and
beat until firm.
7. Remove cake from
refrigerator and run tip
of sharp knife around
inside edge of pan.
Remove side of pan
and place cake on a
plate. Spread cream
over top and side.
Decorate side with
icing comb.
8. Arrange reserved
peach slices in
sunburst pattern on
top of cake. Peel and
slice kiwifruit. Arrange
kiwifruit around top
outside edge of cake;
chill.
9. To make glaze,
combine granulated
sugar, cornstarch and
water in small
saucepan and stir to
blend. Cook over low
heat, stirring, until
mixture thickens and is
clear. Remove from
heat, add flavored
gelatin and stir until
gelatin is completely
dissolved. Let cool to
room temperature.
10. Spoon fruit glaze
over peaches and
kiwifruit, covering top
of cake completely.
Refrigerate 1 hour or
until glaze is set.

Additional Ideas

Substitute lady fingers
for the sponge layer.
Cut lady fingers to fit
in a springform pan
and cover bottom of
pan completely.
Sprinkle lady fingers
with 3 to 4 tablespoons
rum.

Substitute cottage
cheese for yogurt.
Drain cottage cheese
well and process in
food processor or
blender until
completely smooth.
Alternatively, use 2
cups yogurt and 2
cups cottage cheese,
drained and processed
until smooth.

For added flavor, use
fruit-flavored yogurt
instead of plain
yogurt.

Pureed fruit can also
be added to the yogurt
mixture for additional
color and flavor.

To make sure the
whipped cream icing
holds up as long as
possible, stabilize the
cream before
whipping. Place 1/2
cup whipping cream in
a small saucepan and
sprinkle 2 teaspoons
unflavored gelatin
over. Let stand 5
minutes to soften.
Place saucepan over
low heat and cook,
stirring, until gelatin is
dissolved. Remove
from heat and
refrigerate until
mixture is chilled and
thickened. Beat 1/2 cup
whipping cream in
medium bowl until
soft peaks form. Add
gelatin mixture and 2
tablespoons powdered
sugar and beat until
firm. Spread over top
and side of cake.

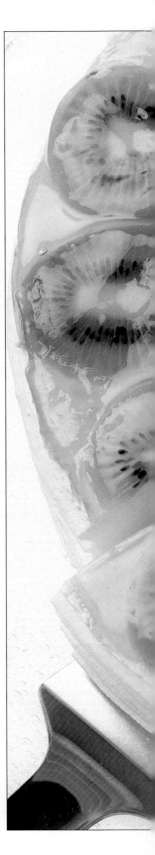

Raspberry-Yogurt Refrigerator Cake

10-12 Lady Fingers,
  split, page 83
1 pint raspberries
1/2 cup orange juice
2 envelopes
  unflavored gelatin
2 teaspoons grated
  orange peel
1 cup creamy-style
  cottage cheese
3/4 cup sugar
1 cup vanilla-flavored
  yogurt
1 cup whipping cream

1. Lightly grease a 10-inch springform pan. Arrange lady fingers, rounded side down, in bottom of pan, cutting to fit.
2. Set several berries aside for decoration. Puree in blender. Strain to remove seeds.
3. Place juice in small saucepan and sprinkle gelatin over. Let stand 5 minutes to soften. Cook over low heat, stirring, until gelatin is dissolved. Stir gelatin and peel into pureed berries.
4. Beat cottage cheese in bowl until smooth; gradually add sugar. Beat in yogurt and raspberry-gelatin mixture.
5. Beat whipped cream in a separate bowl until firm; fold into raspberry mixture. Pour over lady fingers in pan. Chill until set, 3 to 4 hours.
6. To serve, run tip of knife around inside edge of pan. Remove side of pan and place cake on a plate. Arrange berries on top of cake. Chill until ready to serve. Makes 10 to 12 servings.

Meringues—Light, Melt-in-the-Mouth Wonders

Meringue Nests

4 egg whites
1/8 teaspoon cream of
   tartar
3/4 cup superfine
   sugar
1 teaspoon vanilla
   extract
About 4 cups
   strawberries,
   raspberries, dark
   sweet cherries
   or red currants for
   filling

1. Line 2 baking sheets with parchment paper. Draw four (4-inch) circles on each sheet.
2. Beat egg whites and cream of tartar in large bowl until foamy. Gradually sprinkle in sugar, 1 tablespoon at a time, beating constantly. Be sure sugar is dissolved before adding next tablespoonful.
3. Continue beating until stiff glossy peaks form. Beat in vanilla.
4. Preheat oven to 275F (135C).
5. Spoon half the meringue into pastry bag fitted with 1/2-inch open-plain tip. Starting in center of each circle, pipe meringue in a spiral until circles are completely filled.
6. Spoon remaining meringue into pastry bag fitted with 1/2-inch-star tip. Pipe stars around edge on meringue circles.

7. Bake 60 minutes or until firm (meringues should remain white). Turn oven off and leave nests in oven several hours to dry out. Peel off parchment paper when completely cool. Wrap and store nests in an airtight container at room temperature.
8. To serve, fill each nest with 1/2 cup fruit. Makes 8 nests.

Variation
Fill with ice cream or chocolate mousse.

Chocolate Meringues
Prepare Meringue Nests through Step 2. Sift 2 tablespoons cocoa powder over mixture, add vanilla and beat until stiff and glossy. Pipe and bake as directed.

Hazelnut Kisses

1 recipe Meringue
   Nests
1 cup finely ground
   hazelnuts

1. Line baking sheets with parchment paper. Preheat oven to 300F (150C).
2. Prepare meringue through Step 3. Gently fold in hazelnuts.
3. Spoon meringue into pastry bag fitted with large open-plain tip. Pipe walnut-size balls onto baking sheets. Space 1-1/2 inches apart.
4. Bake 35 to 40 minutes or until lightly browned. Cool on baking sheets on wire racks. Peel off parchment paper when cool. Wrap and store in airtight containers at room temperature. Makes about 24 kisses.

According to food historians, meringue was invented in the town of Mehrinyghen in about 1720 by a Swiss pastry chef whose name was Gasparini. It is generally believed that Marie Antoinette was so fond of meringue kisses that she actually went into the royal kitchens and made them herself. This remarkably delicious combination of nothing more than egg whites, sugar and air continues to be one of the most popular sweet treats in the culinary repertoire of pastry chefs everywhere.

Hints and Tips on Making Meringue

Separate eggs while they are still cold. Be sure separated egg whites don't contain even the slightest trace of egg yolk. Let egg whites come to room temperature.

Use a mixing bowl and beaters that are clean and dry.

To be sure sugar has completely dissolved, rub a little beaten egg white between your fingers. If it feels grainy, continue to beat until smooth.

Don't overbeat egg whites. Stop beating when egg whites are thick and shiny and hold stiff peaks.

To find out if egg whites have reached the stiff peak stage, turn the bowl upside down. Stiffly beaten egg whites will not fall out of the bowl.

Use beaten egg whites immediately. They will lose volume if allowed to stand.

Don't try to make meringues when the weather is humid.

Coconut Macaroons

4 egg whites
1 cup sifted powdered sugar
1/2 teaspoon almond extract
1/2 teaspoon cinnamon
2 cups shredded or flaked coconut

1. Preheat oven to 300F (150C). Line baking sheets with foil or parchment paper.
2. Beat egg whites in large bowl until stiff. Beat in sugar and almond extract gradually. Continue beating until stiff, glossy peaks form. Fold in cinnamon and coconut.

3. Drop mixture by heaping teaspoonfuls onto baking sheets spacing about 1 inch apart. Bake 20 to 25 minutes or until golden brown. Cool on baking sheets on wire racks.
4. When completely cool, peel off of lining paper and store in airtight containers. Makes about 3 dozen Coconut Macaroons.

Variation

To make Almond Macaroons, omit coconut and use 1 cup finely ground almonds and 1 cup finely chopped almonds. Increase almond extract to 1 teaspoon.

Almond Tuiles—Crisp, Delicate & Delicious

These special cookies can be served as the perfect accompaniment to sorbet or ice cream. They can also be filled with ice cream, custard, whipped cream or fruit when shaped properly.

Almond Tuiles

2 egg whites
1/2 cup superfine sugar
1/2 teaspoon almond extract
1/2 cup sifted all-purpose flour
1/2 cup finely ground almonds
1/4 cup butter, melted and cooled.

1. Preheat oven to 375F (190C). Grease and flour 2 large baking sheets or line with parchment paper.
2. Beat egg whites in medium bowl until stiff peaks form. Add sugar gradually and beat until stiff. Beat in almond extract.
3. Sprinkle flour and almonds over mixture and fold in. Fold in butter until no streaks remain.
4. Drop mixture, 1 teaspoonful (or tablespoonful—depending on size of cookie desired) at a time, onto baking sheets 3 to 4 inches apart. Spread evenly with small spatula.
5. Bake, 1 sheet at a time, about 6 minutes or until cookies are golden brown.

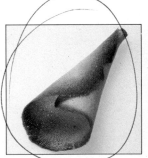

6. Cool on baking sheet on wire rack 1 minute. Remove 1 cookie carefully with wide spatula and wrap it around handle of wooden spoon or rolling pin to shape. Let cookie cool. Slide off and repeat with remaining cookies. Makes 18 to 24 cookies, depending on size.

Horns

(Illustrated above)
Spread mixture on prepared baking sheets in 3-inch circles. Bake as directed. Cool on baking sheet 1 minute. Wrap cookies around metal pastry cream horn and let cool. Slide off mold.

Leaves

(Illustrated above)
Line baking sheets with parchment paper. Draw leaf outlines on parchment. Place 6 tablespoons cookie mixture in bowl. Add 1 teaspoon unsweetened cocoa powder and stir until blended. Set aside. Spread remaining plain mixture on outlines of leaves. Spoon chocolate mixture into small pastry bag fitted with small open-plain tip. Pipe over leaves to make veins. Bake as directed. Cool 1 minute on baking sheet. Remove 1 cookie carefully with wide spatula and drape over rolling pin to curve cookie slightly. Cool and slide off. Repeat with remaining cookies.

Cups

(Illustrated opposite page)
Spread mixture on prepared baking sheets in 4- or 5-inch circles. Bake as directed. Cool on baking sheet 1 minute. Press cookies over bottom of inverted small custard cups or muffin pan and let cool. Remove carefully. Serve filled with fruit, custard, whipped cream or ice cream.

Hints and Tips

Spread mixture as evenly as possible so cookies will brown evenly.

Bake only 3 or 4 cookies at a time so you can shape them before they cool. Once they have cooled, they cannot be shaped.

Moisture softens cookies and soft cookies do not hold their shape. Store in airtight containers to keep them crisp or, better still, serve them as soon as possible.

Berry-Topped Refrigerator Cheesecake

Other than baking the crumb crust briefly, this cake does not require baking. Make it ahead of time and place it in the refrigerator. Spoon fresh berries on top of the cake just before serving and, if desired, have extra berries on the side to spoon over each portion.

For the crust:
1-1/2 cups crushed shortbread cookies
2 tablespoons sugar
6 tablespoons butter, melted

Filling:
1/3 cup water or milk
1 envelope plus 1 teaspoon unflavored gelatin
1 (8-oz.) package cream cheese
2/3 cup sugar
1 cup cottage cheese, drained
1-1/2 teaspoons vanilla extract
1 cup whipping cream
Fresh raspberries, blackberries and blueberries to serve

1. Preheat oven to 350F (175C). Grease an 8-inch springform pan.

2. Stir cookies and sugar in a bowl. Blend in butter. Press mixture onto bottom and halfway up side of pan. Bake 8 to 10 minutes; cool.
3. For filling, place water and gelatin in small saucepan. Let stand 5 minutes. Cook over low heat, stirring, until gelatin is dissolved; cool.
4. Beat cream cheese and sugar in medium bowl until fluffy. Add cottage cheese and beat until smooth. Beat in gelatin and vanilla.
5. Beat whipping cream in a separate bowl until firm. Fold into cheese mixture.
6. Pour into crust. Chill 2 to 3 hours.
7. To serve, remove side of pan. Place cake on a plate; decorate with berries. Makes 8 to 10 servings.

Chocolate-Filled Cookie Sandwiches

This is an inventive way to turn store-bought cookies into a special dessert. If you prefer, you can start from scratch and bake your own cookies. Whichever method you choose, the chocolate filling will make these cookie sandwiches memorable.

1 cup butter, room temperature
2/3 cup firmly packed brown sugar
4 ounces semisweet chocolate, melted and cooled
24 to 30 rectangular butter cookies, bought or homemade
1/3 cup chopped almonds
1/3 cup grated sweet chocolate

1. Beat butter and brown sugar in medium bowl until very light and fluffy.
2. Add melted chocolate and beat until blended.

3. Cover a baking sheet with waxed paper or line a rectangular baking dish large enough to hold 1/3 of cookies.
4. Spread half the chocolate mixture over 1/3 of cookies. Top with cookies. Spread remaining chocolate mixture on top. Sprinkle with chopped almonds and grated chocolate. Top with remaining cookies and press down lightly.
5. Place cookie sandwiches on prepared baking sheet. Cover with waxed paper and refrigerate 1 to 2 hours. Makes 8 to 10 servings.

Crisp & Light Belgian Cream Waffles

Waffles topped with whipped cream and strawberries are a special dessert made popular in Belgium. Serve them for dessert as the Belgians do, or improvise and serve them topped with ice cream, chocolate syrup, any kind of fruit or almost anything else you like.

Mock Trifle

Traditional English trifle is made with custard. However, whipped cream can be a simple substitute for custard. Since the base of a trifle is cake, broken into pieces, keep this recipe in mind if one day a baked cake does not come out of the pan neatly.

1-1/2 cups all-purpose flour
1/2 cup granulated sugar
1/2 teaspoon salt
3 eggs
1/3 cup milk
1/4 cup butter, melted and cooled
1 cup whipping cream
Powdered sugar, whipped cream and sliced strawberries to serve

1. Stir flour, granulated sugar and salt in medium bowl. Set aside.
2. Beat eggs in medium bowl until very foamy. Add milk and melted butter and beat until well blended.
3. Gradually add egg mixture to flour and beat until smooth.
4. Beat cream in a separate bowl until firm. Fold into batter until no streaks remain. Pour into pitcher.
5. Preheat and prepare waffle iron according to manufacturers' directions.
6. Pour about 1/2 cup batter into waffle iron. Close waffle iron and cook about 4 minutes or until waffle is golden brown.
7. Dust with powdered sugar and top with whipped cream and sliced strawberries. Serve immediately. Makes 5 large waffles (25 small hearts).

1 (8-inch) sponge cake, bought or homemade
1/3 cup crushed praline or nut topping
3 tablespoons brandy
1/2 to 3/4 cup sweet cream sherry
1 (16-oz.) can sliced peaches, drained
1-1/2 cups whipping cream
3 to 4 tablespoons powdered sugar
1 teaspoon vanilla extract

1. Break cake into small pieces and place in a soufflé dish or large serving bowl. Set aside 2 tablespoons praline for decoration; sprinkle remainder over cake.
2. Combine brandy and sherry and sprinkle over cake. Toss gently and let stand 30 minutes or until all liqueur has been absorbed.
3. Arrange sliced peaches over cake.
4. Beat whipping cream in medium bowl until soft peaks form. Add sugar and vanilla and beat until firm.
5. Spread or pipe whipped cream over peaches decoratively.
6. Refrigerate 1 to 2 hours. Sprinkle reserved praline over top before serving. Makes 4 to 6 servings.

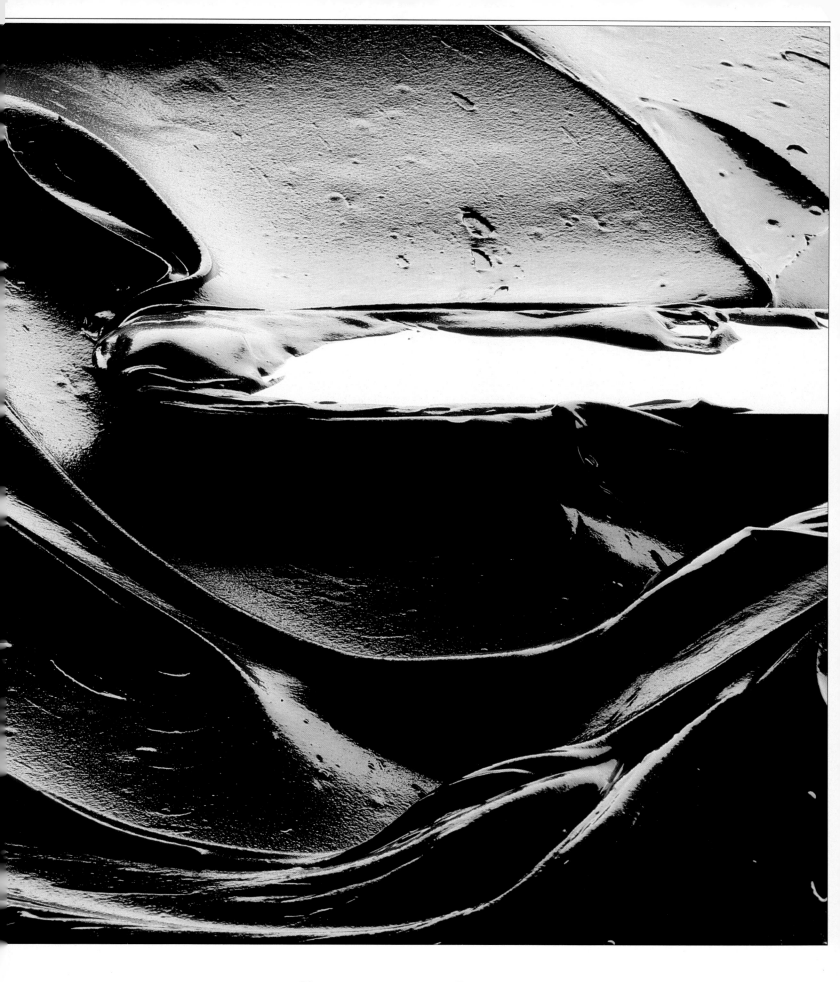

Creams for Filling & Frosting
—Smooth & Delicious

Buttercream— Versatile, Popular & Basic to Good Baking

Buttercream is a well-blended mixture of butter, eggs, sugar, air and flavoring. It can take time to make but the effort is more than worthwhile. A perfectly made buttercream is simply unbeatable.

French Buttercream

French Buttercream is a very smooth buttercream that takes time to make. The eggs and sugar must be beaten constantly over a pan of hot water and then removed from the heat and beaten until cool. The egg mixture cannot be combined with the creamed butter and flavoring until it is cool.

Rich (or English) Buttercream

Rich Buttercream has a delicate balance of egg yolks and butter. It is lighter than French Buttercream and takes less time to make. The custard must not be allowed to boil or the egg yolks will curdle. Once the custard is slightly cooled, it is combined with butter.

Hints and Tips

The main ingredient in a buttercream is butter, and the quality of the butter determines the flavor of the buttercream. Butter must be fresh and unsalted. Don't use margarine in place of butter.

Butter should be allowed to stand at room temperature at least one hour before it is creamed.

It takes patience to cream butter properly. Don't use a hand whisk, your arm will get tired long before the butter is properly creamed. Use a good electric hand mixer and beat the butter several minutes or until it is a very pale color.

The custard and creamed butter must be the same temperature in order for them to be combined properly. If the custard is too hot, it will melt the butter and spoil the texture of the buttercream. If the custard has been refrigerated and is too cold, it will cause the butter to form tiny solid flakes that will prevent the custard and butter from binding together.

Don't add the custard to the creamed butter all at once. Beat the custard into the creamed butter gradually a little at a time.

When piping buttercream, keep the pastry bag as cool as possible. Refrigerate the pastry bag if the buttercream gets too soft and does not hold its shape during piping.

Buttercream can be flavored many ways. Omit vanilla when using another flavoring. If you flavor buttercream with cocoa or coffee, increase the sugar in the buttercream mixture slightly.

Buttercream will keep in a sealed container in the refrigerator for several days. Allow it to come to room temperature before using.

Basic Recipe for French Buttercream

(Illustrated top right)
Equipment:
Double boiler or heatproof bowl fitted over saucepan
Electric hand mixer
Large bowl
Whisk

Ingredients:
5 eggs
1 cup sugar
1-1/2 cups unsalted butter, room temperature
1 vanilla bean, split

Yield:
Enough Buttercream to fill and frost 2-layer 10-inch cake.

Basic Recipe for Rich Buttercream

(Illustrated bottom right)
Equipment:
Medium saucepan
Medium bowl
Whisk
Electric hand mixer

Ingredients:
1 cup whipping cream
1 vanilla bean
6 egg yolks
3/4 cup sugar
1-1/4 cups unsalted butter, room temperature

Yield:
Enough Buttercream to fill and frost 2-layer 10-inch cake.

Preparation

1. Measure ingredients and let stand at room temperature.

2. Break eggs into heatproof bowl.

3. Beat eggs on medium speed until very foamy, about 2 minutes.

4. Add sugar gradually, beating constantly.

5. Place bowl over pan of barely simmering water.

6. Beat egg mixture until thick and creamy, about 5 minutes.

7. Remove bowl from heat and continue beating until egg mixture is cool.

8. Place butter in separate bowl.

9. Beat butter until creamy.

10. Continue to beat butter until very pale, 10 to 12 minutes.

11. Split vanilla bean in half lengthwise.

12. Scrape pith from both pieces of vanilla bean.

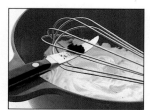

13. Scrape pith off knife into butter with whisk and beat until blended.

14. Gradually add cooled egg mixture to butter, beating constantly.

15. Continue beating until Buttercream is light and fluffy.

Preparation

1. Measure ingredients and let stand at room temperature.

2. Pour cream into heavy saucepan and heat just to the boiling point.

3. Add vanilla bean to hot cream and let stand 10 to 15 minutes. Discard bean.

4. Place egg yolks in heatproof bowl.

5. Add sugar to egg yolks and beat until thoroughly blended.

6. Add hot cream to yolk mixture in very slow stream, beating vigorously.

7. Pour mixture back into saucepan and place over low heat.

8. Cook, stirring constantly, until mixture is thickened. Do not boil.

9. Pour hot custard through sieve set over mixing bowl.

10. Let custard stand at room temperature until completely cooled.

11. Place butter in large bowl.

12. Beat butter on high speed until thick and creamy, 10 to 12 minutes.

13. Butter should be consistency of lightly whipped cream.

14. Gradually add cooled custard to creamed butter, beating constantly.

15. Continue beating until mixture is very fluffy.

Buttercreams —from Chocolate to Pistachio

Flavoring Buttercreams

Regardless of what kind of buttercream you make, you can vary the color and flavor in many ways. But buttercreams are delicate mixtures that cannot be made quickly or carelessly because they may separate. Even flavoring must be added carefully.

When adding a flavoring that must be heated or melted such as chocolate, nougat (praline paste) or coffee, be sure the warm flavoring is cooled to room temperature before it is added to the buttercream.

Liquid flavoring such as liqueur or alcohol should be added to the buttercream gradually, 1 teaspoon at a time. Beat in thoroughly after each addition.

When adding solid ingredients such as nuts, they must be ground to a very fine powder. Large clumps of nuts will spoil the smooth texture of the buttercream and clog the piping tip.

When tinting buttercream with food coloring, add coloring, 1 drop at a time, and beat well.

Nougat (Praline Paste) Buttercream

(Illustrated this page, far left)
Place 3/4 cup nougat in top of double boiler or small heatproof bowl set over pan of barely simmering water. Heat, stirring constantly, until nougat is melted and smooth. Remove bowl from pan and allow nougat to cool completely. Gradually add cooled nougat to Buttercream, a little at a time, beating well after each addition. Refrigerate 30 minutes before using.

When the only extra flavor added to buttercream is vanilla, the color of the buttercream is creamy white. But when ingredients such as chocolate, mocha or raspberry are added, both the flavor and color are dramatically changed.

Chocolate Buttercream

(Opposite page, center)
Melt 4 ounces semisweet chocolate and stir until smooth. Cool to room temperature and add melted chocolate, a little at a time, to Buttercream, beating well after each addition.

Coffee Buttercream

(Opposite page, far right)
Dissolve 1 tablespoon powdered instant coffee in 1 tablespoon hot dark rum or hot water. Let cool to room temperature. Add coffee, a little at a time, to Buttercream, beating well after each addition.

Nutty Buttercream

(This page, far left)
Grind 3/4 cup nuts in food processor or nut grinder until nuts are the consistency of fine powder. Fold ground nuts gently into Buttercream. If desired, add 1 teaspoon almond, brandy or rum extract and stir until blended.

Raspberry Buttercream

(This page, center)
Puree 1 cup fresh raspberries in food processor or blender. Strain raspberry puree to remove seeds. Add 2 to 3 tablespoons raspberry-flavored liqueur to raspberry puree and stir until blended. Add raspberry mixture to Buttercream, 1 tablespoonful at a time, beating well after each addition. Refrigerate or use immediately.

Pistachio Buttercream

(This page, far right)
Grind 3/4 cup pistachios in food processor or nut grinder until nuts are the consistency of fine powder. Gently fold ground pistachios into Buttercream. If desired, add 2 to 3 tablespoons kirsch and a few drops of green food coloring, a little at a time.

Piping Buttercream

With time, patience and practice you will be able to
pipe buttercream as artistically as the piped
cream illustrated on these pages. Practice on waxed paper
and experiment with different tips so you can become
familiar with them and the patterns they make.

Patterns and Piping Techniques

Piping tips come in many sizes. A basic set of tips will provide a good assortment for a novice.

Large fluted, open-star tips are used to pipe fluted strips, swirls, scrolls, borders and flowers.

Small fluted, open- or closed-star tips are used to make small stars, scrolls, rosettes, borders and small flowers. They are also used to pipe all over patterns on cakes and petits fours.

Plain or writing tips have a round opening. They are used to pipe lines, words, dots, beads, stems, numbers and for "string work."

Ribbon tips have a rectangular slit. They are used to make petals, straight ribbon designs and to create a rippled effect.

Assembling and Filling the Pastry Bag

You should have at least 2 or 3 different size pastry bags, preferably plastic coated. It's also helpful to have a coupling ring, but not absolutely necessary.

Slip a piping tip down into a pastry bag pushing it through the opening at the tip. Fold back the top half of the bag to make a cuff and place the bag upright in a tall glass with the cuff resting on the rim of the glass to hold the bag steady. Spoon frosting or buttercream into the bag, pushing it down with a rubber spatula until the bag is half filled. Unfold the cuff, hold the top of the bag tightly in one hand and twist the top half of the bag to force out trapped air.

If you're right-handed, hold the bag so the filled portion rests in your right palm with your fingers grasping it firmly and your thumb on the twisted end of the bag. Hold the piping bag over a piece of waxed paper and exert a small amount of pressure on the bag. Guide the bag by holding it at the bottom in your left hand. Pipe a small amount of buttercream or frosting on the waxed paper to compress the cream and squeeze out any air in the pastry bag. When ready to pipe on a cake, hold the piping bag about 1 inch above the top of the cake and squeeze the cream out of the pastry bag as though it were a tube of toothpaste.

Ganache Cream

Ganache Cream is an exceptional chocolate cream that is surprisingly easy to make. It is a light, melt-in-the-mouth cream made with semisweet chocolate and whipping cream and used to fill and cover cakes and pastries. Once the cream has been made it must be refrigerated at least two hours and then beaten vigorously to make it light and fluffy.

2 cups whipping cream
14 ozs. semisweet chocolate, coarsely chopped

1. Place cream in heavy saucepan and bring almost to boiling over low heat.
2. Remove saucepan from heat and add chopped chocolate. Stir until chocolate is melted and mixture is smooth. Let mixture cool to room temperature.
3. Beat vigorously until mixture is light and fluffy and almost doubled in volume.
4. Refrigerate, uncovered, at least 2 hours.
5. Remove from refrigerator and beat with electric mixer until fluffy. Use immediately.

Lemon Cream

This is a completely different kind of cream. It has a custard base thickened with egg yolks and cornstarch. For extra lightness, beaten egg whites can be added to lighten the cream. Lemon Cream can be used in a fruit flan, as a cake filling or to fill cream puffs.

2 tablespoons cornstarch
3/4 cup sugar
3/4 cup water
3 egg yolks, beaten
1/4 cup lemon juice
1 teaspoon grated lemon peel
2 egg whites (optional)

1. Blend cornstarch, sugar and water in medium saucepan.
2. Add beaten egg yolks, lemon juice and lemon peel. Beat until blended.
3. Place saucepan over low heat and cook, stirring constantly, until mixture is thickened and bubbly. Lower heat and cook 1 minute.
4. Pour into bowl. Place waxed paper over surface of cream to prevent skin from forming. Let cool to room temperature.
5. If desired, beat egg whites in separate bowl until stiff peaks form. Fold beaten egg whites into lemon mixture. Refrigerate several hours or until ready to use.

Crème de la Crème—The Star Creams

These classic creams are unusually versatile and can be served as simple desserts or used as the basis of more complicated desserts. The main thing they have in common is that heat is the means by which they bind and are thickened.

English Custard

English custard is a very rich delicate cream made with whipping cream and egg yolks but no other binding agent. The cream is gently heated and gradually stirred into beaten egg yolks. If the custard is allowed to boil it will separate and the egg yolks will cook, which will spoil the custard. For preparation and ingredients see Rich Buttercream (page 227, bottom photos 2 to 10).

The custard can be used as a dessert, as a base for ice cream (page 210) or as part of Rich Buttercream. It can also be used as a cake filling. With the addition of whipped cream and gelatin, English Custard can even be turned into a Bavarian Cream.

Vanilla Cream (Crème Pâtisserie)

Vanilla Cream is similar to English Custard. Flour is added as a binding agent to make the cream firm. Vanilla Cream is used to fill profiteroles and cream puffs, in fruit flans and on pastry cream slices.

3/4 cup sugar
5 tablespoons all-purpose flour
1/4 teaspoon salt
2 cups milk
6 egg yolks
Seeds of 1 vanilla bean or 2 teaspoons vanilla extract
1 cup whipping cream (optional)

1. Stir sugar, flour and salt in heavy saucepan. Add milk and stir until blended.
2. Place saucepan over low heat and cook, stirring constantly, until mixture thickens and comes to a boil. Remove from heat.
3. Beat egg yolks in bowl. Stir about 1/2 cup hot milk mixture into beaten yolks until blended. Return mixture to saucepan.
4. Cook over low heat, stirring constantly, until mixture thickens and coats back of wooden spoon. (Do not allow mixture to come to a boil.) Remove from heat and pour into bowl. Stir in vanilla seeds or extract until blended. Cover surface of custard with waxed paper to prevent skin from forming. Cool to room temperature.
5. Beat whipping cream in medium bowl until firm. Fold whipped cream into cooled custard mixture. Refrigerate until ready to use.

Variation

To make Chocolate Pastry Cream, add 4 ounces melted and cooled semisweet chocolate to beaten egg yolks and stir until thoroughly blended. Proceed as directed above.

Fruit Mousse

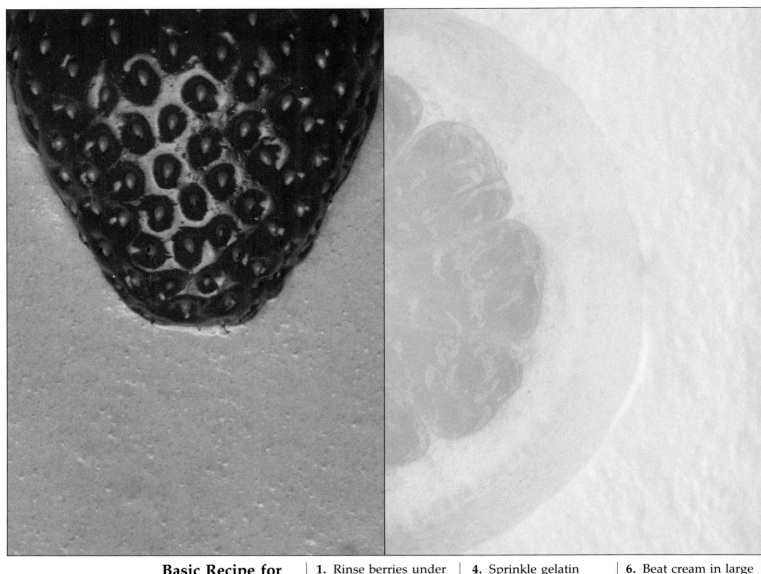

Basic Recipe for Fruit Mousse

1 pint fresh berries (or fruit indicated in specific recipe)

Sugar (depending upon sweetness of fruit)

1 envelope unflavored gelatin

1/4 cup liquid (fruit juice, liqueur, water or milk)

2 cups whipping cream

1. Rinse berries under cold running water. Remove stems and discard any blemished berries. Pat dry with paper towels.

2. Place berries in food processor or blender and process until pureed. Strain puree to remove seeds.

3. Measure puree (you should have about 1 cup) and place in large bowl. Add 1/2 to 1 cup sugar according to taste and stir well. Set aside.

4. Sprinkle gelatin over liquid in heatproof bowl and let stand 5 to 10 minutes to soften. Place bowl over pan of simmering water and cook, stirring occasionally, until gelatin is dissolved. Remove bowl from heat and let cool 1 to 2 minutes.

5. Stir dissolved gelatin into puree. Cool to room temperature and refrigerate until slightly thickened.

6. Beat cream in large bowl until soft peaks form. Add 2 to 4 tablespoons sugar and beat until firm.

7. Stir about 2 tablespoons whipped cream into puree mixture to lighten. Fold in remaining whipped cream and place in refrigerator until set.

8. Spoon into individual dessert dishes and serve garnished with additional berries or use to fill sponge rolls or as cake filling.

Fruit mousse is a delicious dessert and makes a wonderful filling for cakes and sponge rolls. It can be flavored in almost any way.

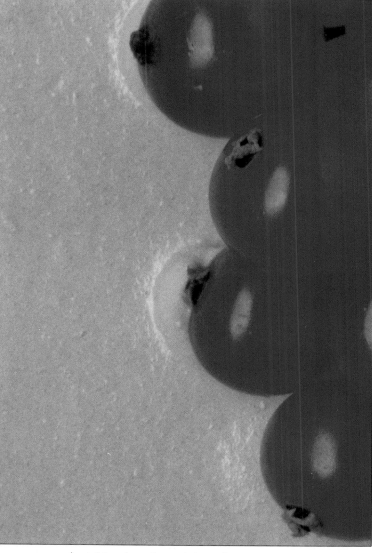

Variations

Strawberry Mousse

(Far left)
Prepare Basic Fruit Mousse as directed. Puree 1 pint freshly hulled strawberries and use 1/4 cup Grand Marnier or other orange-flavored liqueur as liquid in recipe.

Lemon Mousse

(Second from left)
Prepare Basic Fruit Mousse as directed, omitting fresh berries. Use juice of 2 fresh lemons as liquid in recipe. Add 1 to 2 teaspoons freshly grated lemon peel to gelatin mixture and, if desired, add a few drops of yellow food coloring.

Black Cherry Mousse

(Second from right)
Prepare Basic Fruit Mousse as directed. Use 1 (16-oz.) can pitted dark sweet cherries. Drain and puree cherries reserving 1/4 cup cherry syrup. Use reserved cherry syrup as liquid in recipe. Reduce amount of sugar to taste because canned cherries are already sweetened.

Red Currant Mousse

(Far right)
Prepare Basic Fruit Mousse as directed. Puree 1 pint of fresh red currants and use 1/4 cup orange juice or orange-flavored liqueur as liquid in recipe. Add a few drops of red food coloring, if desired.

Hints and Tips

Use well-chilled whipping cream as well as chilled bowl and beaters.

Be sure to whip cream to the soft peak stage before you add sugar or any other flavoring.

The chilled fruit puree mixture should be the same consistency as the whipped cream in order to combine them properly.

Stir the gelatin fruit puree mixture occasionally to prevent the edges from setting completely while refrigerated.

Quick Buttercreams— Versatile & Easy

Delicious buttercreams can be made quickly in a mixer—no cooking required. The trick is to beat the butter until it is very light and fluffy. As with other buttercreams, the quality of the butter is of paramount importance to the flavor of the buttercream. The butter must be fresh and unsalted. Margarine cannot be substituted.

Basic Recipe for Quick Buttercream

1 cup unsalted butter, room temperature
4 cups sifted powdered sugar
3 egg yolks
3 to 4 tablespoons milk, light cream or half and half
1-1/2 teaspoons vanilla extract

1. Beat butter in large bowl with electric mixer until light and creamy, 6 to 8 minutes.
2. Gradually add sugar, 1 cup at a time, beating constantly. Beat until light and fluffy.
3. Beat in egg yolks, 1 at a time, beating well after each addition.
4. Add vanilla and enough milk to make a good spreading consistency, beating until combined.

Variations

Quick Chocolate Buttercream

(Illustrated opposite page, top left) Prepare Basic Recipe for Quick Buttercream. Melt 5 ounces unsweetened chocolate in bowl set over pan of simmering water. Stir until smooth. Remove bowl from heat and cool to room temperature. Add melted chocolate to Buttercream and beat until blended and fluffy.

Caution: Be absolutely certain chocolate has cooled before you add it to Buttercream.

Quick Cherry Buttercream

(Illustrated opposite page, lower left) Prepare Basic Recipe for Quick Buttercream. Coarsely chop 3/4 cup candied cherries. Place cherries in small bowl, add 2 to 3 tablespoons kirsch and stir well. Let stand 30 minutes. Fold chopped cherries and kirsch into Buttercream.

Quick Mocha Buttercream

(Illustrated opposite page, top right) Prepare Basic Recipe for Quick Buttercream, omitting vanilla extract. Dissolve 3 tablespoons powdered instant coffee in 4 tablespoons very hot water. Cool to room temperature. Melt 2 ounces semisweet chocolate and let cool to room temperature. Add coffee and melted chocolate separately to Buttercream. Beat until well combined and Buttercream is light and fluffy.

Peanut-Chocolate Buttercream

(Illustrated opposite page, lower right) Prepare Basic Recipe for Quick Buttercream. Grind 1 cup unsalted peanuts in food processor or nut grinder until nuts are consistency of fine powder. Melt 4 ounces semisweet chocolate and cool to room temperature. Add melted chocolate to Buttercream and beat until blended. Fold in ground nuts.

Lemon or Orange Buttercream

(Not illustrated) Prepare Basic Recipe for Quick Buttercream omitting milk. Substitute 3 to 4 tablespoons orange or lemon juice. Fold in 1 tablespoon freshly grated lemon or orange peel. Tint with a few drops of yellow food coloring. Add 1 to 2 tablespoons orange-flavored brandy, if desired.

Gooseberry Meringue Flan

Shortcrust Pastry:
1-1/4 cups all-purpose
  flour
1/4 cup superfine
  sugar
1 to 2 tablespoons
  cocoa powder
  (optional)
1 egg yolk
1/2 cup chilled butter

Custard:
3/4 cup granulated
  sugar
5 tablespoons
  all-purpose flour
1-1/2 cups milk
5 egg yolks
2 teaspoons vanilla
  extract
1 (15-3/4 oz.) can
  gooseberries,
  drained

Meringue:
4 egg whites
1/4 teaspoon salt
1/2 cup superfine
  sugar

1. Prepare Shortcrust Pastry according to directions on page 101 through step 10. Add cocoa with flour, if using.
2. Preheat oven to 400F (205C). Lightly grease baking sheet.
3. Roll out pastry to a 10-inch circle. Place on baking sheet. Bake 12 to 15 minutes or until lightly browned. Cool completely on wire rack.
4. To make custard, stir granulated sugar and flour in medium saucepan. Add milk and stir until blended.
5. Place saucepan over low heat and cook, stirring, until mixture thickens and boils. Remove from heat.

Hidden Cream in a Meringue-Topped Flan

A melt-in-the-mouth recipe that combines a crisp shortcrust pastry and a fruit-flavored cream, topped by a lightly browned, beautifully piped meringue.

6. Beat egg yolks in small bowl. Add 1/2 cup hot milk mixture to beaten yolks; blend. Return mixture to saucepan.

7. Place saucepan over low heat and cook, stirring constantly, until mixture thickens. (Do not boil.) Remove from heat; and pour custard into bowl.

8. Stir in vanilla extract and fold in drained gooseberries. Cover with waxed paper to prevent skin from forming. Cool to room temperature.

9. Place cooled pastry base on baking sheet. Spoon cooled gooseberry custard over pastry, mounding it in center. Refrigerate until custard is set.

10. To make meringue, beat egg whites and salt in medium bowl until soft peaks form. Add sugar, 2 tablespoons at a time, and beat at high speed until stiff glossy peaks form.

11. Fill pastry bag fitted with large open-star tip. Pipe meringue in decorative swirls over custard-covered pastry base, covering custard completely.

12. Bake in 400F (205C) oven 5 to 6 minutes or until peaks of meringue are golden brown.

13. Cool on baking sheet on wire rack. Remove to serving plate. Refrigerate until ready to serve.

Variations

Substitute cherries, peaches, apricots or blueberries for the gooseberries.

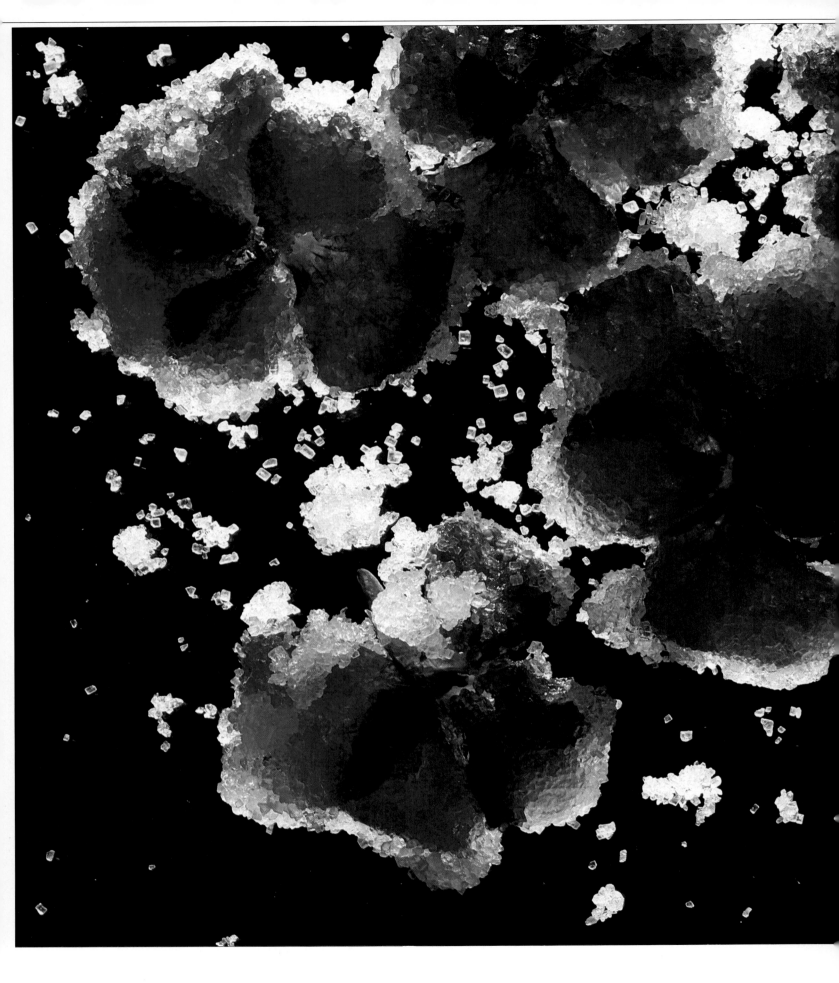

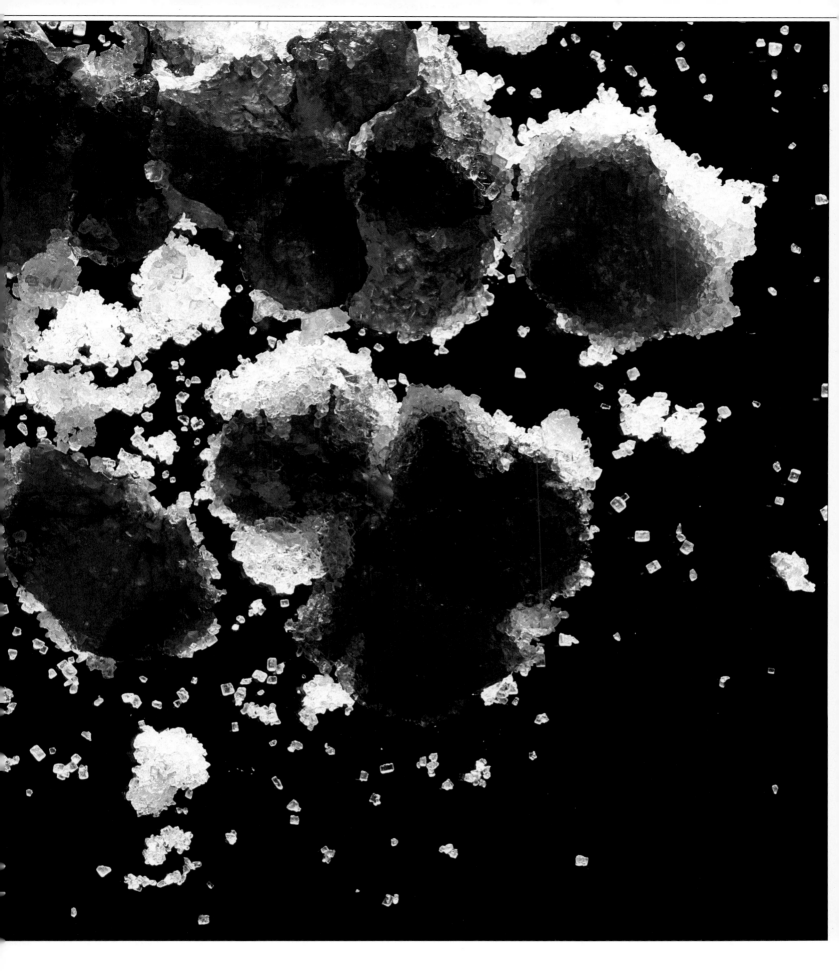

The Fine Art of
Decorating Desserts

From Chocolate Leaves to Pink Roses for Cake Decorating

Preparation: Melting Chocolate

1. Assemble bowl, pan, spatula, chopping board and chocolate.

2. Coarsely chop chocolate with large sharp knife.

3. Place 2/3 of chocolate in bowl. Half-fill pan with water.

4. Over moderate heat bring water just to boiling. Place bowl over pan.

5. Lower heat and melt chocolate, stirring with rubber spatula.

6. Remove bowl from pan as soon as chocolate is melted.

7. Add remaining 1/3 of chopped chocolate to bowl.

8. Stir until all chocolate is melted and temperature is 90F (30C).

9. One way to test for correct temperature is to coat spoon in chocolate.

10. Chocolate should set quickly and have a matte finish.

Preparation: Chocolate Leaves

1. Wash and dry fresh leaves with smooth surface like ivy, rose or bay.

2. Draw 1 side of leaf over melted chocolate, holding leaf by stem end.

3. Remove excess chocolate from edge by drawing leaf over rim of bowl.

4. Place leaf, chocolate side up, over handle of wooden spoon or on flat surface.

5. Let stand until chocolate is completely set. Peel leaf off chocolate carefully.

Preparation: Paper Piping Bag

1. Cut out large triangle of parchment paper.

2. Hold paper in 1 hand and twist corner toward you with other hand.

3. Pull other corner up over cone and pull point in tight.

4. Cut tiny piece off point with scissors to open tip.

5. Fill bag with icing or melted chocolate and fold in top of bag.

Cake decorating can be time-consuming. Set aside time to practice when you will not feel rushed. The art of making beautiful decorations is a skill that must be learned, but once learned it is not easily forgotten.

Preparation: Marzipan Leaves

1. Ingredients: marzipan, sifted powdered sugar, green food coloring.

2. Knead sugar into marzipan. Make well in center. Dilute coloring in water.

3. Knead coloring into marzipan. Roll into rope about 1/2 inch in diameter.

4. Slice rope into 1/2-inch slices.

5. Press slices into ovals; trim. Use a knife to cut veins on leaves.

Preparation: Marzipan Roses

1. Spoon red food coloring or grenadine syrup on top of block of marzipan.

2. Knead marzipan on sugared surface until uniform in color.

3. Shape marzipan into roll 3/4 inch thick.

4. Cut roll into 1/2-inch pieces with sharp knife.

5. Shape a few pieces into cones to make centers for roses.

6. Press some pieces with finger to make thin circles for rose petals.

7. Lift petal from work surface with knife blade or long flexible spatula.

8. Shape petal over your fingertip, bending edges back carefully.

9. Press bottom of petals firmly onto marzipan cone.

10. Set aside to dry at room temperature at least 30 minutes.

Preparation: Crystallized Rose Petals (not edible)

1. Ingredients: 1 teaspoon superfine sugar, 1 teaspoon gum arabic, 1 cup water.

2. Add superfine sugar and gum arabic to water and stir until dissolved.

3. Use tweezers to dip fresh rose petals into sugar liquid, 1 at a time. Drain.

4. Dip petals on both sides in additional sugar to cover completely.

5. Let dry on paper towels several hours. Use for decoration only.

Icings & Glazes—Finishing Touches

Even a perfectly made cake will benefit from a beautiful icing or glaze. And when a freshly baked cake looks less than perfect, the cosmetic imperfections can be hidden beneath a smooth icing or colored glaze, and no one will be the wiser.

Royal Icing

Royal Icing provides a dazzling white covering for a traditional wedding cake (pages 58-59). It is also used as a hard icing on English fruit cakes and Christmas cookies. If desired, the icing can be tinted with food coloring. When made in a smaller quantity than given below, the icing can be used to pipe decorations on cakes, to decorate a gingerbread house and to "write" on cakes. It can also be used to "glue" decorations to cakes.

5 large egg whites
3 (16-oz.) packages powdered sugar
Juice of half a lemon

Beat egg whites in large bowl until soft peaks form. Add sugar and lemon juice gradually, beating constantly until icing is very stiff and shiny. (Be sure to keep bowl covered with damp towel while icing cake to prevent icing from drying out.) Spread thin layer of icing over cake. Let stand until icing is dry; repeat several times. Fill pastry bag with remaining icing and pipe decoratively over cake.

This is enough icing to cover and decorate a large wedding cake made with two 10- or 11-inch cakes.

Apricot Glaze

Fruit glazes, brushed or poured over cakes and tarts, are used to seal in moisture as well as add beauty and flavor. Apricot Glaze is often used because it provides a somewhat neutral flavor that combines well with other flavors.

1 (16-oz.) jar apricot jam
1/2 cup sugar
2 tablespoons lemon juice
4 tablespoons water

Press jam through fine mesh sieve into small heavy saucepan and set aside. Place sugar, lemon juice and water in separate saucepan and bring to a boil. Boil rapidly until reduced by 1/3. Add sugar syrup to apricot jam and bring to a boil. Boil vigorously until mixture is transparent. Spoon or brush warm glaze over cake or pastry.

Variation

To make a red glaze, use red currant jelly instead of apricot jam. It is not necessary to strain jelly.

Glacé Icing

A topping of Glacé Icing is a quick and easy way to add a sweet finish to coffee cakes, Danish pastry, cookies and plain cakes.

1 cup powdered sugar
1 to 2 tablespoons warm water

Sift sugar into small, deep bowl. Add water, 1 tablespoon at a time, and stir until icing is thick and of good spreading consistency.

Variation

Substitute milk, orange or lemon juice, flavored liqueur or coffee for water. Add a few drops of food coloring to white icing.

Chocolate & Cocoa . . .

There are many people whose eyes light up at the mere mention of chocolate. Both chocolate and cocoa are made from cocoa beans, the fruit of the cocoa tree. The botanical name for the cocoa tree is Theobroma cacao; theobroma translates to mean "food of the gods." Brews made from the cocoa bean can be traced back to the Aztec culture, although the original bitter brews bore very little resemblance to the refined, sweet flavor of chocolate drinks popular today.

Chocolate Curls

Chocolate curls make wonderful decorations for cakes and fancy desserts. To make chocolate curls, melt the chocolate and pour it on a smooth, cold work surface such as marble. Spread it out in a thin layer and let it stand until it is set. Push the chocolate forward, scraping it off the work surface with a wide, metal scraper. The chocolate will curl as you push the scraper forward. Lift the curls carefully and place them on a waxed paper-lined plate or baking sheet. Refrigerate until ready to use.

Buying Chocolate in Bulk

Expensive good quality chocolate is less expensive when bought in bulk form. Many kinds of chocolate can be purchased in 5 and 10 pound blocks from specialty shops. If you use a lot of chocolate for baking, it is worth the effort involved to locate a good source for bulk purchases.

A word of caution: chocolate coating, sometimes called summer coating, contains additives and is not pure chocolate. If you buy anything with an unfamiliar name, be sure you understand exactly what you are buying. It may turn out to be something you don't really want!

. . . "Food of the Gods"

Spanish explorers took cocoa beans back to Spain from Mexico. Chocolate was introduced in Spain about 1519 and eventually made its way to London where an enterprising Frenchman opened the first hot chocolate shop in 1657. But it wasn't until 1765 that chocolate was made in the United States. In other words, it took about 250 years for the cocoa bean to make its way from Mexico to the United States by a very roundabout route through Europe!

Special Chocolate Covering

Very few people can resist a cake covered in a smooth shiny coat of chocolate. One way to create a particularly smooth finish is to cover the cake with a thin layer of marzipan before adding the chocolate. Roll out the marzipan to a large, thin circle and drape it over the top and side of the cake. Press all over very gently and trim the bottom edge of the marzipan with a sharp knife. Pour melted chocolate on top of the center of the cake and spread evenly over the top and side with a long, thin icing spatula. Use a generous amount of chocolate to cover the cake completely. Score the chocolate on top of the cake in serving portions before the chocolate is completely set to prevent the chocolate coating from cracking when you cut the cake.

Chocolate Leaves

Cover a cake in marzipan and melted chocolate. Arrange fresh raspberries on the top of the cake and surround the raspberries with beautiful and delicious Chocolate Leaves. Follow the directions for making Chocolate Leaves on page 242. Once you have learned how to make them, you can use them to decorate all kinds of desserts.

Marzipan Shapes—Attractive, Delicious & Fun to Make

Working with marzipan provides an opportunity for every cook to turn into a sculptor. Marzipan can be tinted almost any color desired and, when properly made, is easy to model into all kinds of shapes. Marzipan shapes can be used to decorate a cake or other dessert, can be arranged as a center piece on the table or can be served as candy. Invite the children into the kitchen to help model marzipan and turn your creative cooking and sculpting into a family affair.

Marzipan from Scratch

Marzipan can be bought ready-made or made from scratch quickly and easily. Place equal amounts of almond paste and powdered sugar in a bowl. Add 1 egg white and mix at low speed of mixer. If the mixture is crumbly, add additional egg whites, 1 at a time, until the mixture holds together. A few drops of orange or rose water can be added for flavor and, if desired, corn syrup can be substituted for egg whites. Sprinkle a smooth work surface with powdered sugar and knead the marzipan just until it is smooth. Cover it tightly with plastic wrap and store it in the refrigerator until you are ready to use it. If marzipan is exposed to air before it is shaped, it will dry out and be unusable.

Hints and Tips for Working with Marzipan

Use powdered sugar on the work surface, the rolling pin or your hands in the same way you would use flour when working with pastry.

Be careful not to overknead marzipan. Overkneading may cause the oil in the almonds to separate out and make the marzipan greasy.

If the marzipan has been refrigerated, bring it to room temperature before shaping.

Work with only a small amount of marzipan at a time. Keep the rest of the marzipan covered with a damp towel to keep it from drying out.

When rolling out a large piece of marzipan to cover a cake, roll it between two pieces of waxed paper. Peel off the top piece of paper and invert the marzipan over the cake. Remove the second piece of paper.

If you use a knife or other metal equipment to help shape marzipan, spread a very thin film of oil over the metal to prevent the marzipan from tearing.

If you want to provide a rough finish on the surface of some fruit shapes, roll them gently over a grater.

Color can be added to marzipan either by kneading a few drops of edible food coloring into the marzipan or by brushing color on a finished shape. When food coloring is brushed on, it should be diluted with water. Use a brush with a fine tip rather than a wide pastry brush. Allow shaped marzipan to dry before brushing with dye.

To make small, flat marzipan shapes, roll out marzipan to desired thickness and use cookie cutters to make shapes.

Allow completed marzipan shapes to dry at room temperature.

A Variety of Marzipan Shapes

Mushrooms and Potatoes:
Shape mushroom caps and stems separately and attach while marzipan is soft. Let mushrooms and potato shapes dry. Prepare dark brown food coloring according to directions on box. Brush caps and bottoms of mushroom stems with dark brown color. Dilute dye to lighten and brush on stems and underside of mushroom caps. Brush medium brown color on potatoes and highlight with dark brown.

Cherries, Plums, and Strawberries:
Knead grenadine or red food coloring into marzipan and shape as desired. Use the blunt edge of a knife to make a crease in cherries or plums. Prick strawberries with a wooden pick.

Peaches, Carrots and Oranges:
Combine red and yellow food coloring and tint marzipan as desired; shape. Make a crease in peaches with a knife; use a wooden pick to make lines in carrots; rub the surface of oranges on a grater to make the skin look rough.

Lemons and Bananas:
Use yellow food coloring to tint the marzipan. Shape fruit. Dry bananas and use brown food coloring (see mushrooms above) to make lines on the banana skin and to brush on tips. Rub the surface of lemons on a grater.

Pears:
Tint marzipan with a combination of green and yellow food coloring.

249

Special Piping

The cloth pastry bag used to pipe cake mixtures and buttercreams is too clumsy to use for fine filigree work. It is better to use a small paper piping bag to pipe delicate patterns and for writing. You can make your own piping bags from parchment paper (see page 242), or you can buy them. They are not expensive and once you are finished using them you simply throw them away. The size of the hole cut in the point of the bag determines the thickness of the piped line. If you want to make a pattern with several thicknesses, pipe the thin lines first, enlarge the hole slightly and continue to pipe.

Icing for Decorating

Glacé Icing is an easy icing to pipe, but it must be made somewhat thicker than the icing used to cover pastry. The icing must be thin enough to flow through the hole in the piping bag easily, but not be runny. It must have enough thickness to hold its shape and not break during piping. Combine powdered sugar with a few drops of water, juice or milk to make a thick but workable paste and tint if desired. It's a good idea to strain the icing to remove any small lumps of sugar that might clog the hole in the piping bag.

Piping with a Paper Piping Bag

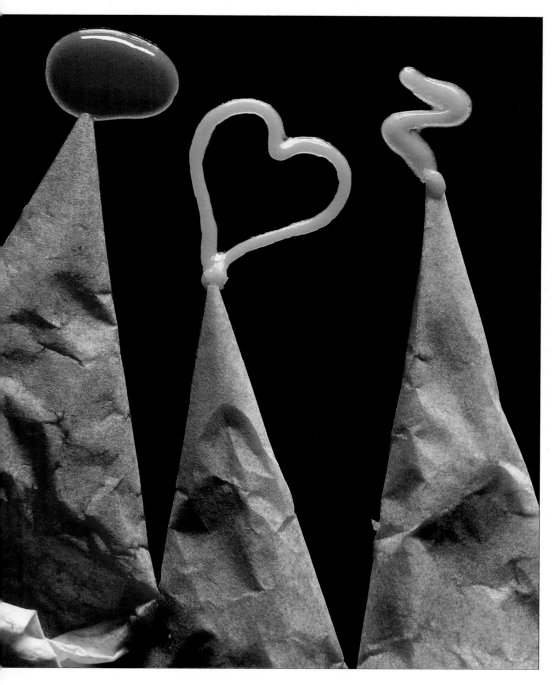

Writing in Chocolate

Thin lines of chocolate can be a bit tricky to pipe. Melt dark semisweet or milk chocolate and stir in enough light corn syrup to give the chocolate a thick and somewhat elastic consistency. Fill a paper piping bag and use it immediately. Practice on waxed paper until you get a good feeling about how to make the chocolate do what you want it to do.

Tips on Using a Piping Bag

Hold the piping bag about 1 inch above the surface you are decorating. If you hold the bag too close you will not be able to draw evenly.

To make very thin lines on small cakes, place the cakes close together and move the piping bag over them quickly from right to left in a zigzag motion. The faster you move the bag, the thinner the lines will be.

Work quickly and don't leave a full bag of icing sitting on the counter as the tip of the bag will dry and clog, and you won't be able to use it.

Tinted Icing

Use food coloring to tint icing. Add it one drop at a time. Be careful not to make the icing too thin. If the icing does get too thin, add powdered sugar to thicken it.

Paper piping bags are used for writing and to make intricate patterns on cakes and pastries.
It takes practice to learn how to pipe with a steady hand.
Work on a piece of waxed paper while you are learning, and use the waxed paper to create interesting designs that can be perfected and then copied on a cake or pastry.

Flan Cases

Flan cases are made with a simple sponge or a crisp and flaky shortcrust pastry. Make the flan case in a flan tin with a removable bottom and fluted rim. The removable bottom makes it easy to get the finished flan out of the tin, and the fluted rim provides a firm and attractive edge for the flan. Bake the flan case far enough in advance to allow it to cool completely before filling.

Fruit Filling

Poached fresh fruit in season, frozen fruit or canned fruit can be used to fill a flan case. Choose 2 or 3 different kinds of fruit that will compliment each other in flavor and color. When fresh fruit is used it should be poached in a sugar syrup and then drained. The sugar syrup can be reduced and used to glaze the flan. Frozen fruit should be thawed and drained thoroughly. The juice or syrup from frozen or canned fruit can also be reduced and used as a glaze. Arrange the fruit directly in the flan case or over a custard-filled case. Cover the fruit with a glaze and let the flan stand until the glaze is set. Refrigerate until ready to serve.

Fruit Flans—Full of Summer Freshness, Even in Winter

Flan cases, ready-made or homemade, can be filled with a custard if desired, and fresh, canned or frozen fruit. It is a quick and easy job to assemble a flan and top it with a shiny glaze and a little whipped cream for a special treat. Make a fruit flan early in the morning and set it aside to cool while you prepare dinner for company.

The Finishing Touch

Flans are finished with a glaze because a glaze holds the fruit firmly in place and adds flavor and a shiny gloss. Use a reduced syrup (see column 1) or make a glaze with jam, sugar and water (see Apricot Glaze, page 244). Allow the glaze to cool 1 or 2 minutes and brush or spoon it over the fruit.

Glaze Made from Jelly

Fruit jelly provides an easy way to make a quick glaze with fine concentrated flavor. Bring the jelly to a boil, stir in a little sugar to taste, cook until the sugar is dissolved, cool slightly and brush over the fruit. The glaze will be firm when set.

A Bed of Custard

Spread Lemon or Vanilla Cream (see pages 232-233) in a flan case before adding fruit. Arrange the well-drained fruit over the custard. A custard filling provides additional flavor and texture to a flan and prevents any fruit juice from seeping into the flan case and making it soggy.

Blueberry-Red Currant Flan

(Opposite, top left) Fill baked 10- or 11-inch flan case with custard. Alternate rows of fresh blueberries and currants or raspberries (about 1 pint of each), starting from center of flan and work out toward edge. Cover with fruit jelly glaze.

Mandarin Orange-Apricot-Grape Flan

(Opposite, top right) Fill a 10- or 11-inch baked flan case with custard. Drain a 14-ounce can mandarin oranges, reserving syrup. Arrange oranges around outside edge of custard. Drain a 16-ounce can apricot halves, reserving syrup. Fill center of flan with apricot halves, cut side down. Fill space between apricots with about a 1/2 pound seedless grapes. Cover with glaze prepared with reserved syrup or fruit jelly.

Strawberry-Pineapple Flan

(Opposite, bottom left Fill a baked 8- or 9-inch flan case with custard. Drain 5-1/4-ounce can pineapple slices, reserving syrup. Place pineapple slices on custard. Arrange 1 pint fresh, hulled small strawberries between pineapple slices. Place a halved strawberry in the center of each pineapple slice. Cover with glaze prepared with reserved pineapple syrup or fruit jelly.

Kiwifruit-Blackberry-Red Currant Flan

(Opposite, lower right) Fill a baked 10- or 11-inch flan case with custard. Peel and slice 3 ripe kiwifruit. Arrange circle of kiwifruit slices on center of custard. Arrange remaining slices around them in larger circle. Fill space between slices of kiwifruit with blackberries. Fill space between kiwifruit and outer edge of flan with red currants. Cover with red currant or apple jelly glaze.

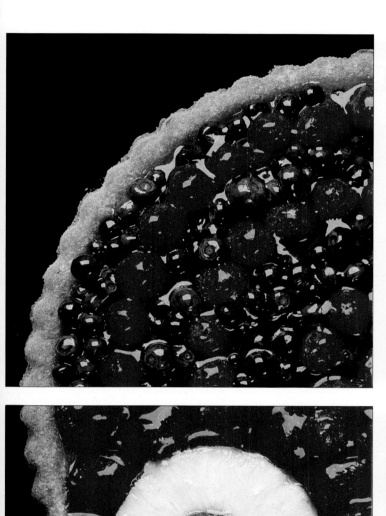
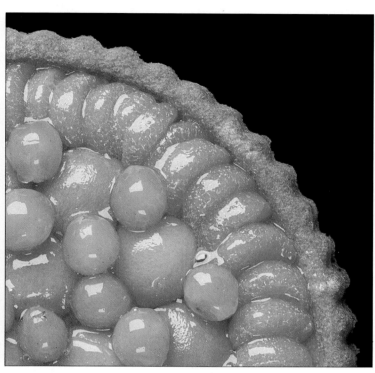

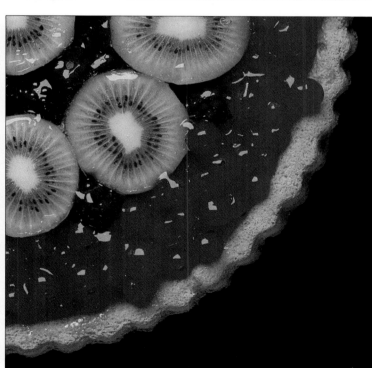

30 Ways to Decorate Desserts

1. Very thin slices of orange, poached in sugar syrup: Brush with Apricot Glaze (see page 244) and use to decorate cakes and soufflés.

2. Marzipan Roses (see page 243): Use on wedding cakes, fruit cakes and special occasion cakes.

3. Chocolate truffles coated with cocoa powder: Use on cakes and chocolate cream desserts.

4. Marzipan numbers decorated with piped chocolate dots: Use for special birthday or anniversary cakes.

5. Crushed meringue: Press onto sides of cakes covered with whipped cream or buttercream.

6. Maraschino cherries: Use in clusters or cut in half to decorate cakes.

7. Shredded or flaked coconut: Use to coat truffles or decorate cakes.

8. Colored sugar balls: Use to decorate cookies or children's birthday cakes.

9. Walnut halves: Use to decorate cookies, candies or cakes.

10. Hazelnut nougat: Use to ice cakes and in candymaking.

11. Spider web icing pattern: Pipe very thin chocolate lines in a spiral on white Glacé Icing. Use tip of sharp knife and draw it from center outward. Move knife and draw next line from outer edge of spiral in toward center. Repeat around circle. Make pattern on cakes and fancy pastries.

12. Cocoa powder: Use to dust cookies, cakes and to coat candy.

13. Piped flowers with candied cherry petals: Use for cake decoration.

14. Raspberry jelly: Use to glaze fruit flans.

15. Marzipan: Roll out and cut to exact size of cake portions. Place on top of cake.

Decoration, the finishing touch for cakes and desserts, can be as simple as a dusting of powdered sugar or an elaborate marzipan rose. Deciding how to decorate a cake may take a bit of imagination, but the execution of an original design provides an opportunity to demonstrate artistic skills along with culinary accomplishments. Try some of the ideas illustrated on these pages, or design your own ways to decorate.

16. Piped swirls of whipped cream or buttercream with pineapple wedge: Place on cakes.

17. Red currants: Use to fill fruit flans covered with red currant jelly glaze.

18. Chocolate shavings: Use to decorate cakes and cream desserts.

19. Nut topping: Use to coat sides of cakes covered with buttercream or whipped cream. Sprinkle on top of frosted cakes or coat candy.

20. Thin squares of chocolate: Use to decorate top of cakes.

21. Colored crystal sugar: Use to sprinkle over cookies, children's birthday cakes or Glacé Icing.

22. Rolled cookies: Stand upright and press onto icing around side of cake to create unusual decoration.

23. Baked meringue: Spread or pipe meringue in peaks over fruit flans or pies. Bake in hot oven just until peaks are lightly browned.

24. Strawberries dipped in pink icing: Dip strawberries into tinted Glacé Icing and use to decorate cakes and cream desserts.

25. Powdered sugar: Place doily or small cardboard shapes on top of cake. Sprinkle powdered sugar over cake and remove doily or cut-outs.

26. Crystallized violets: Sold ready-made. Use to decorate cakes and petits fours.

27. Crystallized brown sugar: Sprinkle over frosted cookies and cakes.

28. Lemon slice and thin strips of curled lemon peel: Use to decorate cakes and cream desserts.

29. Chopped pistachio nuts: Use to decorate edge of cakes covered in buttercream and to coat chocolate candy.

30. Candied coffee beans: Use to decorate petits fours and cakes.

Sweets &
Chocolates—Treats
for Special Occasions

Chocolate Truffles—Tempting, Sinful & Worth Every Calorie

Hints and Tips for Making Chocolate Truffles

Make truffles small enough to eat in one bite.

If you are new to candymaking, you can coat truffles in sweetened cocoa powder or finely ground nuts rather than dip them in melted chocolate. Learning how to dip candy in chocolate takes a bit of practice.

Follow the instructions for handling chocolate on pages 38 and 242. Use a candy thermometer to be sure the melted chocolate is the correct temperature. The temperature must be carefully controlled and never permitted to rise above 110F (45C).

Never cover chocolate when melting it. Even the smallest drop of water or the slightest amount of steam will cause the chocolate to stiffen and you will have to discard it.

When chocolate is overheated it develops grey streaks as it hardens. This does not affect the flavor, but it does affect the look of the chocolate.

Be sure you make enough melted chocolate to work with when coating candy. It is all but impossible to work with a skimpy amount of chocolate, but it is always possible to find a way to use any leftover chocolate. At the very worst, you can have a private chocolate binge and simply eat it!

Semantic confusion abounds when it comes to the subject of truffles. Europeans think of truffles first as a wonderful, rare and expensive fungus. According to some food historians, chocolate truffles are named for their physical resemblance to the "black truffle of Perigord" which is one of the most highly prized truffles found anywhere. On the other hand, "praline" in Germany, Austria and Switzerland is translated to mean "chocolate cream." Therefore, if you want what Americans call a chocolate truffle when you are in some parts of Europe, you must ask for pralines. But if you ask for pralines in the United States you will get the famous New Orleans flat candy made of pecans and caramel or possibly a French candy made with almonds. But, no matter what you call these chocolate sweets, they are absolute heaven to eat.

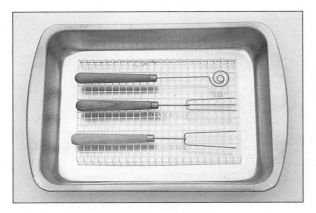

Candymaking Equipment

Special equipment is available to make the job of chocolate dipping as easy as possible. Pictured above: icing rack set over tray; swirl dipping fork; three-prong dipping fork; and two-prong dipping fork.

Storage:

The question of how to store chocolate candies is usually academic because they tend to be eaten almost as quickly as they are made. When absolutely necessary, chocolate candies can be frozen for a short period of time, but freezing will do nothing to improve their flavor. It is a good idea to place chocolates in the refrigerator long enough to harden, but the best storage is at about 65F (20C).

Truffles

Equipment:
Double boiler or heatproof bowl fitted over saucepan
Medium saucepan
15" x 10" pan
Swirl dipping fork (optional)
Paper bonbon cases (optional)

Ingredients:
12 ozs. milk chocolate
12 ozs. dark semisweet chocolate
1 cup heavy cream
10 tablespoons unsalted butter
6 tablespoons dark rum, brandy or other liqueur

Chocolate coating:
20 ozs. milk chocolate or dark semisweet chocolate, broken into pieces
2-1/2 cups superfine sugar

Servings:
70 to 80 Truffles.

Marzipan Centers

Ingredients:
14 ozs. marzipan
Powdered sugar
20 ozs. dark semisweet chocolate
Whole blanched almonds

Servings:
40 to 50 Marzipan Centers

Preparation: Basic Truffles

1. Measure ingredients and let stand until room temperature.

2. Place chocolate in top of double boiler.

3. Melt chocolate over low heat, stirring until smooth.

4. Remove chocolate from heat and set aside to cool.

5. Heat cream and butter in medium saucepan until butter is melted.

6. Stir cooled chocolate and rum into cream mixture.

7. Beat vigorously until mixture is thoroughly blended and cooled.

8. Line 15″ x 10″ pan with plastic wrap. Pour mixture into pan.

9. Let stand until set. Cover with plastic wrap and refrigerate 24 hours.

10. Uncover, invert onto cool work surface and peel off plastic wrap.

11. Cut mixture into small equal-size pieces. Dust hands with powdered sugar.

12. Shape pieces into balls quickly with sugared hands. Refrigerate 2 hours.

13. To make coating, melt 2/3 of chocolate in top of double boiler.

14. Remove melted chocolate and stir in 1/3 of remaining chocolate.

15. Remove 1/3 of truffle balls from refrigerator. Place sugar in dish.

16. Dip balls, 1 at a time, into melted chocolate with spiral dipping fork.

17. Lift out balls and hold over chocolate until excess chocolate drops off.

18. Invert dipping fork and let coated truffle drop into sugar.

19. Repeat until all truffles are coated with chocolate. Cover truffles with sugar.

20. Let stand until completely set. Place in bonbon cases.

Preparation: Marzipan Centers

1. Measure ingredients and let stand until room temperature.

2. Roll out marzipan to 1/2-inch thickness on sugared surface.

3. Cut marzipan into bite-size pieces.

4. Melt 2/3 of chocolate in top of double boiler.

5. Remove melted chocolate and stir in remaining chocolate.

6. Pick up marzipan piece on pronged dipping fork.

7. Dip into melted chocolate and cover marzipan completely.

8. Place on rack set over pan and let excess chocolate drip off.

9. Place almond on top of each piece before chocolate is completely set.

10. Let stand until completely set. Place in bonbon cases.

More About Candymaking

Chocolate Truffles

Once the truffle mixture has been made, it should be covered and stored in the refrigerator overnight. It can be stored for as long as one week before you shape it. Sprinkle your work surface with powdered sugar before you remove the truffle mixture from the pan. If available, a marble work surface is ideal because it remains cool. A Corian work surface will also remain cool. Dust your hands thoroughly with powdered sugar several times while you are shaping the truffles because the heat from your hands will cause the mixture to melt and stick to your fingers and hands.

Marzipan Centers

Marzipan can be purchased in packages or cans and can be kept in the pantry for a long period of time. However, once a package of marzipan has been opened, and exposed to the air, it will dry out quickly. Wrap leftover marzipan tightly and store it in the refrigerator or freezer. Allow it to come to room temperature before using. Sprinkle work surface and rolling pin with powdered sugar and roll out marzipan to about 1/2-inch thickness. Hold the blade of a sharp knife under cold running water briefly, wipe the knife dry and cut the rolled out marzipan into small shapes. Dip the cut marzipan into melted chocolate and decorate as desired (see pages 258-259).

Whether candies are simply chocolate-coated or chocolate throughout, they can be made without too much difficulty if you follow directions faithfully.

Nougat and Caramel Centers

Hazelnut nougat and caramel can be purchased from specialty mail order confectionery suppliers and some specialty stores that sell candymaking supplies. Nougat is sold in 1-pound tub containers and 2-1/4-pound blocks. Block form nougat is the easiest to work with because it is firm enough to be cut with a knife and rolled into a variety of shapes. Handle nougat as you would marzipan, sprinkling the work surface and rolling pin with powdered sugar. Nougat purchased in tub containers has a creamy consistency and should be used to flavor a truffle mixture. If desired, you can omit the liqueur from the truffle mixture and substitute an equal amount of creamy hazelnut nougat.

Caramel in block form is available in both vanilla and chocolate flavors. It can be rolled, cut and shaped.

Both caramel and nougat shapes can be dipped in melted chocolate (see page 259).

Additional Hints and Tips

Truffle mixture must be prepared at least one day in advance to allow it to harden before shaping and dipping. If the mixture is not firm after one day in the refrigerator, place it in the freezer for two or three hours.

Work with cool hands. Rinse them in cold water periodically, dry thoroughly and dust with powdered sugar.

Shape only a small amount of truffle mixture at a time. Keep the mixture you are not shaping in the refrigerator to prevent it from getting soft.

If you have chocolate left over after dipping, add some chopped nuts, chopped raisins, or candied fruit. Drop the mixture in small clusters onto sheets of foil and let stand or refrigerate until set.

Finishing Touches for Candy

The Correct Time to Add Coating

After truffles have been dipped in chocolate, they must "set" one or two minutes before they can be rolled in cocoa or sugar or covered with sprinkles or chopped nuts. But once the chocolate is firmly set, additional decoration cannot be added. Be sure you have a good quantity of coating ingredients ready because you literally want to bury the dipped truffles in the coating rather than roll them around in it. Place coated truffles on a sheet of foil and allow them to stand until completely set.

Chocolate Sprinkle Coating

(Illustrated top left) Place dipped truffles in a deep bowl of chocolate sprinkles and spoon the sprinkles over the truffles. Let stand until the sprinkles are set. When you remove the coated truffles, extra loose sprinkles will fall off.

Cocoa Powder Coating

(Illustrated lower left) Add 1 to 2 tablespoons sifted powdered sugar to 1 cup cocoa and stir until well combined. Place dipped truffles in the cocoa mixture and spoon it over the truffles to coat completely. Let stand until set.

Powdered Sugar Coating

(Illustrated top right) Place dipped truffles in a deep bowl of sifted powdered sugar. Spoon the sugar over the truffles to coat completely. Let stand until set.

White Chocolate & Sugar Coating

(Illustrated lower right) Dip truffles in melted white chocolate and let the excess chocolate drain off. Place dipped truffles in a deep bowl of granulated or superfine sugar. Spoon the sugar over the truffles to cover them completely. Let stand until set.

Dipped candy that is not coated can have a decoration added. Try some of the suggestions shown on the right or make up your own.

Decorating with Nuts

(Illustrated top left) Press small whole nuts or halved nuts onto dipped candy while chocolate covering is still soft.

Sprinkle finely chopped nuts over dipped candy before chocolate sets.

Piped Decoration

(Illustrated top right) Use a color that contrasts the color of the chocolate in which the candy was dipped. Pipe melted dark or milk chocolate on white chocolate candy. Use melted white chocolate to pipe over dark or milk chocolate candy. Pipe in a crisscross, zigzag, swirl, spiral or lined pattern. Allow candy to stand until piped chocolate is completely set. (For additional piping ideas see page 267.)

Other Decorations

(Illustrated lower left)
Chocolate Shavings:
Decorate candy dipped in milk chocolate with shavings of dark chocolate arranged in a fan pattern.

Coffee Beans:
Decorate candy dipped in milk chocolate with dark candied coffee beans.

Lattice Pattern:
Dip candy in chocolate. Just before chocolate is set, roll candy gently back and forth over rack to create lattice pattern in chocolate.

Decorating with Candied Fruit

(Illustrated lower right) Color contrast on candy is very decorative. For example: add candied lemon peel or angelica to candy dipped in white chocolate; add a small piece of dried apricot to candy dipped in milk chocolate; add a piece of citron to candy dipped in milk chocolate; add strips of glacé pear or orange peel to candy dipped in white chocolate.

Toppings as Mystery Solvers

Use your choice of a topping to provide a clue to the filling so you won't have to guess what filling is hidden inside the chocolate. This is particularly helpful when you want to fill a gift box with a balanced assortment of homemade candy.

Candies That Melt in the Mouth

Piped and soft candies provide wonderful variations of taste and texture.

Truffle Creams

Truffle creams contain more butter than the Basic Truffle mixture and therefore will not keep as long. Two basic mixtures are used. One candy is based on the Basic Truffle mixture (see page 258-259) as shown in the photographs on the opposite page, far right column. The other candy is made from a Butter Truffle mixture as shown in the photograph on the opposite page, two left columns. The flavor of both mixtures can be varied by using different kinds of good fruit liqueurs such as raspberry, cherry, pear, plum or apricot.

Centers for Bonbons

Bonbons with fruit-flavored centers are not difficult to make these days because ready-made candy centers are available from mail-order specialty houses and from specialty stores that sell candymaking supplies. Buttercream centers can be bought in 1-pound packages of raspberry, strawberry, lemon, peppermint, cherry, maple nut and whipped chocolate

flavors. These centers can be rolled into balls or formed into a variety of shapes. Dip them in melted chocolate to make truly delicious bonbons.

Pear-Flavored Truffles

(Opposite, far left column)
60 foil candy cups
About 20 ozs. semisweet or milk chocolate, melted

Truffle mixture:
1-1/4 cups unsalted butter
1/3 cup coconut cream
1 cup sifted powdered sugar
9 ozs. milk chocolate, melted
4 to 5 tablespoons pear-flavored liqueur
2 ozs. melted milk chocolate for piping decoration

1. Place foil candy cups close together on large baking sheet. Fill cups with melted chocolate.
2. Invert cups onto draining rack set over large bowl. Let stand until chocolate cups are set. Reserve chocolate in bowl.

3. To make truffle mixture, beat butter, coconut cream and powdered sugar until thick and very light. Add 9 ounces melted milk chocolate and beat until thoroughly blended. Gradually stir in pear liqueur.
4. Spoon mixture into pastry bag fitted with large open plain tip. Pipe mixture into chocolate-lined cups. (If mixture is too soft or runny to pipe, refrigerate 30 to 40 minutes.) Refrigerate filled cups several hours.
5. Remelt chocolate reserved in bowl. Dip tops of filled cups into melted chocolate. Let stand until chocolate is set. Pipe thin lines of melted milk chocolate over tops of candies. Makes 5 dozen Truffles.

Butter Truffles

(Opposite, 2nd column from left)
1 recipe Pear-Flavored Truffle mixture (9-ozs. melted milk chocolate and pear-flavored liqueur omitted)

To decorate:
20 ozs. milk or semisweet chocolate, melted
Granulated or superfine sugar

1. Prepare Pear-Flavored Truffle mixture omitting 9 ounces melted milk chocolate and pear-flavored liqueur.
2. Spoon mixture into pastry bag fitted with large open plain tip. Pipe mixture in small balls on parchment-lined baking sheet.
3. Refrigerate overnight.
4. Dip balls into melted chocolate and roll in sugar. Let stand until set. Refrigerate until ready to serve.

Cognac Truffles

(Opposite, far right column)
1. Prepare Basic Truffle mixture according to directions on page 259. Use cognac instead of dark rum. Refrigerate mixture 2 to 3 hours.
2. Prepare foil candy cups as directed in recipe for Pear-Flavored Truffles. Use milk chocolate instead of semisweet chocolate.
3. Beat Basic Truffle mixture with heavy duty electric mixer until light, about 5 minutes.

4. Spoon mixture into pastry bag fitted with large open-star tip. Pipe mixture into chocolate-lined cups. Refrigerate overnight.
5. Dip tops in melted milk chocolate and refrigerate until chocolate is set. Makes 5 dozen Truffles.

Pistachio Truffles

(Opposite, 2nd column from right)
11 ozs. marzipan
2/3 cup finely ground pistachios
4 to 5 tablespoons dark rum
18 ozs. semisweet chocolate, melted
2 ozs. milk chocolate, melted
Pistachio halves

1. Blend marzipan, ground pistachios, and rum until mixture is a soft consistency.
2. Spoon mixture into pastry bag fitted with large open-star tip. Pipe into small rosettes or mound on parchment-lined baking sheet. Let stand at room temperature 24 hours to dry.
3. Dip candies into melted semisweet chocolate and let stand until chocolate is set.
4. Pipe thin lines of melted milk chocolate over tops of candies and decorate with pistachio halves.

Petits fours are miniature sweets, usually sponge cakes, but are occasionally made with marzipan or another cake or cookie base. They are elaborately iced and decorated and are ideal to serve at a wedding, other special occasion or formal and elegant tea.

Basic Recipe for Petits Fours

1 recipe Swiss Roll, page 82
1 cup (12-oz. jar) apricot jam, pressed through sieve
12 ozs. marzipan

Icing:
4 tablespoons grenadine syrup
1 (16-oz.) package powdered sugar
2 tablespoons light corn syrup
Shelled pistachio nuts to decorate

Makes about 5 dozen Petits Fours.

Variations for Petits Fours

Cover little sponge cakes with vanilla icing. Omit the grenadine syrup and increase the light corn syrup to 4 tablespoons. Add 4 tablespoons hot water and pour over sponge squares as illustrated above. For variety, white icing can be tinted almost any color.

Petits fours can be made in many ways: with a single layer of cake or several layers of sponge cake sandwiched with marzipan, jam or a pastry cream. They can be cut into various shapes such as diamonds, rounds, ovals or triangles.

Hint: When petits fours are made with sponge cake, bake the sponge at least one day in advance so the cake will cut easily without crumbling.

1. Spread jam over cake and trim off about 1/2-inch of cake on all sides.

2. Roll out marzipan and cover top of cake; cut into 1-1/2-inch squares.

3. To make icing, stir grenadine and powdered sugar together well.

Petits Fours—

4. Stir in corn syrup until blended. Icing should run off spoon.

5. Place half the sponge squares on a rack. Pour half the icing over. Repeat.

6. Decorate with pistachio half before icing is set. Let stand until icing sets.

Beautiful & Delicious

Decorating Petits Fours

(Illustrated large photograph, left-hand page, left to right)

1. Pipe a delicate flower outline with dark melted chocolate. Fill in outline with melted milk chocolate. Pipe a dab of white icing in the center.

2. Pipe 2 lines of white icing down the length of the Petits Fours. Decorate with a crystallized violet and a pistachio half.

3. Pipe a flower stem with melted chocolate. Use a Crystallized Rose Petal (page 243) for the flower and pistachio halves for leaves.

4. Use a small tinted, molded marzipan flower and strips of candied citron for leaves. Decorate with piped lines of melted chocolate.

5. Pipe delicate lines of melted chocolate and decorate with a quartered candied cherry. Sprinkle with ground pistachios.

6. Use a strip of candied pineapple and pipe a delicate pattern of melted chocolate.

7. Dip one side of a walnut half in melted chocolate. Dip the chocolate-covered half in ground pistachios.

8. Pipe a delicate lattice pattern of diagonal melted chocolate lines, using both dark chocolate and milk chocolate. Decorate with candied coffee bean.

9. Pipe melted chocolate for flower stem and one leaf. Use a crystallized violet petal for the flower and a pistachio half for the leaf.

(Illustrated large photograph right-hand page, left to right)

10. Use a tinted, cut-out marzipan flower. Decorate the center of the flower with colored sugar.

11. (See 5)

12. (See 4)

13. (See 1)

14. Decorate with clusters of crystallized violet petals.

15. Decorate with a piece of candied orange peel and piped lines of melted chocolate.

16. Place halved candied cherry in centers of Petits Fours. Surround with small dots of melted chocolate.

17. Place a whole hazelnut in center of Petits Fours. Sprinkle ground pistachios around hazelnut.

18. Pipe geometric lines of melted chocolate off-center. Decorate with candied coffee bean.

267

A Sweet Coating for Fresh Fruit

Candy apples are almost synonymous with Halloween.
They may be a bit messy to eat, but the sticky
red smile on the face of a happy child is surely worth the
mess! On the other hand, chocolate-coated cherries
can be eaten neatly in just one bite full of wonderful,
sweet, delicious flavor.

Sweets & Chocolates

Candy Apples

Candy apples are made with a red-tinted sugar syrup and "red hot candies." You will need a candy thermometer to be sure the syrup reaches the proper temperature.

To make candy apples use tart apples with unblemished skins. Golden Delicious, Red Delicious and MacIntosh apples are fine because they keep their shape when dipped in hot sugar syrup.

6 tart apples
6 lollipop or ice cream sticks
2 cups granulated sugar
1-1/2 cups light corn syrup
1 cup water
About 1/3 cup red hot cinnamon candies
Red food coloring

1. Wash and dry apples. Remove stems. Insert lollipop stick in stem end of each apple and set aside.
2. Line baking sheet with foil and set aside.
3. Place sugar, corn syrup, water and candies in heavy saucepan. Cook over moderate heat, stirring constantly, until sugar and candies are dissolved. Tint with red food coloring. Insert candy thermometer and bring to a boil. Boil rapidly, without stirring, until temperature registers 300F (150C) (hard crack stage). Remove from heat.
4. Dip apples quickly, 1 at a time, into hot syrup, swirling apple to coat completely. Remove apple; shake off excess syrup. Place, stick end up, on foil-lined baking sheet. Let stand until set. Makes 6 Candy Apples.

Variation

To make caramel-coated apples, use 1-1/2 pounds vanilla-flavored caramels and 3 tablespoons water. Place in top of double boiler, and cook until caramels are melted, stirring until smooth. Dip apples, 1 at a time, into caramel syrup and proceed as directed above.

Chocolate-Coated Cherries

(Illustrated on pages 256-257)
About 1-1/2 lbs. large, fresh, unblemished, dark sweet cherries or maraschino cherries with stems attached
About 1 cup brandy
20 oz. dark semisweet or milk chocolate (or use half semisweet chocolate and half milk chocolate)

1. Rinse cherries with water being careful not to detach stems or bruise fruit. Place on paper towels; pat dry.
2. Place cherries in tall glass jar with twist cap, large enough to hold fruit comfortably without packing it tightly. Add brandy to cover cherries and close jar.
3. Marinate in refrigerator at least 2 weeks.
4. Drain cherries well and let dry completely on double thickness of paper towels.
5. Melt chocolate according to directions on page 259.
6. Dip cherries into melted chocolate, 1 or 2 at a time, holding cherries by stem end. Cover completely.
7. Place dipped cherries on foil-lined baking sheet. Let stand until chocolate is completely set. Note: To make a thicker layer of chocolate, repeat dipping process 2 or 3 times, allowing chocolate to dry after each dipping.

Index

Metric Chart

Comparison to Metric Measure

When You Know	Symbol	Multiply By	To Find	Symbol
teaspoons	tsp	5.0	milliliters	ml
tablespoons	tbsp	15.0	milliliters	ml
fluid ounces	fl. oz.	30.0	milliliters	ml
cups	c	0.24	liters	l
pints	pt.	0.47	liters	l
quarts	qt.	0.95	liters	l
ounces	oz.	28.0	grams	g
pounds	lb.	0.45	kilograms	kg
Fahrenheit	F	5/9 (after subtracting 32)	Celsius	C

Liquid Measure to Milliliters

1/4 teaspoon	=	1.25 milliliters
1/2 teaspoon	=	2.5 milliliters
3/4 teaspoon	=	3.75 milliliters
1 teaspoon	=	5.0 milliliters
1-1/4 teaspoons	=	6.25 milliliters
1-1/2 teaspoons	=	7.5 milliliters
1-3/4 teaspoons	=	8.75 milliliters
2 teaspoons	=	10.0 milliliters
1 tablespoon	=	15.0 milliliters
2 tablespoons	=	30.0 milliliters

Fahrenheit to Celsius

F	C
200—205	95
220—225	105
245—250	120
275	135
300—305	150
325—330	165
345—350	175
370—375	190
400—405	205
425—430	220
445—450	230
470—475	245
500	260

Liquid Measure to Liters

1/4 cup	=	0.06 liters
1/2 cup	=	0.12 liters
3/4 cup	=	0.18 liters
1 cup	=	0.24 liters
1-1/4 cups	=	0.3 liters
1-1/2 cups	=	0.36 liters
2 cups	=	0.48 liters
2-1/2 cups	=	0.6 liters
3 cups	=	0.72 liters
3-1/2 cups	=	0.84 liters
4 cups	=	0.96 liters
4-1/2 cups	=	1.08 liters
5 cups	=	1.2 liters
5-1/2 cups	=	1.32 liters